BUILDING
EFFECTIVE
MASTERY
LEARNING
SCHOOLS

James H. Block
University of California, Santa Barbara

Helen E. Efthim
School District, City of Pontiac, Michigan

Robert B. Burns
Far West Regional Educational Laboratory

Longman
New York & London

Building Effective Mastery Learning Schools

Longman Inc., 95 Church Street, White Plains, N.Y. 10601

Associated companies:
Longman Group Ltd., London
Longman Cheshire Pty., Melbourne
Longman Paul Pty., Auckland
Copp Clark Pitman, Toronto
Pitman Publishing Inc., New York

Executive editor: Raymond T. O'Connell
Production editor: Halley Gatenby
Text and cover designs: Steven A. Krastin
Text art: J & R Services, Inc.
Production supervisor: Pamela Teisler

Library of Congress Cataloging-in-Publication Data
Block, James H.
  Building effective mastery learning schools.

  Bibliography: p.
  Includes index.
  1. Competency based education—United States.
I. Efthim, Helen E.   II. Burns, Robert B. (Robert
Bounds), 1951–   . III. Title.
LC1032.B58   1988   371.3   87-21344
ISBN 0-582-28552-6

88 89 90 91 92 93 9 8 7 6 5 4 3 2 1

To Benjamin S. Bloom
You continue to teach us, too

Contents

Acknowledgments

Several individuals have provided valuable advice as this volume has unfolded. We thank Benjamin Bloom, Thomas Guskey, William Smith, Tom Rusk Vickery, Glenn Hymel, Kathleen Fitzpatrick, Albert Mamary, John Champlin, Nancy Hill, Patricia LaMarche, and Joan Kozlovsky for their feedback and suggestions on various chapters. While we did not always agree with their observations, we still found them thought provoking.

We express our special thanks to our friend and colleague Lorin Anderson. Many of the ideas and words that appear throughout this volume are his. Indeed, he was one of the original authors of the volume but chose to withdraw to pursue other personal and professional matters. We wish him well.

We are also grateful to the staff of Crofoot School in Pontiac, Michigan, for sharing their experience. They are LeBertha Johnson, Gretchen Parr, Gladys Cifelli, Lois Reynolds, Joy Stimac, Linda Ricks, Sherry Gardner, Myra Burnett, Bertha Johnson, Mildred Garling-Gordon, Irma Johnson, Dolores Mack, Mary Payne, Douglas Bastian, Brenda Street, Mary Elizabeth Roach, Jane Schiebel, Donna Schwartz, Jean MacGillis, Johnnie Wilder, and principal William Counts.

Finally, the senior author, Jim Block, specially acknowledges two individuals for their assistance in drafting this work: Stanley Nicholson served as my right-hand man when issues of word processing arose—and did they ever arise! In an important sense, Stan has been the quiet technical force behind many of my various projects. I am pleased to acknowledge here my past and present debts for his wisdom. If Stan has been the quiet force behind this volume, then Karen Hearn has been the active one. She has provided invaluable secretarial help, and, most of all, that indefinable morale that has helped carry us to conclusion.

Our heartfelt thanks to all of you.

CHAPTER 1

What Is Mastery Learning and How Does It Work?

Recently, public school educators have been besieged with reports calling for fundamental school reforms. Whether these reports will have any general long-term impact on the conduct of American public education remains to be seen. What is certain, though, is the fact that they have had an effect on short-term thinking about our schools and classrooms. Never since perhaps the late 1950s have so many local and national public policymakers been so interested in education.

Policymakers are asking tough questions about issues of student learning excellence. Why, they wonder, are so many students currently leaving our public schools without traditional basic and advanced skills? Some believe that what we teach simply does not prepare students for either their out-of-school or their postschool lives. They want curricular changes ranging from a return to the basics to an advance to high technics. Others feel that the levels at which we teach are too low and that our standards have slipped. They clamor for testing changes ranging from minimum competency tests to maximum graduation requirements.

Public policymakers are also taking a hard look at issues of equity in student learning. Many are concerned with preserving the major student civil rights gains of the 1960s and 1970s. They continue to push for greater equality of educational opportunity. A few, though, are concerned with extending past civil rights gains. These reformers advocate equality of educational outcome as well. As the Reverend Jesse Jackson has reminded them, minority children have been taught to move from the back of the bus to the front and even to the driver's seat; now they must be taught to run the bus company. And both groups of reformers find themselves dealing with a new realization: Issues of equity are not limited to "minority" students; there are issues of equity—for example, tracking—that plague "majority" students as well.

Issues of economy in teaching are uppermost in many educational policymakers' thinking, too. Federal as well as state and local aid for schools has been lacking in recent years. Faced with the reality of no-growth or limited-growth instructional budgets, policymakers are asking hard questions as to where the resources for school reform will come from. Some contend that all-out pushes need to be made to help public schools acquire their fair share of the current economic upturn. They counsel educators to look to traditional funding sources such as legislatures and also to nontraditional ones such as lotteries. Others propose that public schools learn to live with their existing human and nonhuman resources. They advise practitioners to orchestrate current resources more cost-effectively.

Finally, some policymakers are deeply concerned about issues of teacher excitement and renewal. With teacher "burnout" on the rise, they are asking how to create more humane and rewarding teaching climates. Some believe the answer lies in more and better external work incentives. They call for higher teacher salaries and better career benefits. Others believe the answer lies in more and better internal work incentives. They call for strategies to reaffirm teachers' sense of personal worth and power. And all this calling comes at a time when a small but growing number of policymakers fundamentally doubt whether any amount or type of incentives will work. These policymakers are on the brink of stopping the search for a human-dependent technology of teaching. They want a more machine-dependent one instead.

This book chronicles the ideas, research, and practices of a group of educators who for two decades have been addressing matters of excellence and equity in student learning, and economy and excitement in teaching. These educators believe that current district, school, and classroom practices can be restructured so that virtually all students learn as excellently, as swiftly, and as self-confidently as have only our best students in the past. Moreover, they are convinced that this restructuring can occur with largely existing resources if more humane use is made of current human ones. In short, these educators propose that American public school education can be equal *and* excellent for the vast majority of students and can be economical *and* personally exciting for most professionals.

The banner under which these educators march is *mastery learning*. In this chapter we explain *mastery learning*, where it comes from, and how it works. In subsequent chapters we review how well it works and what must be done—technically and ethically—to make it work at the classroom, school, and district levels.

WHAT IS MASTERY LEARNING?

Mastery learning is an old philosophy about teaching and learning with roots deep in both Western and Eastern educational thinking. It asserts that any teacher can help virtually all students learn equally excellently, quickly, and self-confidently; that is, the teacher can help "dumb," "slow," and "unmotivated" students to learn like their "smart," "fast," and "motivated" peers. Such teaching and learning, the philosophy contends, improves most students' and teachers' chances for long-term social and personal prosperity. Students acquire personal competencies that promote lifelong learning. Teachers get professional competencies that generate lifelong effective teaching.

Mastery learning is also a manageable set of individualized instructional ideas and practices that have consistently helped many students learn excellently, swiftly, and self-confidently. Basically, this instruction provides a clear criterion of what constitutes mastery in *all* students' learning. It then provides *each* student with timely and appropriate help when and where learning difficulties arise and, most important, with sufficient time to conquer these difficulties (Bloom, 1974).

As this brief definition hints, mastery approaches to the teaching-learning process have several distinctive characteristics. Although some of these characteristics may be found in major competing instructional approaches such as Rosenshine's (1979) direct instruction, Hunter's (1984) mastery teaching, and Slavin's (1983) cooperative learning, it is rare to find them all.

One characteristic is that mastery learning approaches are philosophically based. They derive from some optimistic beliefs about humans' capacities to learn and to teach, especially the classical humanistic premise of respect for teachers and learners. This premise occasions mastery practitioners to be concerned with student and teacher beliefs (thoughts plus feelings) about the teaching-learning process and with how these beliefs influence their actions. To be sure, we use techniques from behavioral, cognitive, and humanistic psychology to change certain of these actions. However, we are interested in these actions only because they belie some negative beliefs about some humans' capacities to conduct their own teaching or learning affairs. It is these beliefs themselves that are our real targets.

Mastery learning approaches are also holistic. They deal with all aspects of the teaching and learning core in today's classrooms—curricula, teaching, managing, and testing. While mastery practitioners sacrifice some depth for this comprehensive approach to the teaching-learning process, especially relative to approaches that focus on only one aspect (for example, Hunter's mastery teaching), they gain useful scope. This scope provides them a wider perspective from which to evaluate the practical implications of "deeper" developments in each of these core matters. They can then assimilate the most promising and practicable developments.

Mastery learning approaches are aligned. As defined by Cohen (1986), *alignment* simply means that

> These programs consciously strive to match what they want to teach to what they do teach. And they likewise strive to match what they do teach to what they test. Indeed, the alignment of curriculum, instruction, and testing is central to their success. (p. 24)

Whereas their holistic aspect helps ensure that no part of today's teaching-learning core is slighted, their alignment aspect does more. It ensures that one part of the core is always synchronized with the other parts.

Last, mastery learning approaches are individualized. Like their contemporary predecessors—Individually Prescribed Instruction (IPI), Program for Learning According to Needs (PLAN), and Individually Guided Education (IGE) (see Talmage, 1975)—they provide adaptive educational settings that accommodate a diversity of student entry characteristics (abilities, skills, knowledge, attitudes, and values) yet help each student succeed (see Wang & Walberg, 1985). Unlike them, though, they provide a very different *type* and *context* for this individualization (Anderson & Block, 1985).

Rather than individualizing all the time, mastery learning approaches attempt to individualize only as needed. All students take a common course of study rather than different ones. And all students proceed through this course at the teacher's pace, not their own. But once every 10 to 14 days, the teacher checks each student's progress. Students who are not progressing well are provided with supplementary, more personalized instruction. They are offered a variety of alternative learning materials and activities and additional learning time to correct their particular learning errors. Students who are progressing excellently and quickly are provided with additional instruction too, to enrich their learning. After this correction or enrichment occurs, all students return to the root course of study.

Rather than individualizing by using atypical classroom teaching-learning situations, mastery approaches use typical ones. They are specifically designed for situations in which teachers already have a curriculum that must be covered in a fixed period of calendar time, inordinate time cannot be spent on diagnostic or progress testing, and student learning must be periodically evaluated and grades or marks assigned. Moreover, they rely primarily on human beings for their success, rather than on machines and other technological devices. Both teachers and students are responsible for ensuring that they use their time and expertise as well as possible.

WHERE DID MASTERY LEARNING ORIGINATE?

Obviously, neither the philosophy of mastery learning nor many of its ideas and practices evolved from nothing. The evolution of mastery learning falls into several periods. We will call these the Bloom period, the Bloom's Students period, and the Network period.

The Bloom Period

As noted earlier, the idea or philosophy of mastery learning is very old. Block (1971) and more recently Guskey (1987) have traced this idea to early Western educators such as Comenius, Pestalozzi, and Herbart. But discussions with both Western and Eastern scholars and philosophers lead us to believe that its origins are even older.

Every time the idea surfaced to influence educational thinking, however, it floundered due to the lack of a practical sustaining technology (Block, 1971). It was Benjamin S. Bloom who, in the late 1960s, first provided the theoretical basis for such a technology. What Bloom did was transform a conceptual model of school learning developed by John B. Carroll (1963) into a working model for mastery learning.

Carroll's model derived from the observation that a student's aptitude for a particular subject predicted either the level to which the student could learn the subject in a given time or the time the student would require to learn it to a given level. Hence, rather than defining aptitude as only an index of the level to which a student could learn, Carroll also defined it as an index of *learning rate*. A student with a high aptitude for a subject would learn it quickly, while one with a low aptitude would learn it more slowly.

Carroll's view of aptitude as either an index of learning rate (under fixed achievement conditions) or learning level (under fixed time conditions) raised, of course, the intriguing possibility that all students might be able to master a given subject, if they had the time. But how might that time be found? To help resolve this question, Carroll next advanced a model of the "economics" of learning time under ordinary school conditions.

According to this model, if each student was allowed the time he or she needed to learn to some criterion level and if he or she spent the necessary time, Carroll proposed the student would probably attain the level. However, if the student was not allowed enough time or did not spend enough time, the degree to which he or she would learn could be

$$\text{Degree of learning} = f\left(\frac{\text{Time actually spent}}{\text{Time needed}}\right)$$

Figure 1.1. The partial Carroll model (Block & Burns, 1976, p. 5)

expressed as in Figure 1.1. In words, the degree of learning under school conditions is a function of the time the student actually spends in learning relative to the time he or she needs to spend.

According to Carroll, the time a student spent and the time that student needed to spend were influenced not only by learner characteristics but also by school characteristics. In particular, the time spent was determined by whichever was the less, the student's *perseverance* (the amount of time he or she was willing to spend actively engaged in learning) or the student's *opportunity to learn* (the amount of time allocated for learning). If the student's opportunity to learn was greater than his or her perseverance, perseverance determined the time spent in learning. The student would spend no more time than his or her motivation allowed. But if the student's perseverance was greater than his or her opportunity to learn, the reverse would be true. The student might have all the necessary motivation to learn but have it cut off in midstream.

The time needed to learn, by contrast, was determined by the student's *aptitude* for the subject, the *quality* of instruction (including the instructional materials), and the student's *ability to understand* this instruction. If the quality of the instruction was high, the student would readily understand it and would need little additional time to learn beyond that required by individual aptitude. In short, how the student was taught would not unnecessarily interfere with what the student was taught. But if the quality of the instruction was low, the student would need additional time. He or she would have to spend unnecessary time getting through the medium of the instruction to get to the message.

Putting all these observations together, Carroll proposed the complete model of school learning shown in Figure 1.2. In words, the degree of school learning of a given subject is a function of a student's perseverance or opportunity to learn, relative to his or her aptitude for the subject, the quality of instruction, and his or her ability to understand this instruction.

$$\text{Degree of learning} = f\left(\frac{\text{Time actually spent}}{\text{Time needed}}\right)$$

$$= f\left(\frac{\text{1. Time allowed}\quad\text{2. Perseverance}}{\begin{array}{c}\text{3. Aptitude}\quad\text{4. Quality of instruction}\\ \text{5. Ability to understand instruction}\end{array}}\right)$$

Figure 1.2. The complete Carroll model (Block & Burns, 1976, p. 6)

Despite its simplicity and elegance, Carroll's model did not attract the attention of many educational researchers and practitioners until Bloom began to draw out its practical implications (see Carroll, 1985).

From Bloom's perspective, three propositions were central to the model:

1. Aptitude could be viewed as an index of learning rate.
2. The degree of school learning for any student is simply a function of the time he or she actually spends in learning relative to the time he or she needs to spend.
3. The time a student spends, as well as needs to spend, in school learning can be controlled by manipulating certain instructional characteristics alone.

Bloom synthesized these propositions as follows. If aptitude was predictive of the rate at which a student could learn, but not necessarily the level, it should be possible to fix the degree of school learning expected of each student at some high level of mastery. Then, by attending to the variables under school control in Carroll's model, namely, opportunity to learn and quality of instruction, a teacher should be able to ensure that each student attained this level.

Elaborating on this logic, Bloom argued that if students were normally distributed with respect to aptitude for some subject and were provided with uniform opportunity to learn and uniform quality of instruction, only a few students would achieve mastery in their learning. Moreover, each student's aptitude for the subject would be the primary determinant of learning, with high-aptitude students performing well and low-aptitude ones performing poorly. If, however, each student received differential opportunity to learn or differential quality of instruction, a majority of students, perhaps as many as 95 percent, could achieve mastery in their learning. Moreover, each student's learning aptitude should not be a primary determinant of his achievement. We can diagram Bloom's logic as in Figure 1.3.

In accordance with this logic, Bloom next sketched the outline for a mastery learning strategy that might be used in the typical classroom situation. This strategy drew heavily on the ideas of pioneers in individualized instruction, especially Washburne (1922) and his famous Winnetka Plan and Morrison (1926) and his University of Chicago Laboratory School experiments. The strategy's basic elements were these:

1. The learner must understand the nature of the task to be learned and the procedure to be followed in learning it.

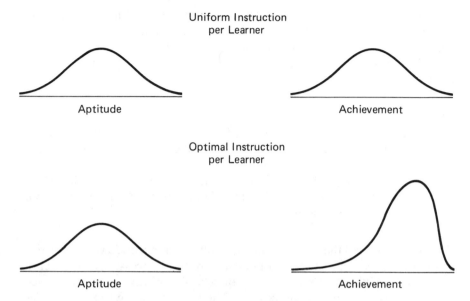

Figure 1.3. A sketch of Bloom's Logic (Block, 1971, pp. 6–7)

2. The specific instructional objectives relating to the learning task must be formulated.
3. It is useful to break a course or subject into small units of learning and to test at the end of each unit.
4. The teacher should provide feedback as to the learner's particular errors and difficulties after each test.
5. The teacher must find ways to alter the time some students have available to learn.
6. It may be profitable to provide alternative learning opportunities.
7. Student effort is increased when small groups of two or three students meet regularly for as long as an hour to review their test results and to help one another overcome the difficulties identified by means of the test. (McNeil, 1969, p. 308)

The Bloom's Students Period

Given his influential position and a mass mailing of his initial "Learning for Mastery" paper (Bloom, 1968) to educators around the world, Bloom was able to disseminate his thinking on mastery learning immediately. Some educators almost immediately branded his ideas a great boondoggle (for instance, Cronbach, 1972), while others viewed them as a great boon (such as McNeil, 1969). However, most practitioners and researchers stood on the sidelines of the debate until they better understood the theory and, in particular, the actual practice and impact of mastery learning (see, for example, Mueller, 1976). While Bloom (1976) turned his attention to extending the theory, a number of his graduate students began to devote their energy to developing the research and practice.

Two major practical developments soon followed. In the process of doing research on the setting of mastery performance standards, James H. Block became acutely aware of the need to elaborate Bloom's now so-called "Learning for Mastery," or LFM, strategy. With the help of Bloom, Carroll, and another of Bloom's students, Peter W. Airasian, Block produced in early 1971 the first book-length exposition of mastery learning, *Mastery Learning: Theory and Practice.*

This book explored some of the practical measurement problems with Carroll's model and provided some testing and teaching solutions. Airasian's (1969) work on mastery testing and Block's (1970) work on mastery testing and teaching were especially highlighted. The former research provided some initial guidelines for the construction of the brief diagnostic progress or "formative evaluation" instruments so central to Bloom's thinking. The latter research added some initial guidelines for using formative test feedback to identify and correct student learning deficiencies.

But these preliminary guidelines on mastery testing and teaching were insufficient for practitioners. So Block and Bloom student Lorin W. Anderson prepared a more detailed how-to book on mastery learning, *Mastery Learning in Classroom Instruction* (1975). This monograph covered how to define, plan, teach, and test for mastery in the typical classroom. It also provided answers to some of the most frequently asked practical questions.

For some readers, however, even the Block and Anderson volume was too short on detail. Consequently, it was quickly followed by a volume by another Bloom student, Kay P. Torshen, *The Mastery Approach to Competency Based Education* (1977). Non-Bloom students also wrote small volumes: Lowell Horton published *Mastery Learning* in 1981, and Jackson Lee, Jr., and K. Wayne Pruitt issued *Providing for Individual Differences in Student Learning* (1984) shortly thereafter. Each book in its own way further developed mastery learning practice. The Torshen work was strong on building mastery learning curricula; Lee and Pruitt, on building mastery learning instruction, especially for younger children; and Horton, on spelling out some of the growing misconceptions about mastery learning among practitioners.

The writing continues. Another of Bloom's students, Thomas R. Guskey, has recently released a much expanded and updated version of the original Block and Anderson volume: *Implementing Mastery Learning*

(1985c) focuses on mastery learning practice at the classroom level. Daniel U. Levine and associates have published *Improving Student Achievement through Mastery Learning Programs* (1985a). This volume begins to concentrate on mastery learning practice at the school and school system level.

The net effect of all this writing has been to bring mastery learning ideas and practices to the forefront of contemporary educational thought and theory. Leading educational publishers (such as McGraw-Hill, SRA, Westinghouse Learning Corporation, and Random House) and new competitors (such as Mastery Education Corporation) have begun to build mastery ideas about curriculum, teaching, and testing into their materials. Some have even developed entire commercial mastery learning reading programs. At the same time, influential national professional organizations, such as the AASA, ASCD, IDEA, and NEA, have begun to include mastery learning ideas and practices in their various programs.

The Network Period

By the early 1980s, mastery learning ideas and practices had become part of the American educational woodwork. Not all the press and professional coverage had been positive, of course. Chicago's board of education, for example, publicly decided to stop mandating its self-developed mastery learning program in reading (see Olson, 1985). But in a discipline where any press and professional coverage is rare, mastery ideas and practices had drawn remarkably sustained attention.

One obvious drawback to these ideas surfaced, though, in the harsh glare of the national school reform movement of the 1980s. Mastery learning had been developed with primarily the classroom in mind. As reform-minded mastery practitioners began to expand successful classroom programs at the school or district level, this drawback became painfully apparent. Only several major mastery learning projects around the country were able to make a smooth transition between mastery learning classrooms and mastery learning schools and districts.

Consequently, a need evolved within the mastery learning movement for some vehicle whereby large-scale implementers might share their trials, tribulations, and insights. This vehicle emerged in the early 1980s spearheaded by William G. Spady, Jr., a longtime mastery learning admirer (see Spady, 1974), and a group of the country's foremost mastery learning practitioners (including Carol Barber of Denver; Beau Fly Jones of Chicago; John Champlin and Albert Mamary of Johnson City, New York; John Hoben of Plymouth-Canton, Michigan; Joan Hyman and Alan Cohen of the University of San Francisco; and Robert Blum of the Northwest Regional Educational Laboratory). Together they formed the Network of Outcome-based Schools under the auspices of the AASA's new national Center for the Improvement of Learning.

The Network's first task was to codify and elaborate the basic philosophical premises undergirding the various schools and districts in which mastery learning ideas were flourishing. A most recent version of these premises appears in Box 1.1. Its second task was to determine the operational essentials of an outcome-based school or district. A recent statement of these essentials may be found in Box 1.2. Its final task was to indicate how these components could be executed at various levels of schooling—classroom, school, and district or state; their implications for instruction and management; and their support requirements. One current statement on these issues occupies Box 1.3.

BOX 1.1   Key Philosophical Principles of Outcome-based Education

The advocates of outcome-based education believe that:

1. *All students can learn and succeed.* Successfully learning the things that lead to literate, self-sufficient, well-informed adults is within the grasp of virtually all students. Schools exist to foster those capabilities, to ensure their accomplishment, and to formally recognize and reward them whenever they occur. Designing and organizing instructional delivery that directly builds on the capabilities students bring with them to the learning situation reinforces their motivation for learning and their opportunity to succeed.

2. *Success breeds success.* How students experience their learning progress affects their self-concept, motivation, and approach to later learning experiences. Providing students with the opportunity to learn and succeed and formally acknowledging and recording their learning success in its own terms encourages students to seek further learning experiences. Learning success is not a scarce commodity reserved for a small group of superior achievers, but the deliberate goal of quality instruction for all students.

3. *Schools control the conditions of success.* Schools directly control the structure and availability of the curriculum, student learning experiences, instructional time, assessment measures, grading and credit options, and opportunities for program advancement—all of which have an enormous bearing on the learning success of students. How schools organize and implement these elements either promotes or inhibits student learning, motivation, and formal success.

Spady, 1985a.

BOX 1.2   Essential Operational Components of Outcome-based Education

Operationally, outcome-based education means:

1. Using clearly defined outcomes for all students
   a. To define and develop curriculum content, structure, and articulation
   b. To establish criterion-referenced measures of student and program success
   c. To establish record-keeping and reporting systems for student progress
2. Organizing instructional delivery based on the performance capabilities and learning needs of students
3. Adjusting instructional time and learning opportunities to enable all students to reach outcome goals successfully
4. Formally acknowledging and documenting student learning and success whenever they occur
5. Modifying the instructional program on the basis of documented student learning results and available data on instructional effectiveness.

Spady, 1985b.

BOX 1.3   Defining Features of Outcome-based Education

A. *Philosophy (definition and commitment to success)*: OBE philosophy states that instruction can be organized so that virtually all students can learn the information, concepts, and skills embodied in the curriculum and have their learning outcomes formally recognized and reported.

B. *Instructional strategy (capacity to deliver quality instruction)*: OBE instructional strategies are long-term plans for organizing, presenting, and monitoring instruction in classrooms. OBE strategies systematize instructional delivery by aligning three components:
   a. *Curriculum component*: The instructional strategy revolves around a curriculum component that consists of: (1) goals and objectives for courses or programs of study, (2) standards of student performance which directly embody the goals and objectives, and (3) curricular materials sequenced in a logical fashion to support attainment of the outcome goals.
   b. *Instruction component*: The instructional strategy uses a delivery system based on mastery learning ideas which (1) divides the cur-

riculum into "units of instruction" that are tied directly to learning goals, (2) focuses instruction explicitly on those goals, (3) adjusts the time needed for instruction based on student goal performance, and (4) uses some form of feedback and correction for students who do not attain the mastery standard established for the unit of instruction.

  c. *Assessment component*: The instructional strategy uses an assessment system capable of providing evidence of student attainment or non-attainment of the mastery standard established for a unit or program of instruction. The assessment component must be able to provide the data base for correcting student learning deficiencies when necessary, making informed instructional decisions about student progress in reaching instructional goals, and recording and reporting initial and improved levels of performance.

C. *Instructional management (school organization and coordination)*: To implement the philosophy and instructional strategy at the school level requires an instructional management system. Together, the philosophy, instructional strategy, and instructional management system produce an *OBE instructional program*. However, since instructional management systems vary, there are different OBE instructional programs. Typically, the type of management system used provides the basis for the particular label or name used for the instructional program or "model." There are two major components to the management system:

  a. *Grouping management component*: The grouping management component refers to how students are organized for instruction and advancement on both a short-term and long-term basis. This may involve between-classroom grouping or within-classroom grouping or both. The three major grouping strategies used by OBE practitioners are whole class, flexible skill-regrouping, and continuous progress.

  b. *Information management component*: The information management component refers to how student information is gathered, recorded, used, and distributed among school personnel and students. Relevant areas of required information management include grouping assignments, daily task assignments, formative evaluation results, unit certification, course grading, program evaluation, and grade-level promotion.

Support Requirements

Schools require resource support from the district and state in order to select OBE programs appropriate to their needs, develop new procedures, acquire new skills, and conduct a coordinated OBE instructional program. The specific kinds of support required depend on the instructional program selected and are directly related to the three components of the instructional strategy and the two components of the instructional management system outlined above:

1. *Curriculum support*: All OBE models require curriculum development work. Schools need support in the definition of outcome goals, development of objectives, establishment of standards, and the design, development, and procurement of materials to teach those objectives.
2. *Instructional support*: All OBE models are based on mastery learning principles. Teachers require in-service training in the use of this classroom pedagogy and ways to group students and organize and use instructional time to enhance both teacher and student success.
3. *Assessment support*: All OBE models are grounded in concerns for student learning. Consequently, the instructional programs require a strong assessment component to provide the necessary information for informed instructional decisions regarding student placement and advancement.
4. *Grouping management support*: Depending on the OBE model implemented, schools may require support in the coordination and organization of students for instruction.
5. *Information management support*: Depending on the OBE model implemented, schools may require support in managing the flow of information between school personnel and students.

Burns, Spady, & Filby, 1986.

The Network of Outcome-based Schools now has a membership approaching 1,500 persons, including many school principals and district-level administrators. In addition to providing a quarterly newsletter, the Network also conducts regional, state, and national conferences on mastery learning (ML) and outcome-based education (OBE). These conferences focus on implementing ML and OBE ideas at the classroom, school, and district levels and are usually held at sites currently using the ideas and staffed with local practitioners and experts.

One important by-product of these conferences has been the further spread of mastery learning ideas. Indeed, states such as Maryland and Missouri have had or now have statewide ML and OBE initiatives in place, and Arizona and Utah seem on the verge of them. Another by-product has been that mastery learning ideas are also being assimilated into other important schooling innovations. For example, many Network members are particularly active in the "effective schools" and "effective teaching" movements. Some are even involved in the "effective management" movement, especially the instructional leader portion.

But with these by-products has also come a growing amount of unnecessary confusion about the relationships among mastery learning, OBE, and many of the other effective schooling, teaching, and managing ideas and concepts. Since we will be using many of these ideas and concepts in this volume, let us try to dispel some of that confusion.

The experience of Carol Barber (1986), one of the country's best-known OBE/ML practitioners, is instructive. She has used the concept of the umbrella to differentiate OBE from ML and other effective schooling ideas and practices.

> The umbrella includes (1) a canopy, (2) a center pole to support the canopy, and (3) a set of hinged ribs radiating from the center pole. . . .
>
> Outcome-based education is represented by the canopy of the umbrella. The OBE ideas represent possible reform of the total school system. Typically when school district personnel implement OBE, they are addressing every aspect of the school organization with the premise that "if it isn't the best that we can do to promote successful teaching and learning, we'll change it!" When a district moves into OBE, it is ready to examine the belief systems of staff, students, [and] parents; placement of students; grading and reporting policies; curriculum issues; certification processes; instructional delivery methods; etc. . . . In other words, OBE means an approach to reform within the *total* school system, i.e., the umbrella under which all practices of school operation will occur.
>
> The center pole supporting the umbrella represents mastery learning ideas. Mastery learning supports the OBE movement in that it is the main vehicle upon which to begin the change process in the belief systems, curriculum organization, and instructional strategies. Mastery learning provides us with the support and the processes needed to begin the total OBE reform in our schools.
>
> The set of hinged ribs radiating from the center pole can be viewed as any of the many effective schools movements and/or strategies available to us. Strategies such as Dr. Hunter's *Mastery Teaching*, [Johns Hopkins's] *Student Team Learning*, Johnson and Johnson's *Cooperative Learning*, Joyce's *Teaching Models*, Good's *TESA*, and many others represent effective practices which are totally compatible and will certainly enhance an OBE/ML program. . . .
>
> In practice the three parts of the umbrella must operate together, otherwise one will not realize its full potential. Realistically, one could implement any one of the above-mentioned strategies without having ML in operation; indeed, one can implement ML without having OBE. However, when OBE is implemented, ML [should] be applied. (pp. 1–2)

HOW DOES MASTERY LEARNING WORK?

How, then, do mastery learning strategies work?[1] Let us illustrate the basic concepts and techniques by outlining Bloom's original "Learning for Mastery" (LFM) strategy (for details, see Block & Anderson, 1975; Guskey, 1985c). This strategy reflects all of these ideas. Moreover, it has proved to be one of the easiest to implement. The strategy is specifically designed for use in instructional situations common in elementary and secondary schools where the calendar time allowed for learning is relatively fixed and students must be taught largely in groups. It minimizes the time students need to learn excellently so that they have sufficient calendar time.

Table 1.1 highlights the basic LFM concepts and techniques. As this table indicates, LFM can be understood at several levels. At the most general level, LFM is a *systematic* approach to instruction. It attempts to build a strong bridge between what the teacher desires to teach and the students who are to be taught. First, the teacher matches his or her instruction to desired learning outcomes for the course. This makes the instruction outcome-based. Then the teacher matches the instruction to the students. This makes the instruction provide multiple ways for each student to attain each outcome.

At a more specific level, LFM is a *proactive* approach to instruction. Much of the teacher's time, effort, and energy is spent in planning outside of class for possible inside-of-class contingencies. Thus when these contingencies occur, the teacher is ready for them. He or she need not waste valuable time, effort, and energy reactively manufacturing solutions on the spot.

Such proactive teaching requires several things. One is a clear and communicable set of expected course learning outcomes. The teacher must consider both what all students will be expected to learn and to what level. Obviously, if a teacher has no clear idea of where or how far the instruction is headed, she or he may get detoured.

The LFM teacher sets expected course learning outcomes in the process of defining mastery. To explicate what all students will be expected to learn, the teacher formulates course instructional outcomes and constructs a special course final or "summative" examination over them. These outcomes can be goals, competencies, objectives, or other benchmarks. To determine the level at which all students will be expected to learn, the teacher then sets some course mastery performance standards on the summative examination, typically standards indicative of A work.

---

[1] This discussion is adapted with permission from Block (1980).

TABLE 1.1. HOW DOES MASTERY LEARNING WORK?

Concepts	Techniques
General	
A. Approach instruction *systematically*: It should provide bridge between whom and what you teach.	
1. Match instruction to outcomes.	Base instruction on outcomes.
2. Match instruction to learners.	Provide multiple instructional methods.
Specific: Extraclassroom	
B. Be *proactive*, not reactive.	
1. Clarify outcomes.	Predefine mastery and make it explicit.
2. Provide for appropriate help in learning.	Preplan instruction for mastery.
3. Provide for appropriate learning time.	Preplan instruction for mastery.
Specific: Intraclassroom	
C. Manage *learning*, not learners.	
1. Provide student orientation.	Orient students to mastery learning.
2. Vary how and how long each student is taught as necessary.	Use preplanned instruction to teach for mastery.
3. Personalize grading.	Grade for mastery.

Source: Block, 1980, p. 69.

In addition to clear expected course learning outcomes, proactive teaching also requires some provision for appropriate help in each student's learning. Current learning problems are often caused by unresolved earlier ones. These earlier problems must be identified and corrected as they occur.

The LFM teacher provides for appropriate help in each student's learning by preplanning classroom instruction. First, the entire course is broken into smaller teaching-learning units. Each unit is long enough (2 to 3 weeks) to convey a number of skills, ideas, concepts, and appreciations but small enough to allow the close monitoring of each student's learning as the unit unfolds. Next these units are sequenced for transfer of learning so that the material in one unit prepares students for the next ones. In this way material taught well once will not be forgotten and will be available for later use. Then the teacher formulates a plan of mastery instruction for each unit. The purpose of this plan is to monitor each student's unit learning and to attain some measure of quality control.

The teacher develops the unit's *original instruction*—that is, the initial lesson plans. Typically, these plans build on her or his customary, whole group instructional methods. They cover the material to be presented, the learning activities in which students will be involved, and the learning encouragements students will need to stay involved until mastery is achieved.

The teacher now constructs a brief, ungraded, unit *diagnostic progress test* or formative evaluation instrument. This test is supposed to be an integral part of the unit's instruction, so each of its items is explicitly keyed to particular unit learning outcomes. The test's results will provide specific feedback about how each student's learning is changing as a result of the original whole group instruction.

Next the teacher specifies a score or *mastery performance standard* on the formative test. This score will indicate each student's mastery or nonmastery of the material. Though this mastery standard may change from unit to unit, typically it ranges from a score of 85 to 95 percent correct.

Then, the teacher develops two sets of *alternative instructional materials and procedures* keyed to each item on the unit's formative test. One set is called *correctives*. Each corrective is designed to reteach certain unit material in ways different from the unit's original whole group instruction. It may present the material in a new fashion, involve the student in fresh learning activities, or provide novel encouragements for learning. The other set is called *enrichments*. Whereas the correctives will be used by students with submastery unit formative test results, the enrichments will be used by those whose results are at or above mastery. Typically, the enrichments will press these students to go deeper into mastered material or to apply it in a wider range of situations.

Last, proactive teaching requires appropriate learning time. Clearly, if each student is to be provided with appropriate help in learning, sufficient time must be found to make use of this help. All students cannot be allowed the same learning time.

The LFM teacher also provides appropriate learning time through preplanned instruction. The teacher's preplan increases the *quantity* of time that each student spends in learning. Essentially, it constrains every student to spend as much time as necessary to master the material in one unit before attempting the next one. The preplan also improves the *quality* of the time that each student spends in learning. It ensures that no student spends unnecessary time learning by methods unsuited to his or her special learning requirements. Any student who cannot learn for mastery from the original instruction can learn from one or more correctives. A student who *has* learned for mastery from the original instruction can extend that learning with one or more enrichments.

At the most specific level, mastery strategies are *management-of-learning* approaches to instruction. They propose that inside the classroom, the function of the teacher is to specify what is to be learned, to motivate pupils to learn it, to provide them with instructional materials, to administer these materials at a rate suitable for each pupil, to monitor students' progress, to diagnose difficulties and provide proper remediation for them, to give praise and encouragement for good performance, and to give review and practice that will maintain pupils' learning over long periods of time. (Carroll, 1971, pp. 29–30)

The LFM teacher manages actual student learning in three phases. In the orientation phase he or she informs students, in a concrete fashion, of how and toward what ends they will be taught. The teacher tells them what they are expected to learn, how they are generally expected to learn it, and to what level they are expected to learn.

In the teaching phase, how and how long each student is taught is varied, as necessary, by using the preplanned instructional units. The teacher teaches the first learning unit using the whole group lesson plans. When the original instruction has been completed, the teacher administers the unit formative test. The test results are used to identify students for whom the original instruction and the initial learning time were sufficient and those for whom they were not. The teacher then certifies the students who have achieved mastery in their learning and identifies those who have not. The former students are challenged to engage in enrichment activities and/or to serve as tutors for their "slower" classmates. And the latter students are encouraged to use the appropriate correctives to complete their unit learning. The teacher then announces when the original instruction for the next unit will commence and gives both sets of students responsibility for making use of their respective learning opportunities. If the teacher desires to postpone the start of the next unit, the students are given in-class as well as out-of-class learning time. If he or she does not, the students must use out-of-class time.

The teacher repeats this teach-test-reteach cycle of original instruction, diagnostic progress testing, certification against the unit mastery standard, and individual correction and/or enrichment, unit by unit, until all units have been taught. The cycle is paced using in-class, in-school, and out-of-school time so that the teacher covers just as much material as would ordinarily be covered.

Finally, in the grading phase, the teacher evaluates students on a personal basis. The course summative examination is administerd, and each student is graded on what he or she has actually learned—that is, graded for mastery. Students whose test scores equal or exceed the predetermined course mastery performance standards typically earn grades of A or its equivalent. Students whose scores are below these standards earn grades of I (incomplete) or its equivalent. Such mastery grading is designed to engage what White (1959) has called "competence motivation," the intrinsic desire to compete against oneself and the material to be learned. It is also intended to disengage what Block (1977) has alluded to as "competition motivation," the extrinsic desire to compete against others. From the standpoint of developing the talent of all students rather than a few, the engagement of the former motivation seems to make much more sense than the engagement of the latter (Nicholls, 1979).

SUMMARY

As you have begun to discover, mastery approaches to learning and teaching dare educators to design instructional systems that meet four specific criteria:

1. They pursue maximums, not just minimums, in virtually all students' learning.
2. They value equality of learning outcomes, not just equality of opportunity.
3. They use existing schooling structures and teaching resources.
4. They prize humans over machines.

We shall now develop and braid these themes. In Chapter 2 we shall review research findings on mastery learning's impact on students. In Chapters 3, 4, and 5 we shall discuss some of the technical how-to's and the ethical whys of implementing a mastery learning program at the district, school, and classroom levels.

Foshay (1973) wisely noted, some time ago, that there are a variety of sources for current American school practices. He writes that "any large social institution," such as the school, "is an amalgam of what it has been, what it is, and what some people hope it will become" (p. 173). We hope that our treatment of mastery learning from a data, a technical, and an ethical perspective will provide you with enough sources of information to dare to become a part of a mastery learning school or district.

CHAPTER 2

How Well Does Mastery Learning Work?

As noted, practitioners initially sat on the sidelines of the boon-boon-doggle debate about mastery learning awaiting clarification of practical matters. Researchers sat, too, awaiting student learning and other data. In this chapter we shall review some of these data. We shall indicate where mastery learning research has been over the past two decades. And we shall speculate about where it is going. But first, a little history is in order.

WHERE HAS THE RESEARCH BEEN?

Recall that Bloom, having set out his initial ideas on mastery learning in 1968, then turned his attention to extending them into a theory of school learning. Not only did he leave the development of mastery learning practice to his students, but he also left the development of most of the initial supporting research. So, paralleling their early work to develop the practice was Bloom's students' related work on the development of the research.

The first attempt to stimulate mastery learning research was Block's (1971) *Mastery Learning: Theory and Practice*. As an addendum to this volume, he developed a brief, annotated bibliography of extant research on the major variables in Carroll's model, on the potential affective consequences of mastery learning, and on the use of mastery learning concepts and practices.

This bibliography was embellished in Block's (1974b) next volume, *Schools, Society, and Mastery Learning*, in which specialists were asked to speculate about the potential economic, social, and administrative implications of mastery learning. But since such speculations made no sense unless it worked, the initial portion of the volume reviewed the fledgling elementary and secondary school research. Block (1974a) concentrated on studies of student learning (especially achievement, retention, and transfer), of learning rate, and of affective development.

His story of mastery learning's impact on students was largely positive but thin and speculative. Accordingly, in 1975, at the invitation of the editor of the American Educational Research Association's yearly *Review of Research in Education*, Block and one of his students, Robert B. Burns, began to prepare a tighter and more comprehensive review.

First, Block and Burns identified the most substantively and methodologically sound studies of two emerging approaches to mastery learning: Bloom's group-based, teacher-paced Learning for Mastery (LFM) strategy and Keller's more individually based, student-paced Personalized System of Instruction (PSI). Then they chronicled four common phases in the research on each approach. The first phase, beginning in the late 1960s, concerned the question "Does mastery learning work?" The second, beginning in the early 1970s, examined the question "If it works, so what?" The third, beginning in the mid-1970s, explored the question "Why does it work?" And the fourth phase, beginning later in the mid-1970s, touched on the question "How does it work?"

On the basis of their review findings, Block and Burns (1976) concluded that mastery learning worked well in terms of promoting student learning. This was true whether the learning was indexed by achievement, retention, transfer, or learning rate measures. They also concluded that mastery learning had some important affective consequences for students. It especially heightened their interest in and attitudes toward subject matter and their academic self-concepts. Block and Burns further reported that mastery learning worked according to certain mechanisms hypothesized in the practical literature, especially the periodic feedback-correction cycle. Finally, they found that these mechanisms could be effectively taught to teachers, especially through in-service staff development efforts.

Their optimistic review did for mastery learning research what Block and Anderson's volume had done for the practice. On its heels came a decade of mastery learning research impressive for both its quantitative and qualitative aspects (Block, 1979).

Whereas in the early 1970s the research had involved few subjects, classes, teachers, and schools, this subsequent research often involved many. Indeed, entire school districts (Chicago; Denver; Johnson City, New York; Philadelphia), states (Maryland), and countries (Indonesia,

Italy, the Netherlands, South Korea) began testing the value of mastery learning for their particular situation.

Likewise, whereas the earlier research had involved few types of subjects, classes, teachers, and schools, the emerging research often involved a wide variety. Mastery learning was now being used in subjects that were intermediate or advanced as well as basic, elective as well as required, open as well as closed, and focused on divergent as well as convergent thinking. These subjects were taught to large as well as small classes, to gifted and "special" (handicapped, disadvantaged, bilingual) as well as to "regular" ones. Their teachers were old hands as well as new, humanists as well as cognitivists and behaviorists, and minority as well as majority group members. And these teachers worked in urban and rural as well as suburban schools, in tertiary and secondary as well as primary and elementary schools, in technical and professional as well as academic institutions, and in private as well as public settings.

By the early 1980s, therefore, Hymel (1982) was able to supplant Block's initial annotated bibliography on mastery learning research with a new one containing about 1,000 entries. Some entries appeared as chapters in books on American education (for example, Bloom's [1976] *Human Characteristics and School Learning*) and international education (see, for example, Husen & Postlethwaite's [1985] *International Encyclopedia of Education: Research and Studies*). Others appeared as articles in major research journals (such as the AERA's *Review of Educational Research*) and professional journals (such as the *Phi Delta Kappan* and the ASCD's *Educational Leadership*). And still other entries were presented at national professional meetings (ASCD, AASA, AERA, APA). Indeed, a special-interest group was formed within the American Educational Research Association to provide a yearly scholarly forum for mastery research.

What story, then, does this large body of accumulated research really tell? Much of this research has already been reviewed by Block (1974b), Block and Burns (1976), Bloom (1976), Burns (1979, 1986), Carroll (1985), and Guskey and Gates (1985, 1986), among others (such as Mueller, 1976). So let us concentrate on only the Block and Burns and Guskey and Gates reviews. Each covers relatively nonoverlapping bodies of LFM research—the former for roughly the period 1970–1976 and the latter 1976–1985. Each was comprehensive and rigorous in selecting appropriate studies for review. And both used a review technique called *metanalysis* (see Glass, McGaw, & Smith, 1981; Hedges & Olkin, 1985; Light & Pillemer, 1984). This technique allows us to quantify and summarize their respective results in a common metric called an *effect size* (see Box 2.1). We can tell whether and how well mastery learning strategies work.

BOX 2.1   A Primer on Effect Sizes

An effect size is an easy statistic to learn. It is simply the difference between the average scores on some outcome measure of an experimental group and of a control group divided by the control group standard deviation on that same measure. In our case, the experimental group would be the mastery-taught students, the control group would be the nonmastery-taught students, and the outcome measure would be some index of student learning, learning rate, or affect. Thus the effect sizes we report will tell us how far the average score of the mastery group is above or below the average score of the nonmastery group in the standard deviation units of the nonmastery group.

$$\text{Effect size} = \frac{\text{Mastery group average score} - \text{Nonmastery group average}}{\text{Standard deviation of the nonmastery group}}$$

Traditionally, effect sizes are reported in terms of the Greek term *sigma* since this is the name used in statistics to refer to measuring units based on standard deviations. A study with an effect size of 1.0 might be said to have demonstrated a "1-sigma" effect. Using the nonmastery standard deviation as the yardstick, the average score of the mastery group was one standard deviation (sigma) unit above the average score of the nonmastery group on some learning measure.

To develop this concept further, consider three examples. Suppose that both groups had the same average score on an achievement test. In this case the effect size would be zero since the numberator in the formula would be zero, indicating that the mastery instruction had no effect. Now suppose that the average difference in achievement scores between groups was 5 points and that the standard deviation of the nonmastery group's scores was 10. In this case the effect size would be .50 (5 divided by 10), or a ½-sigma effect, implying that the average mastery student scored at about half a standard deviation unit higher than the average nonmastery student. Finally, consider the case where the nonmastery group achieves higher scores, on the average, than the mastery group. In this case the effect size will be negative, suggesting that the average nonmastery student achieved higher scores than the average mastery student.

In a metanalysis each study is characterized by one effect size for each outcome measure of interest. These effect sizes are then averaged across all studies for a given measure or class of measures (say, achievement or interest). The resulting average effect size is taken as the best summary of the effect of the experimental treatment on the measure or class of measures of interest.

Caution should be exercised in interpreting the meaning of a mastery learning effect size. For example, effect sizes should not be confused with mastery test criterion scores (such as 80%), percentage of students passing a mastery test (86% passed a criterion score of 80%), or percentage of objectives passed (95% of the objectives were passed). Effects sizes and these other commonly used statistics related to student test performance are *not* the same.

Furthermore, confusion sometimes arises when effect sizes are interchanged with percentage of students. The confusion emanates from the fact that a common interpretation of an effect size is obtained by relating it to the bell or normal curve. Only when test scores are distributed normally or approximately normally can one interpret an effect size as moving the average mastery group student to the percentile of the nonmastery group indicated by the effect size. If this condition holds, then, for example, since 1 sigma above the mean is the 84th percentile and 2 sigmas above the mean is approximately the 98th percentile, a mastery effect size of 1.28 might be interpreted as suggesting that the mastery treatment could be expected to take the average student to the level achieved by the student at the 90th percentile in the nonmastery treatment group (the effect size of 1.28 corresponds to the 90th percentile). To repeat, though, it does not mean that 90% of the students achieved mastery or that 90% of the mastery objectives were passed.

For reporting purposes, we shall assume that the test scores from the various studies under review are roughly normal and use the effect size indicator presented here. Although this indicator ignores the basic premise that student learning under mastery conditions should be skewed and nonnormally distributed, conceptually more appealing effects size indicators (see Ziomek & Wilson, n.d.) have yet to gain widespread acceptance.

Student Learning

General Achievement.   Student achievement is the criterion most often used by our schools to evaluate instructional innovations (Brownell, 1948). Let us begin our review, therefore, by focusing on it. Most of the achievement results we shall review come from locally constructed achievement tests; however, several studies used standardized ones. All the results come from common examinations in common courses typically taught by the same or similar teachers using similar students.

From the Block and Burns review based on 13 studies, 52 achievement effect sizes were obtained; the average effect size was .83. Some 31 additional effect sizes were obtained from the Guskey and Gates review based on 22 studies; the average effect size was .82. So our metanalysis is based on 83 effect sizes from 35 different studies. Two additional "outlier" studies reporting very anomalous positive (3.04, Arlin & Webster, 1983) and negative ($-.55$, Guskey & Monsaas, 1979) effect sizes have been excluded.

Figure 2.1 presents the combined results in what is called a "stem-and-leaf display." Although such displays are not common in education, they are quite useful in examining the distribution of data (see Leinhardt & Leinhardt, 1980; Tukey, 1977). This particular display allows us to examine the entire distribution of 83 effect sizes across both reviews (see Box 2.2).

What, then, does Figure 2.1 tell us about the general student achievement effect sizes for mastery learning studies? First, the distribution of effect sizes is bimodal, with one mode at the stem of 4 and the other at the stem of 8. The significance of this apparent bimodality is unclear. On

---

BOX 2.2   A Primer on Stem-and-Leaf Displays

Stem-and-leaf displays are graphic ways to represent discrete data points in a batch of information. In many respects, they are a modern version of the old histograms.

Each display consists of a long vertical line with numbers to the right and left. Each number to the right of the long vertical line represents a leaf. The number to the immediate left of the vertical line is the starting point for a given leaf. All leaves with the same starting point form a stem. Although this may sound somewhat complicated, the stem-and-leaf display qualifies as one case where the explanation is more difficult than the concept being explained.

Every data point in a batch of numbers is represented by a starting point and a leaf. Looking at Figure 2.1, consider the first starting point, 2.6, and the first leaf, 4. To construct this data point, put the starting point and the leaf together: 2.64. This is a single effect size, which, because we have ranked all data values, also turns out to be the largest effect size in the entire batch. Now find the starting point of 1.7. This stem contains three leaves, 0, 1, and 2, which means three different effect sizes, 1.70, 1.71, and 1.72.

To the left of the stem-and-leaf display is a column of "inwardly cumulating counts." This is a cumulative count of the number of data points, the only tricky thing being that it starts at both ends of the distribution and proceeds inward to the stem where the median score occurs (the median score is the score that divides the ranked set of scores in half). The cumulative count where the median occurs is represented in parentheses and reflects only the number of leaves in that stem.

Thus the stem-and-leaf display is an economical way of presenting a batch of data so that the distributional properties of the batch can be readily seen. The extreme values are also apparent, as is the median. Perhaps more important, turning the display counterclockwise 90 degrees allows one to examine visually an approximation of the frequency distribution of the batch of numbers. Along with the cumulative count, the stem-and-leaf display provides an extremely detailed view of the data being examined.

1	2.6	4
2	2.5	0
	2.4	
	2.3	
3	2.2	0
4	2.1	5
6	2.0	0 0
	1.9	
	1.8	
9	1.7	0 1 2
11	1.6	4 9
12	1.5	9
14	1.4	4 9
15	1.3	4
16	1.2	8
22	1.1	1 1 2 5 7 8
24	1.0	0 6
28	.9	5 5 7 8
39	.8	0 1 2 3 5 6 8 8 9 9 9
(7)	.7	0 3 5 5 6 8 9
37	.6	1 4 8
34	.5	1 2 5 5
30	.4	0 0 1 2 2 2 6 6 6 9 9
19	.3	0 6 7 7 9
14	.2	1 5 6 7 8 9
8	.1	0 8 9
5	.0	1 2 2
2	.0	1 6

$$\bar{x} = .834$$
$$SD = .593$$
$$SE = .065$$
$$Mdn = .76$$
$$n = 83$$

Figure 2.1. Stem-and-leaf display of mastery learning achievement effect sizes (After Burns, 1986, p. 7)

the one hand, we might reasonably expect the effect sizes to be normally distributed if all the studies are samples from the same population of mastery learning treatments and students. Thus bimodality may be an indication that there are actually two different types of mastery treatments or students being sampled in these studies, each one with its own effect size. On the other hand, the bimodality may simply be a result of not having enough effect sizes to obtain a good characterization of the distribution.

Another possibility is that the bimodality is indicative of some systematic factor in the studies reviewed. We examined duration of the study, sample size, subject matter, and grade level. But none of these variables accounted for the bimodality. The bimodality issue will have to remain unresolved for the time being. We will treat it as being a function of too small a sample of effect sizes. This will allow us to use measures of central tendency to summarize the average effect size.

Second, turning to measures of central tendency, the mean effect size (.83) is higher than the median (.76) because the distribution is skewed— there are six effect sizes of 2.00 or larger. Because of this skew, the median is probably a better measure of the central tendency of the effect sizes than the mean.

Third, the batch of effect sizes may be summarized by five numbers: .01, .40, .76, 1.17, 2.64. These are the minimum and maximum effect sizes and, between them, the 25th, 50th, and 75th percentiles of effect sizes. For example, 50% of the effect sizes fall between the values .40 and 1.17.

Taken as a whole, then, Figure 2.1 tells two basic stories. One is that mastery learning approaches seem to work comparatively well almost all of the time. That is, they typically produce effects that are greater than or equal to a nonmastery approach. The other is that mastery learning approaches have comparatively strong effects on general student achievement. Assuming normality of scores, a median effect size of .76 means that the typical LFM application should move the average 50th-percentile student to about the 77th percentile in achievement.

There are no absolute effect size criteria or scales that can be applied across the board, but this is a sizable effect. Indeed, the median effect size of over ¾ sigma is one of the largest effect sizes currently reported for any instructional strategy (see Bloom, 1984; Walberg, 1984). Waxman, Wang, Anderson, and Walberg (1985), for example, report an average effect size of only .39 for 32 studies of "adaptive education" (see Wang & Walberg, 1985). And Bangert, Kulik, and Kulik (1983) report one of only .10 for a whole host of other "individualized systems of instruction" in grade 6–12 secondary schools.

The impressiveness of this median effect size is even more apparent when the middle 50% of effect sizes are considered. The effect sizes of .40 and 1.17 correspond to the 65th and 88th percentiles, respectively. In other words, the middle 50% of effect sizes suggest that mastery methods will move the average 50th percentile student to at least the 65th and perhaps to the 88th percentile.

Specific Achievement.   The foregoing statistics are impressive regarding how well mastery learning works in general, but they are less informative about how it works in given subjects, at various grade levels, and over various periods of time. Fortunately, some of this information is contained in the Guskey and Gates review, though it is sometimes based on very few studies. Their findings appear in Tables 2.1, 2.2, and 2.3.

As is clear from Table 2.1, mastery learning ideas seem to work better for elementary school students than secondary ones and for secondary students than tertiary ones. Even for tertiary students, however, their effects are still strong.

TABLE 2.1. LFM EFFECT SIZE BY GRADE LEVEL

Level	Grades	Number of Studies	Mean Effect Size
Elementary	1–8	13	.95
High School	9–12	12	.72
College	13+	10	.65

Source: Guskey and Gates, 1985, p. 55.

TABLE 2.2. LFM EFFECT SIZE BY SUBJECT

Subject Area	Number of Studies	Mean Effect Size
Science	9	.49
Mathematics	20	.72
Social studies	8	.72
Language arts	9	.77
Psychology	4	.83

Source: Guskey and Gates, 1985, p. 56.

TABLE 2.3. LFM EFFECT SIZE BY DURATION OF STUDY

Duration	Number of Studies	Mean Effect Size
1 week	6	.93
2–12 weeks	14	.76
13+ weeks	15	.74

Source: Guskey and Gates, 1985, p. 57.

Guskey and Gates offer two possible explanations for these differential grade-level effects. One involves learning histories. They argue that elementary students simply do not have as long a history of acquired learning deficiencies to correct as secondary and especially tertiary students. The problem with this interpretation, however, is that one would expect tertiary students to be some of the best of the secondary school graduates. They should be relatively free of these deficiencies.

Their second, and more reasonable, explanation is that LFM strategies are simply more effective for elementary school students and learning conditions. As Guskey and Gates note, several studies have shown that elementary school students seem to need more direct guidance from their teachers to establish an appropriate learning pace. LFM provides such guidance. Elementary school teachers and administrators, on the whole, also often seem to have a somewhat clearer view of what they want their students to master, a somewhat greater openness to new ideas about how to teach for mastery, and a somewhat greater commitment to mastery in all their students' learning than their secondary or tertiary school counterparts.

In Table 2.2 we also find that LFM strategies work better in some subjects than others. Their effects in mathematics (basic, general, and consumer math; matrix and regular algebra; geometry), social studies (social studies, economics, government, history, and humanities), and language arts (English grammar and vocabulary; reading; foreign language) are generally in the range of .72 to .77. Only in science (biology and chemistry) do they fall off to .49.

At first glance these findings provide some fuel for critics (such as Cronbach, 1972) who have long contended that mastery learning ideas simply cannot work as well in open and relatively unstructured curriculum areas such as science. This fuel should be handled carefully, though.

First, as Guskey and Gates note, there is evidence that the relatively low effect sizes in science may be an artifact of grade-level differences. Almost all the science studies were conducted at the secondary and tertiary levels, where, as we have seen, the effect size for mastery learning is weaker.

Second, if mastery learning does not work as well in open and unstructured areas such as science, why did it work well in social studies? There is a considerable amount of openness and lack of structure (sequence) in this curriculum area, too.

Third, even the somewhat weaker science effects are still comparatively large effects. Willett, Yamashita, and Anderson (1983), for example, report an average effect size of only .07 for "instructional systems" in science, an instructional system being defined as a "general plan for conducting a course over an extended system of time." The systems examined included audio-tutorial instruction, computer-based instruction, individualized instruction, LFM, PSI, programmed instruction, and team teaching, among others. Mastery learning, by the way, demonstrated the largest effect size—.50—of all these systems.

Obviously, given the current interest in science, the issue of mastery learning in science bears more study. Some of the earliest research in mastery learning was conducted in science (see, for example, Okey, 1974; Walbesser & Carter, 1968), and mastery learning has attracted many science teachers' attention (see, for instance, Dunkleberger & Heikkinen, 1983). But there has not been much follow-up, and there should be more. After all, mastery learning proponents have long proposed that the real power of mastery learning should lie in its capacity to help teachers of open and unstructured subjects such as science to become clearer about their instructional objectives and more systematic in attaining them (see White, 1979, for example). Walberg (1985) estimates, in fact, that mastery learning effect sizes of .80 or more may become routine in science.

Finally, in Table 2.3 we find that mastery learning's effect size does seem to depend on the duration of the project. Short-term studies produced larger effect sizes than long-term ones.

Again, Guskey and Gates offer several explanations. One is the novelty of the mastery instruction. As any administrator, teacher, or student knows, enthusiasm for and fidelity to a given instructional innovation usually begins high and then fades. But if only novelty is the explanation for mastery learning's larger short-run achievement effects, why have not other recent instructional innovations had similar large short-term effects? After all, some practitioners have repeatedly suggested that many of our teaching techniques are far less novel than many of our competitors'. Indeed, they perceive mastery learning as nothing more than time-honored techniques of good teaching.

Another of their explanations is the novelty of the subject matter. In the shorter mastery learning studies, students were taught new and unfamiliar school topics, for example, matrix arithmetic or imaginary science. In the longer studies, though, they were taught more traditional ones such as reading and mathematics. Consequently, students would have entered the former subjects under conditions that have long been hospitable to mastery learning. That is, they would have come to them intellectually fresh and eager to learn. But, once again, if the novelty of the subject matter is the explanation for mastery learning's larger short-run effects, why would other instructional innnovations not have had similar effects on the same novel subjects? Merrill, Barton, and Wood (1970), for example, taught the same imaginary science used in Arlin's (1973) mastery learning research and did not have similar learning effects.

Accordingly, let us offer a third explanation for the stronger short-term effects of mastery learning. Whereas Guskey and Gates's explanations focus on issues of *innovation*, ours focuses on issues of *institutionalization*. As tough as innovation of ideas and practices is, institutionalization is tougher (Miles, 1983). We suspect that many of the longer-term mastery learning studies may have fallen into the some of the usual traps encountered in institutionalizing any educational idea—lack of energy and commitment, lack of resources and technical assistance, or change of key personnel. Shorter-term studies (especially doctoral dissertations), of course, are often calibrated and monitored to avoid these traps. Teachers, for instance, are typically given time to plan and often conduct this planning on school time. In the longer-term studies, they must find this time on their own. We shall return to this issue of innovation versus institutionalization repeatedly, so keep it in mind.

Taken as a whole, therefore, Guskey and Gates's specific achievement findings add an important practical footnote to the more general research on student achievement. This footnote should alert you to the fact that although mastery learning has had strong general effects on student achievement, its effects have been stronger in some subjects, at some grade levels, and over some time periods than others. Issues of subject matter, grade levels, and duration should therefore be of concern in getting your mastery program off the ground. Based on the available data, you should expect the effects of mastery learning to be stronger in the elementary grades than the secondary or tertiary, in language arts, math, and social studies than in sciences, and in shorter subjects than longer ones.

That such issues can be effectively addressed and that mastery learning strategies can have compelling long-term and short-term effects on students achievement at the elementary and secondary school levels and in all subject matter areas is evident in the following example. It comes from Johnson City, a largely blue-collar district near Binghamton, New York. Johnson City Central Schools have been implementing mastery learning ideas and practices for some 15 years. Over the course of these years, school staff have been able to implement mastery learning district-wide in all subjects at the elementary, middle, and secondary levels.

The elementary program has been totally validated by the National Diffusion Network and adopted by nine districts from the states of Virginia, New York, Michigan, Texas, and Utah. Indeed, since about 1980 in mathematics and 1982 in reading, at least 75% of elementary students have been at 6 or more months above grade level on standardized achievement tests, compared to only about 42% in mathematics and 37% in reading when the project started (see Table 2.4 for some recent test data). And usually the elementary district continues to make achievement gains not only from year to year but from grade level to grade level.

Johnson City's secondary program is also being considered for total validation across subject matters. Currently, some 80% of the district's secondary students, compared to 44% statewide, receive New York State Regent's Honors Examination Certificates in tested subjects.

Retention.   So far we have seen that mastery learning has a positive effect on student achievement, though the size of its effect seems to vary with grade level, subject, and study duration. Much of school learning is cumulative, however, in the sense that the things that students learn at one point must often be used at later points. And it simply does not follow that if a student has mastered the material once, it will be available later (Brownell, 1948). No school person is unaware of the forgetting that occurs not only over the summer but over vacation, between grading periods, over weekends, and sometimes overnight!

A second important criterion by which we can review the mastery learning research, therefore, is retention. Are mastery-taught students, compared to others, better at retrieving past information when needed for

TABLE 2.4. CALIFORNIA ACHIEVEMENT TEST RESULTS FOR JOHNSON CITY, NEW YORK

Grade	National Norm	1977	1978	1979	1980	1981	1982	1983	1984	1985	1986	1987
Reading												
1	1.8	1.7	1.9	2.0	1.9	2.1	2.1	2.1	2.2	2.3	2.2	2.1
2	2.8	3.0	3.0	3.2	3.1	3.1	3.2	3.4	3.6	3.4	3.8	3.2
3	3.8	4.1	4.1	4.1	3.9	4.0	4.1	4.5	4.2	4.4	4.7	5.6
4	4.8	5.5	5.7	5.6	5.7	5.7	5.6	5.8	5.8	6.3	6.3	6.1
5	5.8	6.6	6.7	7.3	7.8	7.6	7.1	7.0	7.2	6.9	7.5	7.6
6	6.8	7.7	8.3	8.0	8.1	8.5	8.3	8.3	8.2	8.4	8.6	8.6
7	7.8	8.7	8.8	9.3	9.4	9.7	10.0	10.0	10.0	9.6	10.0	9.4
8	8.8	10.1	10.0	10.2	10.8	10.6	11.0	11.1	11.1	10.7	10.6	10.4
Math												
1	1.8	1.8	2.1	2.2	2.0	2.1	2.2	2.3	2.4	2.6	2.5	2.3
2	2.8	· 3.2	3.3	3.5	3.3	3.3	3.2	3.3	3.4	3.4	3.5	3.1
3	3.8	4.1	4.3	4.4	4.3	4.4	4.3	4.6	4.4	4.6	4.7	5.6
4	4.8	5.3	5.6	5.8	5.7	5.5	5.4	5.5	5.9	5.9	6.2	6.0
5	5.8	7.0	6.8	7.4	7.5	5.5	5.4	5.5	5.9	7.2	7.5	8.2
6	6.8	7.5	8.2	8.0	8.1	8.4	8.2	8.1	8.1	8.3	8.7	9.1
7	7.8	8.5	9.0	9.3	9.2	10.0	10.0	9.8	10.0	9.4	9.9	12.9
8	8.8	10.7	10.0	11.1	12.5	11.9	12.5	12.5	12.5	11.6	11.1	12.3

Source: Vickery, 1987, p. 3.

future applications? After all, achievement retention theory suggests that they should be, simply because they learned it better in the first place (Block, 1974a).

There have been fewer studies of student retention than of achievement. The Block and Burns and Guskey and Gates reviews contain the basic findings. The former reports results from seven studies, the latter from four. Since three of these studies were common to both reviews, the net number of retention studies is eight.

These few studies are also favorable to mastery learning methods. In virtually every one, the retention scores of the mastery students are, on average, greater than those of the nonmastery students. Indeed, Block and Burns report an effect size of .67 based on both LFM and PSI studies, and Guskey and Gates report one of .62 for LFM studies alone. Though these effects sizes are somewhat smaller than for achievement, they are still considerable. They suggest that a 50th-percentile student could be moved to the 73rd to 75th percentile in retention using mastery methods.

These general effect sizes are again influenced, though, by a whole series of specific factors, especially the length of the retention interval. Whereas Block and Burns (1976), and Block (1974a) even earlier still, have reported studies in which learning for mastery helped prevent forgetting for several weeks to several months, Guskey and Gates (1986) find that this prevention effect weakens somewhat over time. Retention effect sizes range from about .62 over a 2-week period to about .52 over a 4-month one for elementary and secondary school students. Still, 2 weeks corresponds to the length of many major holidays in the public school calendar, and 4 months is more than the length of the summer vacation.

So even though their retention effects wear off somewhat over time, mastery methods still appear to be one potent way to prevent students from forgetting. Obviously, more studies of student retention are needed before educators rush to use mastery methods as one way to stem the "brain drain" that so frequently occurs over most major school breaks. Studies that vary the retention intervals to break periods common to schools, particularly overnight, weekends, national holidays, and summer vacation, are especially needed.

Transfer.   As important as student achievement and retention are in their own right as indices of student learning, these days most public school educators are interested in them for other reasons. They are interested in achievement and retention because of what they portend about student transfer of learning. Educators believe they signal the students' capacity to take what they have learned and eventually to apply it elsewhere in school and in life.

Transfer, however, is typically the criterion of student learning least used in evaluating the impact of various instructional strategies (Brownell, 1948). This statement is as true for mastery strategies as for others. Still, a few transfer studies exist. These studies test mastery students' ability to apply their achievements to the solution of new problems or learning. They also test LFM's capacity to teach the higher-order critical thinking skills widely assumed to be essential for new problem solving or learning.

Block (1974b), for example, reported three studies in which mastery learning transfer effects were experimentally tested. These were studies of listening comprehension of Spanish for nonnative Spanish-speaking sixth graders by Smith (1968), of matrix arithmetic concepts for eighth graders by Block (1972), and of upper-division history for college undergraduates by Block and Tierney (1974). In each study there were positive transfer effects, but only if students were held to "high" mastery performance standards throughout their learning. We shall say more about what we consider "high" in Chapter 4.

Block (1974b) and Guskey (1985a) also report two additional studies wherein mastery learning transfer effects were explored as part of larger evaluation studies. In the first of these studies, Walbesser and Carter (1968) examined the cumulative impact of the first 4 years of a mastery learning curriculum project in science. Specifically, they compared the effects of exposure to the kindergarten program on grade 1 learning, of exposure to the kindergarten and grade 1 programs on grade 2 learning, and of exposure to the kindergarten, grade 1, and grade 2 programs on grade 3 learning. Mastery learning had positive effects on students' future learning. While much cumulative mastery learning was better than less, some was better than none.

In the second of these studies, McDonald (1982) evaluated the effects of the New York City schools' Mastery Learning Program. He found that mastery classes scored 3 to 4 times higher on statewide Regents Honors Diploma examinations than similar nonmastery classes in the same subject at the same school. These tests were designed to measure higher-level thinking skills—problem solving, applying, analyzing, synthesizing, and evaluating, skills long believed to be key for future learning.

Studies by Block and Tierney (1974), Anderson (1976a), Glasnapp, Poggio, and Ory (1975), and Poggio (1976) have also experimentally studied whether mastery learning strategies can be used to teach these higher-level skills. Their findings are mixed. Apparently, the strategies can be used successfully. There are some real questions, however, whether the positive results on locally constructed tests would be replicated on standardized tests of problem solving or concept learning (see Anderson, 1976a). There are also questions as to whether the positive higher-level learning can be retained over several months (see Poggio, 1976).

Less mixed are the findings of a recent study by one of Bloom's students, Zemira Mevarech (n.d.; see also her similar 1980 study). In this study, groups of fifth graders were taught either by tutoring, LFM, or conventional group-based instructional techniques. Half learned lower-order mental processing skills such as answering knowledge questions asked by the instructor, using mechanical problem-solving strategies, and answering lower-order mental process test items. The other half learned higher-order skills such as answering application and analysis questions, engaging in heuristic reasoning, and answering higher-order mental process test items.

Mevarech's results indicated that the mastery-taught students performed only slightly less well than the tutored students and much better than conventionally taught students on a final examination testing for both lower- and higher-order mental processes. Indeed, they achieved both lower- and higher-order mental processes, on the average, at a level above approximately 90% of the students who received the conventional, nonmastery instruction. Moreover, they did so regardless of whether their mastery instruction was targeted toward lower- or higher-order thinking. Apparently, mastery methods can promote better higher-order mental processing even if the curriculum does not.

Even with studies such as Mevarech's, though, there are still too few studies to permit any solid conclusions about the student transfer effects of mastery learning programs. The transfer issue, like retention, demands more study. Clearly, unless one makes the drastic assumption that the exams used in most of the research test for just lower-order thinking skills, it is hard to believe that mastery students can attain such comparatively high degrees of achievement and retention without engaging in higher-order thinking. Perhaps projected projects on the use of mastery learning ideas to teach for critical thinking, problem solving, and other higher-order skills will provide some answers. We are thinking especially of those in East Islip, New York (W. J. Smith, personal communication, 1987), and Baltimore County, Maryland (J. D. Kozlovsky, personal communication, 1986).

Variability in Learning

As we have seen, mastery learning raises student achievement and may improve retention and transfer of learning. In short, mastery learning seems to affect student learning regardless of how it is measured.

But central to the theory is the hypothesis that mastery learning can also generate less variability in learning. Obviously, if mastery learning only increased the average level of student learning but did not decrease the variability, we might have a situation such as in Figure 2.2. Here, the absolute level of learning has increased for all mastery students, but some students are still learning poorly relative to others. This comparative poorness in learning might have the same negative emotional consequences as it does in conventional nonmastery instruction (Bloom, 1971). The question, then, is can these "poorer" students be taught to learn more like

Before   After

Figure 2.2. Hypothetical achievement distribution before and after mastery learning (Adapted from Idstein, 1984, p. 12)

Figure 2.3. Hypothetical achievement distribution before and after mastery learning (Adapted from Block & Anderson, 1975, p. 7)

their "better" classmates? Can mastery learning help reduce the variability in learning excellence? And can it do so without dragging the "better" students down? If it can, Figure 2.2 should start to look like Figure 2.3.

Unfortunately, only the decade-old Block and Burns (1976) review has directly addressed the question of variability in student learning under mastery learning conditions. Their data, based on 4 studies and 10 comparisons, hint that such conditions can reduce the spread in learning between the best and the poorest students. In particular, mastery students exhibited less variability in their achievement about 74% of the time and in their retention about 85%. How much less? Block and Burns judge it to be about 52% and 53%, respectively.

For the reader for whom such numbers have no practical meaning, let us give two concrete examples of what increased student learning and decreased variability in learning may mean for your school or district. Example 1 comes from a rural elementary school of 950 students in a small Texas border town. The exact site must remain anonymous. Suffice it to say that 65% of its students are Mexican-American, 6% are black, and 29% are Anglo. Most of these students come from low-income homes (58%) and have limited English proficiency (60%).

In Figure 2.4 we have recorded the quartile distributions of student achievement on the California Test of Basic Skills for grade 1 students in reading, language, and mathematics prior to (1982–1983) and following (1983–1986) the implementation of mastery learning. Note how the distributions change under mastery learning conditions. Not only did mastery techniques raise the average levels of student achievement in all three areas, but they also homogenized student achievement around these high levels. Whereas in 1982–1983 about 1 out of every 3 students was *below*

38

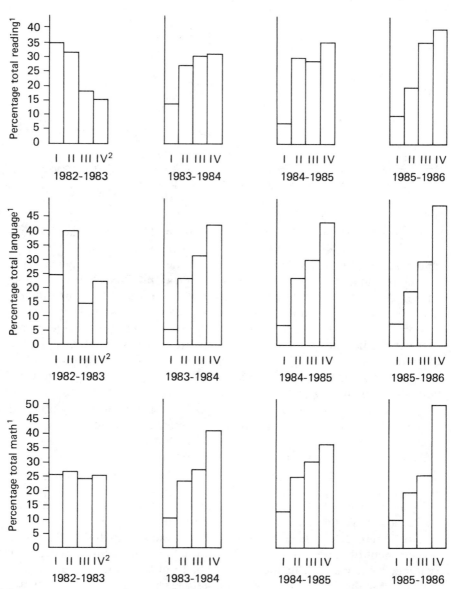

[1]California Test of Basic Skills
[2]I = First quartile (1-25); II = Second quartile (26-50); III = Third quartile (51-75);
IV = Fourth quartile (76-99)

Figure 2.4. Some achievement results in a bilingual school

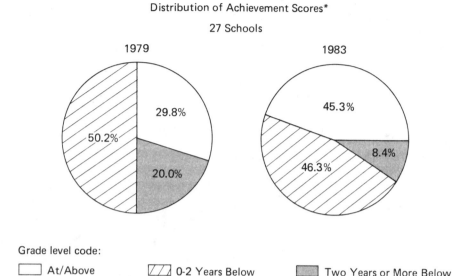

Distribution of Achievement Scores*

27 Schools

Grade level code:

☐ At/Above   ▨ 0-2 Years Below   ▧ Two Years or More Below

*California Achievement Test; Form D; results presented without limited English proficiency students

Figure 2.5. California Achievement Test results for District 19, Brooklyn, New York (Adapted from Mastery Education Corp., 1985)

the 50th percentile in reading and language and 1 out of 2 in mathematics, by 1985–1986 about 3 out of every 4 students were *above* it in all three areas. Likewise, whereas about 1 out of 4 to 7 students was in the top quartile in each subject in 1982–1983, about 1 out of 2 or 3 was there by 1985–1986.

Example 2 comes from a large urban school district in New York City. District 19, Brooklyn, is the city's third largest district. It serves nearly 25,000 students, most of whom are black or Hispanic, through 21 elementary and 6 intermediate schools.

In Figure 2.5 we have reproduced the distribution of achievement scores for the district prior to the implementation of mastery learning ideas in reading and 4 years later. Interestingly, these scores have been attained using the unjustly maligned Chicago Mastery Learning Reading program. Note the shrinkage of the proportion of students below and far below grade level.

Though we know it is dangerous to draw inferences from just two cases, both of these examples suggest an intriguing scenario for schools and districts that might choose to try mastery learning. The increases in student learning and the decreases in variability in learning under mastery conditions should lead to several consequences:

- An increase in the proportion of students reaching higher percentiles or grade levels in their learning
- A decrease in the proportion of students remaining at lower percentiles or grade levels in their learning
- The chance for greater excellence in learning for a larger proportion of the students, especially blacks and Hispanics

Moreover, these effects should be apparent on standardized tests as well as locally constructed ones. (See also Table 2.4.)

Some colleagues, confronted with data as in Figures 2.4 and 2.5, raise an important caveat. They wonder whether such reductions in the variability of student learning have not come at a very dear price. While they acknowledge that mastery learning ideas do seem to help traditionally "poorer" students to learn more like their "better" classmates, they intimate that perhaps the best students have been "held back" and not allowed to distance themselves from their weaker academic peers (see, for example, Good & Stipek, 1983). Either the better students have not been allowed to proceed as fast as they might, or they have not been given tests that reflect their greater learning. Since we will address the student learning rate issue shortly, let us deal with the test ceiling issue here.

There is probably some truth to the charge that certain of the reductions in the variability of mastery students' learning have been due to test ceiling phenomena. We are not convinced, though, that all of them can be so easily explained away. Our doubts stem from a rather elegant Australian study that evaluated the effects of mastery learning on early elementary school students' reading comprehension.

Chan (1981) used Rasch item analysis procedures to create essentially ceilingless tests of achievement and retention in reading comprehension. By ceilingless we mean that students could score as high as they desired; there were no arbitrary score limits set beyond which they could not proceed. These tests were then used to evaluate the effects of learning for mastery under higher and lower mastery performance standards. Her results showed that learning for mastery produced greater student achievement and retention *and* less variability in achievement and retention than conventional nonmastery instruction on these essentially ceilingless tests. Apparently, learning for mastery had helped poorer students to learn more like better ones, and these results were not an artifact of the tests.

Learning Rate

So far we have seen that mastery learning apparently affects both the level and the variability in student learning. These days, however, many educators are concerned not only that more students learn well but fast, too. Since time to learn has always been at the heart of the theory and practice, let us now examine the effects of mastery learning on student learning rates. Once again, some history is in order.

One of the earliest mastery learning propositions was that virtually all students could learn, given sufficient time. While many practitioners interpreted this proposition to mean that they ought to accept individual differences in student learning rates as a given and to build instructional systems that allowed for individual rates of progress (for example, self-paced or continuous-progress programs), Bloom's earliest mastery learning protégés took a different tack. They began to explore whether these rates could be altered so that all students could still be taught for mastery using ordinary group-based, teacher-paced classroom techniques. This meant bringing the learning rate of "slow" students up to that of the "fast" ones, that is, reducing the ratio of individual differences in learning rates between fast and slow students from roughly 6 to 1 to about 1 to 1.

To this end, Block (1970), Anderson (1973), Marshall Arlin (1973), and William Garner (1973) began to examine the total time costs of learning for mastery. They also began to explore what economists call the *marginal* time costs, the time it takes students to master the next unit of instruction, given prior mastery of earlier units. Educational economists had long realized that there are always some fixed time costs in getting any instructional innovation off the ground. Bloom's students' concern, therefore, was whether the fixed time costs of starting to implement mastery learning would eventually pay off. Marginal time costs were one way to explore this payoff issue. Anderson (1973, 1975, 1976b) began to make some crucial distinctions between elapsed time to learn and active time to learn. These distinctions would later lead to notions of "time on task," "academic learning time," "allocated learning time," "opportunity to learn," and other concepts central to mastery time research (see, for example, Bloom, 1974).

This research hinted that mastery learning could improve student learning and student learning rates as well. Specifically, it indicated that the early and consistent use of mastery learning procedures could eventually help slower students to learn more like faster ones. Indeed, the research hinted that individual differences in learning rates might be cut from about 6 to 1 to about 1.25 to 1 (Block, 1974a). These cuts occurred because mastery learning seemed to press slower students, like their faster classmates, to spend sufficient time on task.

On the basis of these findings and after almost a decade of claiming that mastery learning could only help most students learn *better*, Bloom began to claim that their consistent use could also help them learn *faster*. This shift in his thinking was well captured in the preface to Bloom's (1976) book *Human Characteristics and School Learning*:

When I first entered the field of educational research and measurement, the prevailing construct was:

1. There are good learners and there are poor learners

This was considered to be a relatively permanent attribute of the individual. It was also the prevailing view that individuals possessed it in different amounts and that a quantitative index of it could be made by the use of an appropriate intelligence, aptitude, or achievement test. Furthermore, it was believed that good learners could learn the more complex and abstract ideas, while poor learners could learn only the simplest and most concrete ideas. School systems throughout the world have been organized on the basis of this construct and the selection systems, grading systems, and even the curriculum has been built on the basis of it.

During the early 1960s, some of us became interested in the Carroll Model of School learning, which was built on the construct:

2. There are faster learners and there are slower learners

While we were not entirely clear whether or not rate of learning was a permanent trait of individuals, we dedicated ourselves to finding ways by which the slower learners could be given the extra time and help they needed to attain some criterion of achievement. In this research, in both educational laboratories as well as classrooms in different nations, it became evident that a large proportion of slower learners may learn as well as faster learners. When the slower learners do succeed in attaining the same criterion of achievement as faster learners, they appear to be able to learn equally complex and abstract ideas, they can apply these ideas to new problems, and they can retain the ideas equally well—in spite of the fact that they learned with more time and help than was given to others. Furthermore, their interests and attitudes toward the school subjects in which they attain the achievement criterion are as positive as those of faster learners.

During the past decade, my students and I have done research which has led us to the view that:

3. Most students become very similar with regard to learning ability, rate of learning, and motivation for further learning—when provided with favorable learning conditions

This research questions the first two constructs, especially about the permanence of good-poor learning ability or fast-slow learning characteristics. However, the research does demonstrate that when students are provided with unfavorable learning conditions, they become even more dissimilar with regard to learning ability, rate of learning, and motivation for further learning. (pp. ix–x)

Despite recent data that continue to show that student learning rate is an alterable characteristic under mastery learning conditions (see, for example, Guskey & Gates, 1985), critics continue to contend the reverse.

As one colleague put it in a conversation at a national educational research meeting, "There are fast kids and slow kids and you can't do anything about it. Bloom's learning rate proposition is just plain wrong, and anyone who believes it is not playing with a full deck."

To be sure, some of this criticism had been expected and came from respected scholars such as Cronbach who had a long history of questions regarding mastery learning (see Cronbach & Snow, 1977). What had not been expected was similar criticisms within the mastery learning movement itself. The rallying point for this fire has been the notion that mastery learning "holds back" the faster students.

One of the most articulate proponents of this theory has been Bloom's former student Arlin. He contends that both Bloom and Block have neglected the real time issue in mastery learning. Mastery strategies must trade *depth*, the "degree, level, or intensity of learning," for *breadth*, the "amount or extent of learning" (Arlin, 1982, p. 335). This trade-off makes the learning rates of students different, not similar, over time, and creates a condition constantly "requiring the teacher's managerial consideration" (p. 339). He writes:

> The positive gains evidenced in most mastery learning programs come mainly from continually providing greater amounts of learning time for students who are experiencing problems or difficulties. This time spent helping the slower students essentially holds back the learning rate of the better students. And even if the rates of the slowest and fastest students can be eventually made equal, still the differential amount of time spent early on slow relative to fast learners seems unconscionable. (p. 351)

Another articulate proponent of the "hold back" theory has been S. Alan Cohen (1983), a leading individually based, self-paced mastery learning advocate. He charges that Bloom, Block, and Anderson have fundamentally misinterpreted Carroll's model:

> Perhaps no other component of mastery learning generates as much intrafamily strife as the issue of differentiating instructional time. Within the mastery learning family are those who insist that mastery learning is by definition a group-taught pedagogy, and differentiating instructional time is merely a matter of organizing classrooms in the traditional modes. Students are grouped for instruction (canaries, pigeons, vultures—three different rates). Stragglers are picked up rather haphazardly with individual attention. Eventually real time emerges dominant; a whistle is blown and some must flunk.
>
> Accepting the traditional classroom organizational structure avoids the realities of differentiated learning rates that have always plagued the teacher even before Mastery Learning entered the educator's vocabulary.

Exactly how the teacher matches allowed time to individual variations in required time so that every student learns everything required, and at the same time presents lessons to 30 students (or three groups of ten students) is blatantly ignored by Bloom. The same issue is obfuscated, perhaps sidestepped, by Block and Anderson in the original exposition of Mastery Learning (Block & Anderson, 1975). There is no question that the University of Chicago group originally perceived Mastery Learning as an approach that fit the time-based, assignment-driven (Spady, 1981) graded and group-taught American school. And it is understandable that those who view Mastery Learning as beginning with the work of Bloom's students think of Mastery Learning as a procedure that differentiates, but "not too much." (pp. 21–22)

What does some of the most recent mastery learning data say about the brouhaha over Bloom's learning rate proposition? Does mastery learning necessarily hobble the fast students while helping the slow? Several studies have focused on the hold-back issue.

Arlin (1982) makes perhaps the strongest case that LFM techniques hold back faster students. He turns to some data from one of his own mastery implementation studies in 7 schools and 10 classrooms from two semirural school districts in south-central British Columbia. These data, he contends, clearly show that "differences between the fast and slow learners remained stable across time" and "the extra time needed to bring slower students to mastery remained stable across the course of time" (Arlin, 1984, p. 116). Arlin writes elsewhere:

Under mastery learning depth is constrained at mastery levels, so there are fewer variables that can be adjusted to accommodate individual differences in aptitude. Individual differences . . . are reflected primarily in differences in learning time or finishing rates. The primary focus of the teachers' managerial concerns was directed toward keeping the faster students meaningfully occupied while assisting slower students in their review toward mastery. Student cooperation may have been achieved because slower students felt that instruction and the teacher's attention were directed toward them. Faster students did not seem to object to missed learning opportunities. Even when teachers abandoned their "enrichment activities," the basis of the cooperation of the faster learners seemed to be an implicit arrangement by the teacher—"If you're quiet and don't bother me or the rest of the class, you can do what you want with your free time." Although the workable environment may be different in the mastery case, it may be achieved in both cases at the expense of faster students. A workable environment seemed to be achieved by timing instruction to the needs of students with lower aptitude. (Arlin, 1982, pp. 351–352)

Three other studies come to a different conclusion, however. The first is an experimental study conducted, surprisingly, by Cohen (see Cohen, Hyman, & Stone, 1985). Cohen and colleagues taught low, average, and gifted junior high school graduates Feuerstein's (1980) adolescent thinking skills program under group-based mastery learning conditions. They then observed learning rate differentials between the fastest and slowest students across a sequence of learning units. Students had been intellectually and emotionally equated so that any observed learning rate trends had to be primarily due to their learning for mastery.

As one might expect, on the earliest units, individual differences in learning rate immediately appeared, with some students learning much faster than others. But much to the researchers' surprise, as the mastery learning procedures took hold, so did the Bloom learning rate hypothesis. By the last units of the course, the learning rates for the initially faster and slower students had become almost identical.

The second study is an evaluation of Philadelphia's highly successful mastery learning program (see, for example, Conner et al., 1985). As part of their evaluation for the 1982–1983 school year, project developers looked into the question "But what about the top students?" A comparison was made of the performance of the top five and the bottom five students entering each of some 22 Chapter 1 first- through sixth-grade classes. Their data did not reveal a hold-back effect. The best-prepared students averaged more than a year's growth, a third of them more than a year and a half. Virtually none of them fell back in their learning, and 2% even increased it.

The final study is also an evaluation of a mastery learning program, conducted by Fitzpatrick and Charters (1986). Block (1983), in a essay review of Arlin's research, had been especially critical of the fidelity of his staff development procedures. He raised the possibility that Arlin's findings were an artifact of sloppy classroom implementation. So Fitzpatrick and Charters paid special attention to this issue and developed a research-based Time for Mastery staff development program that concentrated on classroom management and organizational issues. They then tried the program with 40 secondary teachers from 10 schools and 6 districts and observed the differences it made in their teaching.

Their data led them to conclude that mastery teachers could help "slow" students to learn like the "fast" and still not rob the "fast" students of appropriate learning opportunities. For example, they found, contrary to Arlin, that with appropriate staff development, teachers did not have to shorten their original instruction so as to provide appropriate time for feedback or correction—indeed, they could allocate more time. They also found that teachers could do a significant amount of the correction in class and that teachers did not have to keep the "faster" learners simply "busy" while this correction occurred but could enrich their learning.

In short, their results indicated that teachers did not have to adopt a "Robin Hood" philosophy to teach "slow" and "fast" students for mastery. They write:

> Our results suggest that instructional time within a group-based instructional setting can be positively altered to accommodate implementation of the principles of mastery learning without sacrificing the amount of content presented and without placing one group of students at a disadvantage while increasing the benefits of instruction for others.... The combination of the research findings on classroom management and on the principles of mastery learning appears to offer teachers a set of effective and efficient strategies that can enable them to assist all their students in achieving higher levels of mastery of their learning within the scheduling and time constraints of most secondary school classrooms. (Fitzpatrick & Charters, 1986, pp. 75–78)

What, then, can we really say regarding mastery learning's effects on student learning rates? While we are inclined to say that the "hold back" theory for explaining mastery learning's equalizing effects on students' learning rates is shaky, let us demur. Instead, let us echo the substantive, practical, and ethical observations of Cohen, Hyman, and Stone (1985) on the whole issue. Substantively speaking, they contend that "the relevant literature is long on opinion and inference and short on empirical data derived from directly testing the proposition" (p. 2).

Practically speaking, they point out that even if Bloom's proposition holds, there are serious issues involved in the real-life school learning environment where teachers implement mastery learning:

> That environment has already confounded the affective and cognitive status of the lower achievers who are suddenly subjected to mastery learning strategies, and the results often contradict the Bloom proposition, not because it is invalid, but because typical school conditions have already affected the confounding. It is highly unlikely that affective patterns of "failure" and "superiority" are so easily and quickly eradicated with the implementation of a mastery learning program. It is equally unlikely that the typical mastery learning sequence is as tight and as valid as the Feuerstein curriculum used in the present study. (p. 4)

And ethically speaking, they note:

> On the one hand, the gap between faster and slower learners exacerbates the general social problem of haves vs. have nots. Across the broad range

of factors that define the disadvantaged social status of have nots, this school achievement discrepancy contributes significantly to locking them permanently into their disadvantaged condition. Thus, anything that helps reduce the gap contributes to the amelioration of a serious social and human problem.

On the other hand, consciously curtailing the faster learner's pace while the lower achiever catches up, and doing this for the "common good," poses an ethical dilemma of real import. This dilemma is not a hypothetical issue; it involves decisions curriculum designers face when deciding how to structure mastery learning programs. (pp. 3–4)

We shall return to the practical aspects of these comments later in this chapter and again in Chapter 4 and to the ethical aspects in Chapter 5. Suffice it to say now that the question of mastery learning's impact on student learning rates remains an open and highly controversial issue. That mastery learning can help more students learn better is relatively clear, but whether it can do so without practically or ethically holding back the learning of so called "better," "faster," or "more motivated" students is not. What is definitely needed in mastery learning research are more joint tests of level and variance relationships in student learning and learning rate.

Student Affect

We have seen that mastery learning programs influence student intellectual development. They seem to help most students to learn well and, perhaps, fast. But what are their side effects, especially on student emotional development? Can they promote students' interests, attitudes, self-concepts, and self-esteem? After all, the problems of emotional development engendered by non–mastery learning approaches to instruction had been the starting point for the development of the whole mastery learning idea. As Bloom (1968) wrote in his introductory paper on the subject:

Each teacher begins a new term or course with the expectation that about a third of his students will adequately learn what he has to teach. He expects about a third to fail or to just "get by." Finally, he expects another third to learn a good deal of what he has to teach, but not enough to be regarded as "good students." This set of expectations, supported by school policies and practices in grading, is transmitted to students through the grading procedures and through the methods and materials of instruction. This sytem creates a self-fulfilling prophecy such that the final sorting of students through the grading process becomes approximately equivalent to the original expectations.

This set of expectations, which fixes the academic goals of teachers and students, is the most wasteful and destructive aspect of the present education system. It reduces the aspirations of both teachers and students, it reduces motivation for learning in students, and it systematically destroys the ego and self-concept of a sizable group of students who are legally required to attend school for ten to twelve years under conditions which are frustrating and humiliating year after year. The cost of this system in reducing opportunities for further learning and in alienating youth from both school and community at large is so great that no society can tolerate it for long. (p. 1)

Researchers have been examining the effects of mastery learning strategies on student affective development since the early 1970s. Since much of their research has already been reviewed by Block (1974a), Block and Burns (1976), Guskey and Gates (1985), and others (such as Dolan, 1986), let us again concentrate on the Block and Burns and Guskey and Gates reviews to outline the essentials. The former review examined mastery approaches' effects on students' interest in and attitudes toward the subject matter, their academic and general self-concepts, their attitudes toward cooperation in learning, their academic self-confidence, and their attitudes toward the mastery learning approach. The latter review reexamined some of Block and Burns's studies of student subject matter–related affect and academic self-concept. Moreover, it covered new studies of students' feelings toward the subject, their grade expectations, and their attributions for learning outcomes.

These reviews paint a generally favorable picture. Mastery-taught students, compared to non-mastery-taught peers, nearly always had better interest in and attitude toward the subject matter learned, better self-concept (academic and general), and higher academic self-confidence. They were also more confident of their abilities in the subject taught, felt the subject was more important, and accepted greater personal responsibility for their learning. And they had more positive attitudes toward their instruction, especially its cooperative learning aspects.

The effect sizes for these affective outcomes were positive (except in the case of "grade expectations," which was −.05), ranging from .11 to .53. Though these effect sizes are generally smaller than the aforementioned achievement and retention ones, they are still considerable. Even instructional techniques designed explicitly to foster student affective development (such as humanistic education) have had small, no, or inconsistent effects (see, for example, Simpson, 1976).

When combined with the cognitive findings, these affective findings may help address at least some of the practical issues raised by Cohen and colleagues regarding the implementation of mastery learning programs. Recall, in particular, that Cohen and coworkers posit that one major practical drawback to these programs lies in the fact that students seem to enter each phase of schooling different in terms of intellectual and emotional readiness. The cognitive and affective findings suggest that if mastery learning strategies are used early enough in the each student's career, perhaps some of these differences can be minimized.

Before we place too much stock in these affective findings, however, several research issues raised by both Block and Burns and by Guskey and Gates have to be addressed. One is that most of the studies have been so short (one to several weeks) that some affective effects may be attributable simply to the novelty of the mastery learning techniques. Longer-term studies such as those of the Philadelphia (Conner et al., 1986) and Johnson City (Vickery, 1987) public schools are sorely needed to determine whether these effects are temporary expressions of enthusiasm or more permanent ones that carry over into students' subsequent work. The second is that most of the studies have come from relatively small-scale applications of mastery learning ideas. Larger-scale studies are needed, for promising affective developments on the small scale may not imply similar developments on the larger scale (see, for example, Barker & Gump, 1964). The third is that most of the studies have focused on student affective development in only the most general sense. Welcome would be studies that concentrate on some of the more specific affective traits that mastery learning might influence. For example, mastery learning methods may have important positive effects on a student intrinsic motivational state that adults call "flow" and that students call "play" (see Block, 1984; Block & King, 1987). It would be interesting to test whether they can indeed make school learning more playlike for many students.

WHERE IS THE RESEARCH HEADED?

The past two decades of research paint an intriguing picture of the effects of mastery learning on student intellectual and emotional development. Sometimes this picture is sharp and positive, as in the case of student achievement. Sometimes it is fuzzy but positive, as in the case of student retention, transfer, variability in learning, and affect. Sometimes it is just plain fuzzy, as in the case of student learning rate. Still, the net impression is that mastery learning works rather well. Let us now examine where contemporary research is headed to make mastery learning work even better in the future. Four themes seem to capture the spirit of this research: (1) the pursuit of 2-sigma, (2) self-determination, (3) prevention, and (4) functionality.

The Pursuit of 2-Sigma

From the outset, theorists such as Bloom and Block have proposed that mastery procedures should help 90% to 95% of students learn like the best students under conventional instruction. If they are correct, these procedures should produce effect sizes on the order of 2.0. As we have just seen, however, the typical effect size falls below 1.0.

This gap between theory and data has spurred researchers to explore the kinds of ideas that must be added to mastery learning practice to generate consistent 2-sigma differences in student learning. Bloom and a new generation of University of Chicago graduate students, in particular, have been studying how to better approximate the effects of 1-to-1 tutorial instruction, where 2-sigma effects are common, under ordinary 30-to-1, group-based instructional conditions. Six ways have now been identified to make conventional group-based instruction more tutorlike (Bloom, 1984):

1. Improve student processing of conventional instruction
2. Improve instructional materials and technology
3. Improve the quality of teaching to provide effective learning cues, more equal participation and reinforcement, and systematic diagnosis and correction of errors
4. Improve the teaching of higher mental processes
5. Improve the home environment to encourage good work habits, adequate stimulation and academic guidance, language development, and academic goals
6. Control the peer group

As Jones and Spady (1985) note, mastery learning programs can be "enhanced" to generate 2-sigma effects routinely by mixing and matching any of the first four of these ways. The use of strategy 1 will help control students' "entry characteristics," while the use of strategies 2 through 4 will enhance the "quality of the mastery instruction." Not only is each of these strategies under direct educator control, but each also tends to be a relatively more powerful way of promoting student learning than strategies 5 and 6. Moreover, their systematic inclusion in mastery learning programs has repeatedly produced 2-sigma effects or better (see Bloom, 1984; Hyman & Cohen, 1979; Jones & Spady, 1985).

A variety of resources exists for routinely including these enhancements in mastery learning programs. First, there are various commercial reference books such as *Improving Student Achievement through Mastery Learning Programs* (Levine, 1985a), *Providing for Individual Differences in Student Learning: A Mastery Learning Approach* (Lee & Pruitt, 1984), and *Implementing Mastery Learning* (Guskey, 1985c). Then there are various commercial and noncommercial training manuals and programs, such as those originally assembled by Carol Barber (1985) for use in the Denver public schools, by Kathy Conner and her colleagues for the Philadelphia public schools (1980), and by James Okey and James Ciesla (1975) for the Indianapolis public schools. Next there are a host of functioning mastery learning programs such as those in Johnson City and Brooklyn, New York; Philadelphia, Pennsylvania; Baltimore County, Maryland; Mt. Prospect, Illinois; Jackson, Mississippi; Wheatland, Wyoming; Colstrip, Montana; Tok, Alaska; and Campbell, Norwalk, and Santa Barbara, California. And, naturally, there are people. Beau Jones and her colleagues (1985), for example, provide a wealth of information about the improvement of instructional materials. Richard Miller of the Port Hueneme, California, public schools and Robert Bortnick of Arlington Heights, Illinois, elementary schools do likewise for the integration of technology. Joan Kozlovsky of the Baltimore County, Maryland, public schools and William Smith of the East Islip, New York, public schools have interesting ideas regarding the addition of higher-order thinking skills to mastery learning programs. Conner and her colleagues in the Philadelpia public schools, Kathleen Fitzpatrick in the Mount Prospect, Illinois, school district, and Albert Mamary in Johnson City, New York, have additional ideas on how to improve student participation and reinforcement.

All of these resources are but a sample. They and others are listed in the Appendix.

Self-determination

Over the years a whole variety of explanations have been raised about why mastery learning works. Most have focused on mastery learning's effects on student's intellectual attributes. Bloom (1976) and others (such as Jones & Spady, 1985) have repeatedly argued, in particular, that mastery learning works because it consistently provides students with the cognitive characteristics necessary to enter the next unit of instruction. Not only does Bloom (1986) insist that mastery learning yields such characteristics, but he also hints, echoing an earlier discussion by Anderson and Block (1977) on the relationship between mastery and proficiency, that it makes students "automatic" in the use of these characteristics, too.

There is, however, another possible, albeit less well known, explanation for why mastery learning works. This one is more motivational than intellectual, namely, that mastery learning promotes student self-determination.

As originally developed by Deci (1980), there are two aspects to self-determination. One is competence; the other is self-control. Deci argues that a person can be competent (can do something) and yet not be under self-control (not want to do it), or vice versa.

Mastery learning has long been proposed to have effects on the development of personal competence. Indeed, Block (1978a) has developed a whole model of human competence in which mastery learning plays a central part. But that mastery learning can have similar effects on self-control is another matter. Yet central to the notion of self-control is precisely the notion of automaticity with which Bloom is currently playing.

Two lines of research should shed light on the role of mastery learning in self-determination. Obviously, one line will be the research on mastery learning and prevention. Integral to this research are concepts that bear on mastery learning's capacity to generate self-competence and self-control.

The other line will be the one now developing within the field of student motivation that concerns the impact of goal structures on student learning. These structures are "pervasive features" of classroom life that define "the goals students are to accomplish, how students are to be evaluated, and how students are to relate to each other and to the task" (Ames & Ames, 1984a, p. 535). They are of three basic types: competitive structures in which one student's winning at learning must come at the expense of another student's losing; cooperative structures in which one student's winning helps other students to win; and an individualistic structure in which one student's winning has no bearing on other students' winning or losing.

Mastery learning programs set up essentially individualistic goal structures in the classroom, structures that encourage as much student-student and student-teacher cooperation in learning as possible (see Block & Anderson, 1975). The research of Covington (1984), Nicholls (1984), and Ames and Ames (1984a, 1984b) concurs that individualistic goal structures should have great impact on elementary, secondary, and tertiary students' perceptions of self-control and self-competence.

Nicholls (1983) points out, in particular, that in individualistic structures students are primarily concerned with task mastery rather than with their comparative abilities. They find that "learning is more inherently valuable, meaningful, or satisfying, and attention is focused on the task and the strategies needed to master it rather than on the self" (p. 214), and they "choose tasks of suitable difficulty levels, perform on them effectively, ask for help when they need it, and have a continuing interest in learning" (pp. 224–225). And Ames and Ames (1984b) add that such students, rather than comparing themselves against others with regard to their learning, compare themselves against themselves and the material to be learned. They attribute their success or failure in learning to their effort rather than their ability. Instead of asking "Am I smart enough?" and "Can I do this?" they ask "Am I trying hard enough?" and "How can I do this?" Such "can do" and "want to do" attitudes are, of course, central to self-determination.

Prevention

Historically central to mastery learning research has been the concern, "If it works, so what?" (Block & Burns, 1976). Out of this concern, especially for student affective consequences, has come a growing suspicion that the real power of mastery learning may lie in its power to promote educational "wellness"—that is, the prevention as well as remediation of student emotional and intellectual difficulties.

Block (1979), in particular, has called on mastery learning researchers to begin viewing mastery learning as a preventive tool of public educational health. He writes:

> Although from the outset mastery learning theorists have been concerned with the development of talent rather than its selection, we have tended to attack only part of the talent development issue. Specifically, we have formulated our theory in terms that tell the practitioner or researcher what to do only *after* misdevelopments in learning occur. Remediation of misdevelopments, however, is only one way to develop talent. Prevention of misdevelopments in talent in the first place is another way. It is time, I believe, that we add to our present remedial formulations of mastery learning theory some new preventative ones. These new formulations would tell the practitioner and researcher what to do *before* misdevelopments in learning occur.
>
> Note that I said we must add to our present theoretical formulations. I am not saying that our current formulations are passé. Clearly, schools throughout the world have many students, especially older ones, who have already failed to learn excellently, and we must find ways to *discontinue* their failure. However, schools throughout the world also have many students, especially younger ones, who have not yet failed to learn excellently. Mastery theorists must also find ways to *continue* these students' success. (p. 117)

Central to Block's (1983) view about mastery learning and prevention is that besides producing certain student learning products such as achievement, retention, and transfer, mastery learning strategies should also produce certain learning processes. One set of these processes is what are commonly called *learning-to-learn* skills. Block has proposed, in particular, that mastery learning programs should first generate certain self-care skills so that students know that they are ultimately responsible for their own learning. These programs should also yield certain self-treatment skills, especially those of goal setting, teaching, testing, and correcting or enriching, so that students learn that they are "response-able" to take care of themselves in the absence of others. Finally, mastery learning programs should produce certain self-assessment skills so that students learn that they are "respond-able" and can gauge how they are changing not only in learning terms but also in learner ones. In short, the self-care skills generate a student who wants to learn; the self-treatment skills, one who can learn; and the self-assessment skills, one who will learn.

Block also proposes mastery learning strategies should teach so-called *learning-to-be* skills (Faure, 1972). Whereas learning-to-learn skills may be viewed as generally preparing students to learn to work, these latter skills are commonly viewed as central to their learning to play. Recent research (Block & King, 1987) indicates that from the perspective of students, most common school learning activities, especially assignments, homework, and tests, are perceived as work rather than play. That is, they are perceived as tasks that one must do, whether one wants to or not, because they are graded, rather than tasks one does not have to do but wants to do because they are fun. But as Dewey (1938) observed long ago, when you take the fun out of work, the work becomes hard labor and drudgery to most students. Block believes that unless we teach students how to find fun in their instruction, they will be forced to find fun outside it and in spite of it. Mastery learning procedures, he contends, should have the capacity to make ordinary school "work" activities seem like "play."

Solid research on mastery learning's preventive power in general, and its learning-to-learn or learning-to-be effects in particular, is just beginning to emerge. Reports of mastery learning's effects on learning-to-learn skills such as self-care, self-treatment, and self-assessment appear in DelSeni (1981), Duby (1980), and Guskey (1985a). Its effects on learning-to-be skills such as students' perceptions of their classrooms as places to work and play may now be tested with a new scale by Hartwig (1986).

We are especially awaiting the results of a large-scale test of the whole idea of mastery learning as prevention currently under way in the Baltimore public schools. Researchers from Johns Hopkins University's Prevention Intervention Research Center are exploring the long-term preventive effect of mastery learning procedures (see Dolan, 1986). Their fundamental hypothesis is that the early and successful application of mastery learning ideas can effectively immunize students against future mental health problems by teaching them certain learning-to-learn skills. These are skills of high-level self-management and self-regulation "closely related to the competencies involved in successfully coping with significant social tasks outside the school environment" (p. 23). The researchers believe that one important consequence of successful mastery learning will be

> students' obtaining a greater sense of self-efficacy concerning their in-school as well as their out-of-school behavior. Self-efficacy, as defined by Bandura (1977), points to the student's self-perception that he has the basic skills to succeed in life. The greater his sense of self-efficacy, the less vulnerable and distressed the individual feels in light of his perceived ability to cope with stress. (p. 23)

Preliminary findings after 1 year of this project are very encouraging (Dolan & Kellam, 1987).

Functionality

The final new area of mastery learning research, involving the concept of functional analysis, has evolved out of continuing concern by mastery learning pioneers, especially Anderson (1981), over growing disputes between advocates and critics over what was and was not a "true" mastery learning program of instruction. Among mastery learning advocates these disputes took the form of claims that there were right ways and wrong ways to do mastery learning and that some forms of mastery learning were simply more "faithful" than others. Among critics they took the form of charges that mastery learning was simply a special version of more general ideas in teaching. Certain critics, for example, had repeatedly charged that mastery learning was simply a rehash of old ideas in "behavioral" or "programmed" instruction (see, for example, Groff, 1974).

The net upshot of these debates was a disconcerting lack of articulation within the mastery learning movement and between this movement and other significant teaching and schooling innovations. Even within the umbrella of the Network of Outcome-based Schools, mastery learning practitioners from one camp rarely drew on the ideas and practices of another camp. And new commercial and noncommercial programs appeared without fail to lay their claim to fidelity as the best approach to mastery learning. Moreover, mastery learning advocates rarely drew on the larger field of teaching research. The net effect was that mastery ideas and practices continued to sit at the sidelines of teaching research. The recent *Third Handbook of Research on Teaching* (Wittrock, 1986), for example, gave scant attention to mastery learning at all, save as part of a chapter by Stallings and Stipek (1986).

Anderson's (1981) functional approach to understanding mastery learning is designed to stimulate this within and across movement articulation. It explicitly recognizes that there is not one right way to do mastery learning but many ways, each consistent with one's own values and each functionally accurate and effective. Rather than concentrating on teacher personality variables or teacher behaviors per se, the approach focuses on *what* teaching tasks or "functions" (see Brophy, 1981; Rosenshine, 1983) the mastery teachers must perform to improve student learning, *why* they must perform them, and *when* they must be performed. It recognizes that teaching for mastery is a craft whose execution requires the accomplishment of a specific set of tasks, with appropriate behaviors and in an appropriate sequence.

TABLE 2.5. A FUNCTIONAL ANALYSIS OF THE KEY COMPONENTS OF MASTERY LEARNING

Components	Functional Analysis
1. Assumptions and propositions	1. Estimating feasibility of proper planning and execution of program
2. Objectives, tests, teaching [and] learning activities, mastery performance standards	2. Communicating expectations to students, teachers, administrators and parents
3. Learning units	3. Teaching of new content/objectives within larger context; presenting interrelationships among content/objectives
4. Sequence of learning units	4. Teaching content/objectives which are at appropriate levels of difficulty; relating new learning to prior learning
5. Formative tests, performance standards	5. Monitoring student learning; making instructional decisions based on evidence
6. Correctives	6. Helping students overcome errors and misunderstandings before they accumulate and interfere with future learning
7. Summative tests, performance standards	7. Gathering cumulative information to use in grading students; grading relative to learning, not relative to other students

Source: Anderson, 1981, p. 2.

Table 2.5 provides Anderson's initial functional analysis of mastery learning. Note that the table provides both a rationale for the inclusion of the various components of a mastery learning program and a description of the components per se. Further note that in developing this rationale Anderson has used many ideas and concepts that are general to the field of teaching research. Rosenshine and Stevens (1986), for example, suggest that that there are six fundamental instructional functions: daily review and checking homework, presentation of new content and skills, guided student practice, feedback and correctives, independent student practice, and weekly and monthly review. Anderson (1986) proposes eight: planning instruction, assessing students, clarifying behavioral rules and routines, organizing the classroom, creating a learning set, teaching to objectives, providing student practice, and maintaining student involvement in learning and disciplining inappropriate behavior. Clearly the craft of mastery learning asks teachers, as we shall see especially in Chapter 4, to execute all of these functions in their classrooms. Various mastery learning practices differ in only *how* they execute them.

Research is just beginning to emerge analyzing mastery learning from a functional perspective. Some of it compares various features of mastery learning with features of other well-known instructional strategies such as direct instruction and cooperative learning (see, for example, Rosenshine, 1985; Slavin & Karweit, 1984). Some of it compares various features of one mastery learning program with other mastery learning programs (see, for example, Block & Burns, 1976; Hyman & Cohen, 1979). Some even compares mastery learning with effective schooling and outcome-based schooling (see, for example, Hymel, 1986). And, of course, there is Bloom's 2-sigma research, which treats mastery learning as an instructional program consisting of a series of components, each of which can be systematically enhanced to make the entire program functionally more effective.

Perhaps the best example of functional analysis in mastery learning, however, will be the remainder of this book. Herein we shall take a functional view of mastery teaching at the classroom level and of mastery administrating at the school or district level. We hope thereby to access the general literature on effective teaching, managing, and schooling as well.

SUMMARY

It is common in education to refer to students who are 2 standard deviations above their peers as being talented. And one hears much talk in educational circles these days about the development of talent. But most of these discussions focus on the development of talent in only a small part of the student body.

The past two decades of research on mastery learning has offered educators hope that there is a pool of potential learning talent in virtually all of our students that conventional approaches to instruction do not begin to touch. The next 20 years of mastery learning research may provide educators with the high human teaching technology for developing that talent in the vast majority of our students. Just as Bloom's recent work (1985) raises hope that this dream can be realized at home, contemporary mastery learning research does likewise that it can be realized at school. Functional views of teaching should yield preventive approaches to education that encourage a whole generation of students to become self-determined. Self-determined people always have and will continue to pursue 2-sigma in their learning.

CHAPTER 3

How Do I Implement Mastery Learning in My School or District?

The research findings on mastery learning are so appealing that many school administrators have been tempted to mandate its wider use. Indeed, the appeal of mastery learning is that it can turn the ordinary classroom around without turning the ordinary school or district upside down. No major organizational or structural changes, greatly increased resources, or time allotments are required to begin the process, although some special needs may develop as a program grows in size.

The literature and some unmarked graves, however, indicate the fate of programs too widely, hastily, grudgingly, or mechanistically applied. Since it will be difficult to regain the interest of school communities where this has occurred, we will recommend in this chapter a "think big, start small" approach to schoolwide and districtwide implementation that is based on voluntary participation and not fiat. At the heart of this approach will be the fundamental belief that it is the skills, judgment, and informed decision making of educators, coupled with their concern for their particular students, that make excellent and equitable learning possible. If mastery learning is viewed as an enabling approach to what educators want to accomplish as professionals and as human beings, we will have the right perspective on involving them. In this perspective, teacher-centered staff development will always take precedence over a materials-based curriculum development.

Our voluntary, teacher-centered, "think big, start small" approach to staff development will require that each implementer have sufficient understanding of mastery learning to begin to transfer it into his or her own setting and sufficient willingness to "tinker" with it until convinced it will work or will not work. This suggests an incremental, evolutionary approach to schoolwide and districtwide adoption of mastery learning.

Just as we shall see that the practice of mastery learning has been strengthened by new findings on effective teaching, so has the implementation of mastery learning on a wider scale been informed by the research and practice in outcome-based education and effective schooling, leadership, and staff development. These implementation experiences indicate that a change toward mastery learning can begin anywhere in a system, but it must eventually root itself and become part of the belief system and behavioral norms of an individual school if it is to survive and grow.

This chapter is therefore addressed to anyone in or near a school system who wants to promote high achievement for virtually all students, regardless of background. We draw on research and practice in outcome-based education and in effective schooling, leadership, and staff development *and* on our own experience to suggest what may be essential to begin a schoolwide or districtwide mastery learning program, what is desirable to extend and improve it, and what is undesirable or has been shown to decrease or destroy the effectiveness of a program. Remember, though, that the irreducible minimum in implementing mastery learning in your school or system may be you. Our chapter is organized into steps that may be followed from introduction to institutionalization of mastery learning, but it is your considerations that accompany each step that are key.

SOME LESSONS

Because schools are complex, living systems, there is no implementation model for mastery learning that can be uniformly applied to each school. There are, however, some common problems, mistakes, and solutions that emerge as themes from the experience of others. Let us begin, therefore, with several horror stories and one success story to set the tone for what follows. The themes and cautions we will draw from these stories are meant to provoke you into thinking concretely about your own setting and its "ordinary people," who, when conditions are right, can achieve extraordinary results (Peters & Waterman, 1982).

Horror Stories

Levine (1985b) has captured so well the negative aspects of several attempts to install outcome-based/mastery learning ideas and concepts that we include his descriptions in their entirety. He notes that each system described is trying to correct its initial errors and move on and, importantly, that districts without equivalent "horror stories" are just not trying hard enough and are probably still content with "bashing" teachers and administrators for low student scores.

(1) *District A* attempted to initiate a comprehensive instructional improvement process in which data on student performance would be used to identify learning objectives requiring emphasis at the school, grade, classroom and individual-student levels. Decision makers (both teachers and administrators) would monitor and self-monitor the preparation and implementation of a schedule for teaching and assessing these objectives, and the resulting data and monitoring would feed back into the process to ensure successful modification and development. Blessed (cursed?) with one of the largest research and development units in the United States, this district also attempted to assess and monitor teachers' attitudes and implementation efforts, school climate and culture considerations, administrative and pedagogic obstacles at the school and classroom levels, and other aspects of school operation bearing on the success of outcomes-based instruction.

However, the systematic effort delineated above did not appear to have much impact in terms of improving students' and teachers' performance, especially in inner-city schools enrolling high proportions of poverty students. Asked about reasons for the apparently discouraging results, the district's director of research and development stated (in a confidential, personal communication) that the major reason was because the whole operation was built on a "foundation of sand." Stating the reason more specifically, he said that "political and historical considerations" dictated use of the "wrong tests" for assessing student performance, i.e., the established norm-referenced tests which could not be used effectively for redesigning instruction in accordance with students' most important skill deficiencies. Thus victimized by non-mastery tests, numerous personnel skilled in instructional design and development wasted several hundred thousand dollars in an unsuccessful attempt to install outcomes-based instruction.

(2) *District B* attempted to install outcomes-based instruction by identifying approximately 1,200 objectives in reading for grades K–8. Utilizing the latest computer technology then available for monitoring student performance on a biweekly basis, teachers were required to prepare records showing each student's performance through the reading program's sequence of objectives. The resulting flood of records and paper not only left teachers with little time for instruction, it also encouraged, indeed practically required, destructive distortion of the reading program toward: (1) overemphasis on narrow decoding skills (regardless of whether students already had mastered them); (2) utilization of record-keeping chores as an excuse allowing teachers and administrators to say that they had fulfilled all of their responsibility to students when appropriate data had been submitted; (3) over-testing of students; (4) reinforcement of building-level educators' view that they were governed

by "idiots" in the central office and (5) diversion of attention from difficult issues such as rearranging classes to provide slower learners with sufficient time for mastery.

(3) *District C* attempted to install outcomes-based education by aligning the reading curriculum so that instruction would be based (the jargonized term seems to be "driven") on data reflecting students' mastery or non-mastery of the most important learning objectives. The implementation design depended on the availability of either validated [criterion-referenced tests] CRTs or precise and laborious re-analysis at the classroom level of item-response patterns on standardized tests. When neither validated CRTs nor appropriate item-analysis data could be made available in time for implementation of the curriculum alignment process, central office administrators ignored this fact and proceeded to tell school-level educators that they should align their reading curriculum, thereby repeating the mistake of District A. Worse, District C proceeded to reinforce the "relentless march" of students and teachers through the basal readers—the very problem that curriculum alignment is supposed to overcome. This mindless dependence on the basal reader was reinforced by:

- Preparing progress charts to show whether teachers were proceeding linearly through the basal readers
- Instituting a student promotions policy (grade-to-grade) partly based on students' progress in the basal readers
- Providing a majority of schools with a second (excellent) set of mastery-based reading materials that could be used (i.e., misused) to place still more emphasis on narrow skills already taught in the basal readers
- Sending schools a directive telling teachers at some grades to teach all of both these sets of reading materials

(4) *District D* launched one of the nation's best-organized efforts to align curriculum, instruction, and testing through: (1) preparation and administration of mastery tests; (2) arrangements for teachers to meet by grade level in using these data to identify their students' most important skill deficiencies and to prepare a schedule for teaching appropriate objectives; (3) assessment of materials available in the school for teaching specific skills; (4) identification of skills for which new or different teaching materials are required and (5) linkage of the previous tasks through a computerized information system.

The pilot schools participating in the project received significant assistance from resource personnel who worked with teachers to help them implement this approach to outcomes-based education. When students in some of these schools made large and rapid achievement gains, other schools throughout the district clamored for a chance to participate in the project. The project then went system-wide, but without an adequate amount of resource personnel to help teachers at building level learn to implement it effectively. In addition, an excellent approach to computerized management which had been developed successfully at the pilot schools was not included as part of the project expansion. Along with other impediments, this led to the usual outcome of no significant achievement gain at many participating schools.

(5) *District E* is a national leader in development of a criterion-referenced testing system for initiating outcomes-based instruction in the classroom. After several expensive years of hard work expended in developing appropriate learning objectives and test items, the district moved to install continuous progress learning based primarily on individual and small-group instruction. Monitoring sheets and arrangements also were developed to ensure that teachers used a mastery approach and seldom, if ever, utilized whole-class or large-group instruction. However, little was done to address the enormous demands involved in effective delivery of individualized and small-group instruction. (These demands include need for small classes, large amounts of daily planning time for teachers and extensive amounts of appropriate instructional materials easily available to teachers.) Two years after installation of the new system, student achievement had improved very little.

(6) *District F* prepared, validated and introduced an excellent set of objectives and CRTs for teaching reading and math in elementary schools. So far, so good. Unfortunately, implementation was fouled up in some schools by attempting to organize the school improvement process partly on a bureaucratic approach to monitoring teachers' and principals' utilization of the outcomes-based curriculum. Teachers were told to implement the outcomes-based system with emphasis on a formalized sequence of steps for planning and delivering whole-group lessons. Principals were directed to spend much of their time in classroom observations and conferences focusing on the delivery of such lessons. Weekly logs were prepared and scrutinized to ensure that principals spent much of their time discharging this responsibility.

Had this process been designed in a less technocratic manner with sophisticated attention to the diversity of teaching and administrative tasks required to install outcomes-based instruction successfully, it might well have been widely productive. Instead, it operated in many schools to divert principals from the proactive supervisory responsibilities involved in effective implementation of outcomes-based instruction ... [see Ryan, 1983]; and it also served to provide weak and ineffective principals with a bureaucratic monitoring form to "demonstrate" that they indeed had "succeeded" in observing and conferencing with teachers, just as the central office had required them to do. The result, in some schools, was to divert attention from student outcomes on important skills to principal and teacher compliance with a bureaucratic monitoring system. (pp. 15–17)

A Success Story

Now consider not another horror story, but a success. The only characteristic that distinguished this Michigan elementary school (Efthim, 1987) from others in its district in the mid-1970s was its design as an open school and the attraction it had for principals and teachers interested in that concept. It is possible that a small core of innovation-prone staff still remain at the school. This may partly explain their success, although they could now be said to be at the opposite pole from open education. That approach was called a dismal failure for the school's students.

In family income, the school ranks at the bottom in a poor, recession-ridden industrial city; close to 90% of students receive free lunch. Because of unemployment, student mobility is high, with 40% annual student turnover. About half the students come from single-parent homes. Since 1971 the proportion of minority students has ranged between 40% and 60%. The district, desegregated by court order, has recurring financial problems. Class sizes are large, and few support services remain.

In the mid- to late 1970s the school ranked about average in the district on state assessment tests of essential skills—that is to say, among the lowest in the state, in line with the well-known relationship between community income levels and student achievement scores. There was a high concentration of low achievers and nonreaders.

In the late 1970s the school district contracted with Michigan State University for the services of Dr. Wilbur Brookover. He and his associates were to present their research findings on effective schools and help all school staffs begin to translate the findings into action. Later, federal funding was obtained for a more concentrated program. The case study school firmly resisted involvement and "outside interference." The teachers and principal did decide, however, to explore on their own. They began to study and discuss the new findings.

With no help from outside except for this information (later published; Brookover et al., 1982) and with no observers in the school, their state assessment scores jumped in 1 year to around 90% of students demonstrating adequate skill mastery in math and over 80% in reading. This is not too surprising, except that scores have remained at or well above that level for more than 7 years now, comparing well with affluent communities around the state. Generally they have moved all children out of the lowest quartile, and few remain below the 50% mastery level, suggesting that there are no more nonreaders at third and fourth grade.

After scores had jumped up, the school became a part of the federally funded program and did participate in staff development activities. This lasted only a year; federal funds were cut and the program was eliminated 2 years early. The school also elected a building leadership team, which included the principal. It is hard to tell now who is *not* on this team since all staff members are equally outspoken and reflective about their history.

This steady state of higher achievement for all students has survived two new building administrators who were quickly socialized into the new building norms; one has become an outstanding example of instructional leadership. Even more significantly, perhaps, some of the teachers re-assigned here who would not or could not observe these norms, after adequate time and socializing efforts by the combined staff, are no longer at the school, without official action. Staff members are demonstrating their concern for all their students—through example and peer pressure—by reviewing schools for graduates.

Several other schools in the district have taken similar paths, and some have achieved even higher scores, including 100% on state assessment. The stability and continuing refinement of the innovation at this school have special interest, however. Here, student achievement goals arrived at by consensus, flexible instructional calendars at each grade level for the core curriculum, and shared staff development are the basis of genuine staff collegiality and coordination. Student achievement data serve as the language.

Like most effective schools (schools with high achievement in which family income plays no role), this one uses mastery learning according to Anderson's (1981) "functional analysis" of mastery learning. They did not set out to use mastery learning with fidelity. It was the fact that they set mastery goals for each grade level that moved them to reinstruction and rechecking for mastery on specified learning outcomes. Each teacher, group, or dyad of teachers may do this somewhat differently. The only specified formative testing occurs quarterly, when all students take cur-riculum-sensitive, criterion-referenced tests keyed to the instructional calendar. The quarterly tests parallel the district's grade-level skill tests, used summatively at the end of each school year along with norm-referenced tests.

These quarterlies do not sit on the principal's desk or vanish into individual classrooms, never to surface. At first, teachers posted test results in the faculty lounge for their comparative self-monitoring. By agreement, they are now the basis for at least four formal meetings each year by the total staff and principal. The reporting format for the quarterlies was designed to draw attention to individual students, class-rooms, and grade levels not making adequate progress toward the mas-tery goals established.

The staff first recognizes classes performing up to standard or beyond. Discussion then focuses on individuals and classes that are not. This discussion centers on how extra instructional time and school resources can be brought to bear on any problems. Staff members trade information, ideas, and corrective materials or offer to swap or "adopt" certain students temporarily. The compensatory and special education staffs are part of the discussion and part of the solution since their students, with some excep-tions, are expected to reach the same mastery levels. This staff interaction is overwhelmingly positive, offering encouragement and direct support to teachers having trouble. Occasionally there is criticism. This is infinitely more powerful coming from peers who face the same classroom problems than from a more distant principal, however respected.

Students are heterogeneously grouped, with an eye toward maintaining ethnic integration, and are instructed on grade level. Most teachers react in shocked disapproval to the notion of between-class ability or achievement grouping. They have not, however, given up the basal readers, and most group for part of the daily reading instruction in the primary grades. The use of basals plays a subordinate role to daily whole class instruction on grade-level skills and materials. The amount of time spent on basals is generally agreed to have lessened; frequently the whole class uses a single basal level for instruction on a new or prerequisite skill. Any labeling of students or any derogatory comments about them are vocally discouraged by staff.

The affective status of students has flowed from the emphasis on achievement goals and the academic success that students experience, not the other way around. The atmosphere of the school is one of relaxed friendliness, purposeful classroom activity, high time on task, and continuous informal communication between teachers. Teachers decided long ago to cut down on meetings, which seemed only to delay problem solving and the flow of information. They have even turned the noisy disadvantage of wall-less classrooms into an advantage: No classroom doors impede their ability to settle things swiftly, efficiently, and cooperatively between themselves.

Cooperation pervades the school. Although the teachers have not formally used cooperative learning teams with competitive games, students feel free to ask for or offer help to others, and teachers frequently suggest it. Parents are kept fully informed of the school's expectations and their children's progress, and many ways to help at home are suggested. The parent organization is not strong, nor is attendance at school functions heavy.

There has been little recognition of the school's accomplishments, even, until recently, by the district. The teachers are uncomfortable at being singled out, for two reasons. The first is that they resist unnecessary intrusions into working or personal time because they are so focused on what they are trying to accomplish. The second is that they are still short of the goals they have set for themselves. They express the kind of dissatisfaction with present performance that Brookover and Lezotte (1979) say characterizes effective or improving schools and have a common determination to do whatever is necessary to get the achievement outcomes they want for students. "We will do whatever it takes to get the job done," says the school's principal.

Like all case studies, this one represents idiosyncratic development in a particular time and place; it should not be considered a guideline for others. Nevertheless, it indicates what is possible under circumstances that most researchers would say militated against success. Most of all, it illustrates that a building staff that has discovered its professional strength can roll right over many research-identified obstacles to reach its goals.

Lessons

There are lessons to be learned from these horror and success stories. Levine (1985) drew the following ones from his horror stories:

(1) *You cannot install outcomes-based instruction successfully if you drive instruction in opposite directions at the same time.* This lesson is perhaps most apparent in the description of District C, which took several steps to encourage teachers to go page-by-page through the basal readers at the same time that it told them to adopt a mastery approach in teaching the most important skills. It also is apparent in District A's dependence on norm-referenced tests and in District F's efforts to install an outcomes-based system while simultaneously directing principals into an unproductive overemphasis on a traditional supervision approach.

(2) *You cannot install outcomes-based instruction successfully unless you address its major implications for instructional organization and support.* This lesson is most apparent in District D, which expanded its approach system-wide without providing sufficient resource personnel to assist teachers at the school and classroom level. It is also evident in District E, which took too little account of the enormous problems and demands involved in successful implementation of individualized and small-group continuous-progress instruction.

(3) *You should not pretend that a vital prerequisite for outcomes-based instruction has been accomplished if it has not.* This lesson is apparent in the history of District C, which did not have adequate CRTs to initiate its outcomes-based approach but went blithely ahead anyway, telling teachers to align objectives, instruction and testing as if they would or could do this in the absence of a fundamental component.

(4) *You cannot depend on technology to solve problems which are nontechnological.* This is apparent in the description of District B, which identified too many of the wrong reading objectives and then computerized the whole mess in the hope that printouts would somehow enable teachers to help students learn to read in a mastery framework. It also is apparent in District F, where an excellent set of objectives seemingly was devised but where the installation approach emphasized an administrative/management technology for bureaucratic monitoring of teacher implementation. Technocrats won't save you if you move in the wrong direction in trying to design and install an outcomes-based system for

delivering instruction; rather, they will multiply your problems and ensure your failure.

(5) *You cannot install outcomes-based instruction successfully unless you recognize that organizations have a (largely unintelligent) mind of their own and are prone to incompetence.* Upon hindsight, the decisions and actions in my mini-descriptions appear unintelligent. The people involved in decision making generally were dedicated, professional, hard-working and capable, yet their actions appear unintelligent. Partly this is because hindsight is, of course, much easier than actual decision making, but to some degree the decisions and actions were attributable to typical organizational processes that result in incompetent design and implementation of instructional programs. Each of the districts might have been more successful if adequate attention had been devoted at the beginning to implementation problems in the field, resulting in immediate redesign of their overall approaches to outcomes-based instruction.

Why are unworkable and misguided plans not corrected before they are widely put into practice? Why do not decision makers admit to problems early on and take adequate steps to correct them? Why do resources get spread too thin to allow for effective implementation? You know the answers as well as I do. I will only add that these types of organizational issues point to the invidious kind of organizational stupidity which I will define as the design and initiation of plans for improvement which are fundamentally divorced from the realities that must be faced to ensure successful classroom implementation. (pp. 17–18)

Likewise, Efthim has drawn some additional lessons from her success story:

- A school staff working together is more powerful, productive, and creative than the sum of its teachers working in isolation.
- Complex innovations can be developed, maintained, and strengthened over time if the staff is given or seizes ownership and if the innovations fit or can be modified to fit school priorities.
- Some things can be mandated, such as goal setting, planning for improvement, and staff development activities; others cannot. The details are best worked out by those in the trenches and must certainly not be part of performance evaluation without staff agreement. (Could anyone have mandated the public test score comparisons in the school described, for instance?)
- Modern educators are rightly suspicious of "miracle cures." They need access to all relevant strains of research and experience that address their priorities. Outside experts and facilitators can be very valuable when the staff wants their help, if they are credible, and if they treat staff members as fellow professionals.

- Instructional leadership may begin with, but should not remain with, any single person. The most developed leader does not have all the skills, or the unflagging energy and enthusiasm, to carry such a burden year after year. Instructional leadership and management must become a shared responsibility between administrators and teachers and between teachers, too.
- Endless meetings are not necessarily the indicator of change. The nature of informal, ongoing staff interaction and actual classroom behavior are better clues. However, meetings on designated topics and with definite structure are essential to beginning the process.
- Most important, some schools, after several years of mastery learning use, opt for increased student heterogeneity in the classroom and more rather than less uniformity of core content, taught at generally higher levels to all students simultaneously.

How, then, does one go about building a successful mastery learning, outcome-based program that builds on these lessons, a program that cares for kids and for academic excellence, that builds unity and purpose by participatory planning and decision making, that allows goals and outcomes to drive curriculum planning and instruction, that treats planning as a continuous process and uses time in flexible ways (Hagans, 1986)? We believe the answer lies in the following processes.

GETTING STARTED: AN INFORMAL DISCUSSION OF VALUES

The original initiative for instructional improvement has come from all sectors of various school communities—from single individuals or groups at the classroom teacher level and from unions, building or central administration levels, R&D departments, universities, and intermediate district or state department of education levels—as well as from outside the schools. Whether you, the initiator, consider yourself to be in a relatively powerless or powerful position, the first objective is to get "elbows" around you—to get other people as interested, excited, and informed about the possibilities of mastery learning as you are.

Finding Some Literature

Initiators often overlook a fairly obvious and nonthreatening first step. Instead of bringing in a high-powered presenter at the beginning, consider circulating a series of well-chosen mastery learning articles to people who may already be interested or whose interest you wish to gain. Whatever your position, colleagues will be flattered by this intellectual attention. Articles should be chosen to match concerns of the receivers as much as possible. This matching may have to do with position, subject, grade level, type of district, or any number of other possibilities. If you know who they are, include natural opinion leaders in your circle of readers.

If the initiator has some budgetary control or can tap the school's "kitty," subscriptions to journals and newsletters can be purchased for sharing. The Appendix lists some of the best of the articles on mastery learning as well as addresses for publications and organizations you may wish to contact. Three of the most useful general sources for these articles are ASCD's *Educational Leadership*, the Network for Outcome-based Schools' *Outcomes*, and Kelwynn's *Effective Schools Newsletter*. These are all "bridging" publications between research and practice.

Any professional or university library can also direct you to books and articles in your special-interest areas, or consult the mastery learning bibliography compiled by Hymel (1982). The American Educational Research Association has a special-interest group on mastery learning. The regional educational laboratories (especially the Far West, the Northwest, and the Central-Midwest) and the new national research centers on school effectiveness can also be contacted for recent publications and for information about activities occurring in your area. Of course, the intermediate school districts, state departments of education, and district R&D departments will also provide assistance in finding materials.

Forming Study Groups

Fielding, Schalock, Christensen, and Schalock (1986) make a good case for ensuring that "conceptual grounding" in the premises underlying a new program comes before any actual training of participants. This does not prevent challenges and criticism, nor should it, but it does minimize spurious attacks.

From discussions between senders and receivers of mastery learning articles, it is just a step to a study group. Because a catalyst for change is being created, the group should begin after a while to look like a planning team; it should be cross-hierarchical and representative of its setting to the extent possible.

Organization of a study group moves participants from awareness to consideration of local possibilities, but this is still exploratory and there is no commitment. Organization of a study group also sets a pattern of studying the whys of mastery learning and other innovations of interest, not just the how-to's. This helps you to be as sure of what mastery learning is *not* as of what it *is*. For example, many people assume that mastery learning is a rigid and restrictive system that cramps teachers' styles, bogs them down in record keeping, and limits their creativity. Others confuse it with minimum competency programs, some of which, according to Pringle (1982), have tended to depress general learning and lower teacher expectations (although one suspects that some expectations have been raised, too). Mastery learning is, in fact, an open-ended approach based on setting very high standards and aimed at having virtually all students attain those standards.

We believe that the study group, once formed, should have three basic functions: (1) to establish a data base, (2) to establish the conceptual grounding that will culminate in a statement of philosophical commitment, and (3) to develop a "brief" in anticipation of possible resistance.

Establishing a Data Base.   Reading and discussion by the study group across a broad spectrum of research findings should form a solid basis for school or district consideration and implementation of mastery learning. The discussion group must be able to convey this data base to others, however. This simply means that group members must organize their reading findings into a presentable form for future participants, for future decision making, and for adding future findings.

Blum and Butler (1985a; see also Northwest Regional Laboratory, 1985) report a synthesis of effective schooling practices that is a useful model of a data base because of its clarity and organization. They reviewed nearly 300 studies and categorized results as follows: school effects research, teacher effects research, research on instructional leadership, curriculum alignment research, research on program coupling, and research on educational change. These categories are conveniently placed in three sections, with applicability for school improvement at the classroom, school, and building levels.

The importance of developing such an initial data base cannot be overstressed. John Champlin (1983), former superintendent of the remarkably successful Johnson City, New York, system, has described the importance of a data base there. All educational decision making, at all levels in Johnson City, had to be passed through the data screen. This use of the best available data for decision making instilled a whole new spirit of professionalism in the staff and helped them confront their often non-data-based, personal belief systems. Champlin writes:

> Biased misbeliefs prohibit and restrict program improvement. Whatever effective tools we can muster to dispel the mysticism and destructive influence of prevalent educational belief need to be aggressively sought. The task of demystifying education begins by codifying what is known. Our current belief system emphasizes distortions, prohibitions, and restrictions about student learning and is one of the most powerful weapons employed by the vocal negative group found in the informal

structure of every school organization. This influence can be managed and eventually dispelled through effective utilization of the data screen. . . .

I cannot recall a single bad instructional decision being made in Johnson City after we insisted that this procedure be in place. Even a sound decision implemented clumsily is a significant improvement over professionally invalid decisions which, at best, produce more and more of what we want to move away from. (p. 33)

It is significant that by using such a data screen to inform decision making, Johnson City has moved deliberately over time from individualization and homogeneous grouping to increased student heterogeneity and "best shot" whole class instruction, using a variety of team-teaching approaches. The needs of virtually all special education students are now being met in regular mastery learning classrooms (personal communication, 1986; see also Mamary & Rowe, 1985).

Formulating a Statement of Philosophical Commitment. A statement of philosophical commitment is a statement of mission or purpose critical to mastery learning. It is related to the mission statement research identifies as being characteristic of effective schools. Such a statement serves as a touchstone for the whole school community, giving direction, meaning, and relevance to decision making and action. The study group may want to pay particular attention to it, partly because the statement defines their work and partly because it may later be adopted officially.

Preparation of a statement should begin with consideration of school and district goal statements already in place. Most of these reflect worthy goals, priorities, and community input over time, but they may also be too abstract or idealistic to be of much practical use. (A good test of the value of existing statements is checking a sample of teachers and administrators to find out how many know of the existence of such statements; how many can quote from them or know where to find a copy; and how many consider them useful to their decision making.) Therefore, existing statements may have to be amended, clarified, rephrased, or abandoned.

Boxes 3.1 and 3.2 provide examples of philosophical statements. Box 3.1 is drawn from Johnson City's public schools, and Box 3.2 is drawn from Mariner Public High School in Mulkiteo, Washington. The latter statement differs from the former in that it deals extensively with staff relationships, roles, and responsibilities during a period of change, as well as a philosophically based commitment to outcome-based education. Only part of the school's long statement is shown in Box 3.2; the remainder goes on to deal with criteria for decision making, formal and informal methods of communication, cooperation and support, issues of loyalty, and staff rights to professional disagreement.

BOX 3.1   Johnson City's Philosophical Principles and Practices

1. Almost all students are capable of achieving excellence in learning provided that students:

- Have sufficient time to learn
- Experience challenge with little threat
- Make decisions without fear of irreversible failure or criticism
- Have a supportive learning environment
- Have favorable learning conditions and quality instruction
- Have increased time on learning through active involvement in the learning process
- Have their performance expectations and be expected to achieve them

2. The instructional process can be changed to improve learning, provided that teachers:

- Improve planning procedures and clearly define expected outcomes and prerequisites
- Systematically control the learning process by teaching the stated objectives and providing the help necessary to achieve them
- Systematically manage change so that improvement will be evolutionary and revolutionary

3. An essential function of schooling is to ensure that all students perform at high levels of learning and experience opportunities for individual success, provided that teachers:

- Reduce competition and encourage cooperation in learning
- Create a trust environment
- Understand that it is no longer appropriate for society to accept the fact that only 30% of the students now learn what is expected
- Eliminate the elitist notion of schooling
- Value all human beings
- Provide an affirming classroom
- Expect all students to learn and learn well
- Develop self-directed learning through opportunities and modeling

4. An effective instructional process varies the time for learning according to the needs of each student and the complexity of the task, provided that teachers believe:

- Learning is a continuous yet irregular process
- Aptitude is not defined as the ability to learn, but as the time necessary to learn
- Most students can learn what is expected, provided that they have the necessary time to learn
- The time to learn can vary

- The time necessary for students to learn a task need not be different, but [must be] appropriate

5. Success influences self-concept; self-concept influences learning and behavior, provided that teachers believe:

- The key to building a positive self-concept lies largely in what the teacher believes and communicates to his or her students
- When students come to view themselves as important, valued, and respected by their teachers and accept that they can learn, they will develop a healthy self-concept
- Students will build positive self-esteem when the classroom atmosphere is based on success rather than unnecessary failure
- Lack of success may make for a negative self-concept, alienate the student from the learning process, and foster negative behavior
- When schools provide successful learning experiences, students are more likely to develop positive self-concepts, which in turn facilitate learning and success
- Testing and reporting should be criterion-referenced, emphasizing individual growth and development and not the relationship of one individual to another
- A student's self-image is based upon his or her experiences in mastering certain tasks
- The more positive the self-concept the higher one's learning expectation and levels of performance

6. Staff and students share responsibility for successful learning outcomes when students and teachers believe:

- Learning is an active process requiring active participation of students and teachers
- Teachers should share the responsibility for learning by planning instruction carefully
- Students should share responsibility for learning by actively processing information to be learned and by interacting with the teacher, others in the class, and the instructional materials
- Students should also share the responsibility for learning by preparing for homework assignments and examinations

7. Assessment of learning is continuous and directly determines instructional placement, provided that teachers believe:

- The appropriateness of the instruction can only be determined by continuous diagnosis of individual student skill attainment
- The diagnostic information resulting from the assessment enables them to prescribe the appropriate level of beginning instruction as well as determining when one skill has been mastered and instruction for the next skill should begin
- Assessment, feedback, and reporting should emphasize individual

growth and development. It also should be used to determine how well students have learned what is expected, how well initial instruction and the instructional process are working, and also as a basis for determining necessary correctives

- Assessment should not be norm-referenced, but rather should be self-referenced
- Students should be assigned to groups by demonstrated performance

8. Credit is awarded and recorded when learning is assessed and validated, provided that teachers believe:

- Mastery learning varies the time necessary for learning
- Credit is awarded when the material is mastered, rather than at formal arbitrary periods during the student's school career
- Students should be encouraged to continue to learn by awarding them additional credit as they increase their learning
- Grades can be altered to reflect new learning and achievement

Champlin and Mamary, 1982, pp. 22–23.

BOX 3.2   Mariner High School's Operating Principles

Introduction

The one major attribute that sets a successful organization apart from an unsuccessful one is effective, satisfied, and dynamic personnel. To guarantee a quality education for students, a school must have staff members who agree on some philosophical ideas and practical ways of working together to achieve the goals of the organization.

The purpose of any school is to provide quality education. Our team believes that *schools are for kids* and *schools belong to the people.*

Further, we are committed to having our decisions measured and tested against these fundamental beliefs and goals. Our team also is committed to developing the intellectual, vocational, physical, creative, cultural, and social capabilities of the students and staff.

Operating principles and ground rules are beliefs, values, and practical ways of working together for a common goal. As a team we have agreed to adhere to the following operating principles and ground rules:

Positive Approach

Each member of the team will strive to bring about the best in people and recognize that every student and staff member is unique. We will consistently strive to improve our feelings of self-worth through positive commendations (strokes) for each other whenever possible. We will work to acknowledge and reinforce others' successes—both students and staff. We will accentuate the positive! We will ask ourselves, "What can I do to improve the situation or better implement the decisions?"

Initiative

The success of Mariner High School is dependent upon each individual assuming his/her responsibility to create and maintain a positive and valuable learning experience. [All staff members] (both vertical and horizontal in the organization) shall concern themselves with each school situation.

Initiative should be encouraged in all people through realistic, attainable goal-setting that provides avenues for success. Each of us will take the initiative to:

- Suggest improvements for each other's classes, the school, the program and its management, as well as for our own classes
- Voice our feelings and opinions in a straightforward and clear manner to each other
- Hold ourselves accountable for our well-being and the well-being of our peers
- Keep students objectively informed of matters pertinent to their education
- Consistently during the school year try to make MHS a better place to live
- Communicate right (and inform about inconsistent) standards, goals, expectations, and views
- Encourage ourselves to openly and realistically deal with important problems, even when risky
- Be involved in change, considering philosophical consistency throughout the program

The administrative team will take the initiative to provide quality leadership to the staff and to be creative.

Accountability

Each of us is accountable for his/her actions and will help be accountable for the total team's actions. We will communicate our personal expectations to each other. We will be accountable to realistic demands, share responsibilities, admit mistakes and work as a team to reach our goals during the normal school day or during co-curricular activities.

Simonson, 1982, pp. 17–21.

As these boxes indicate, a statement of philosophical commitment or purpose may be as detailed as the study group considers appropriate for the setting. If the statement is very long, it is wise to give wide publicity to key phrases and concepts from it. For example, many schools and classrooms now sport the simple slogan "All Children Can Learn" on posters, stickers, buttons, and flags.

Developing a Brief.   The study group has now collected widely applicable research generalizations in a number of areas. They have also explored their school or district's goals and beliefs as well as their own in light of these research findings and have developed a preliminary philosophical commitment or purpose statement. If these experiences have been positive and supportive, the group, anticipating possible resistance, will now prepare to present its case and argue its merits. In short, the study group will develop what lawyers call a brief for mastery learning. Central to this brief will be answers to the question "Why mastery learning?"—more specifically, "Why group-based, teacher-paced mastery learning instead of individualized, continuous progress?"

Two mastery learning superintendents, Lewis Grell (1984), currently in Hamburg, New York, and Champlin (1981), provide some interesting briefs on why their staffs chose to adopt mastery learning. Grell's brief was developed by first defining what staff believed to be the basic philosophical premises of mastery learning and then comparing them to various lists of research generalizations about what effective schools should be. This brief centered on mastery learning's capacity

> for using all those school and classroom practices that have been shown to be most effective. Mastery learning provides an organized model, under the control of the school staff, which encourages and helps *all* teachers to use those practices used by the most *effective* teachers, thus potentially making every teacher an effective teacher. (p. 15)

The details of this brief can be found in Box 3.3.

Champlin's (1981) staff, by contrast, compared mastery learning ideas and practices not only with other critical educational practices but also with their own beliefs about professional growth. Their brief centered around mastery learning's "omnibus approach to education which mandates bringing together and fusing many critical educational practices," requiring a renewal process and professional growth, with continual reassessment "but never a typical win-lose evaluation" (p. 5).

Anticipating and Dealing with Resistance

The order of the next steps is a function of local circumstances. In many locales, school improvement plans are now required. Structures or

---

BOX 3.3   Example of a Brief

1. Almost all students are capable of achieving excellence in learning the essentials of formal schooling. This is sometimes stated ninety percent of the students can learn ninety percent of the material.
2. Success influences self-concept; self-concept influences learning and behavior. Success leads to higher levels of maturation, more initiative, and stronger academic self-concepts. That is to say, success directly influences learning and behavior.
3. The instructional process can be changed to improve learning, i.e., if we focus on the dynamics of what happens between the teachers and the students in the teaching-learning situation, means of improving those dynamics can be discovered.
4. Schools can maximize the learning conditions for all students by:
   a. Establishing a school climate which continually affirms the worth and diversity of all students. If the school sees the student in this light he will soon see himself in the same light.
   b. Specifying expected learning outcomes. The student must know what is expected in order to be truly aware of his progress.
   c. Expecting that all students perform at high levels of learning.
   d. Ensuring that all students experience opportunities for personal success. Opportunities are at the heart of any school program.
   e. Varying the time for learning according to the needs of each student and the complexity of the task. As mentioned above, time is a resource which should be used more wisely.
   f. Having staff and students both take responsibility for successful learning outcomes. Notice it is not either/or but both who are responsible.
   g. Determining instructional assignment directly through continuous assessment of student learning.
   h. Certifying educational progress whenever demonstrated mastery is assessed and validated.

Grell, 1984, pp. 15–16.

---

processes may already be in place for planning. If the initiators are working from a state or district level, the objective should be to "stimulate" individual schools to change, as Louis (1986) puts it, by providing them with appropriate assistance. If already working at the building level, the objective of the study group is to create a planning team (or transform or add to an existing one) to consider mastery learning an associated or supportive innovation for that school. Building-level planning teams are needed whether districtwide or school-by-school adoption is anticipated.

Generally speaking, it helps to overcome resistance if the study team's initial feelers to staff make the following points clear:

1. Mastery learning will be a voluntary program.
2. There will be an adequate time line and sufficient support for the teachers and administrators involved.
3. Decisions will be based on what Levine (1985) calls "organic adaptation and monitoring." In contrast with bureaucratic implementation and monitoring in which every detail is specified in advance and teachers are held accountable for precisely observing each of them, adaptation is organic when "teachers not only depart from but are encouraged and assisted to depart from guidelines when necessary to achieve the overall purposes of the instructional program" (p. 282). (Note, however, that there *are* guidelines.) Monitoring is organic when "forms and checkoff sheets are reduced to a minimum, in favor of collegial teacher planning and decision-making, with close and personal support from administrators and supervisors" (p. 283).

If the study team's attempts are met with hostility or are stonewalled at any level, it is wise to pull back and regroup. The study group may have to assume some functions that otherwise would belong to the planning team. The first of these would be to identify the sources of conflict and hostility. What is the history of recent innovations, if any? Is there a misunderstanding of the group's intent, or do its proposals suggest interference with current priorities, activities, or leadership roles? Do the group's proposals adequately address the concerns potential implementers will surely have?

Whereas in some cases retreat is a useful strategy, in other cases it may be important for the study group to come from a stronger but still nonadversarial position. You can increase the numbers on your side by steadily providing more information and attracting new people. You can also join a network that exists for this purpose. You could form a coalition that reaches new sectors of the school community. In one Michigan district the teachers' and administrators' unions endorsed and formed a joint committee that successfully pressed central administration formally to adopt effective schools principles. And you can form a coalition that reaches into the local community itself. Many community coalitions have records of success in stimulating and supporting school improvement. Another interim step, again one that the planning team would use if it existed, is visits to or from successful implementers. Since occasionally outsiders have made a bad situation worse, the most careful kind of advance work should be done in engaging presenters. If possible, these implementers should be selected on the basis of familiarity with your kind of setting. Some mastery learning implementers are strong on stirring interest, others on putting out brushfires; some concentrate at the secondary level, others at the elementary level; and some specialize in working with teachers while others work well with administrators, board members, and the public. Some help in selecting acceptable implementers might be found in the personnel directory in the Appendix. Funding for employing them, for visiting other sites, and for attendance at mastery learning conferences can be raised by a coalition if other funds are not available.

The study group may also have to move into some local needs assessment. Many teachers are quite surprised to learn that their classes exhibit low time on task (Stallings, 1980); many schools or districts are surprised and embarrassed when evidence indicates that their low-income students are systematically denied access to quality education. We are certainly not suggesting a negative approach that places blame or makes people defensive; this would defeat our purpose. There are times, though, when the difference between what is and what could be must be brought to the attention of the people who can make the changes.

Whatever course the study group takes in dealing with resistance, it is essential that it appreciate some of the common reasons for resistance. One reason is stubborn complacency. Teaching has been called a static profession, where teachers can return after years of absence and be expected to pick up right where they left off, without any retraining (Vickery, 1984); where teachers are often reassigned to unfamiliar grade levels outside their primary disciplines, with no in-service training provided to make the transition, as if they were interchangeable machine parts. Teachers, for lack of other assistance, therefore, often teach as they were taught when children, from their own classroom trial and error, and with tips from the more experienced teachers down the hall. Change may be seen as threatening to hard-won routines and great personal autonomy.

Resistance is more than stubborn complacency, however. It is often quite rational. "Thinking" resisters include those who doubt that adequate support and commitment can be gained from the school board or administration to carry through a mastery learning program. They may be accustomed to frequent shifts in priorities and personnel. They may be afraid of being evaluated prematurely on new instructional techniques, with no assistance provided. They may see such a plethora of conflicting programs and guidelines already in existence that one more would just add to the confusion. They may worry about any extra time required by mastery learning or about losing their own efficiency by being forced to work with others. They may think mastery learning will hurt high achievers, or they may be so steeped in normal-curve ideology that their own experiences have convinced them that many students cannot learn (Miller, 1983). They may worry that independent seat work ("purple passion" days) will not be allowed or that any personal inadequacies may be revealed in more "public" instruction. Or they may be concerned about violating negative building norms and bringing upon themselves sanctions from other teachers. Some can feel so burdened already that any extra move is painful.

Remember that the volunteer groups and the resister groups may both contain successful and unsuccessful teachers and that persuasion and example work better than bludgeoning. Some thoughtful resisters will later become champions of the new practices.

Forming a Planning Team

Eventually the resistance, if any, will be sufficiently overcome to form an accepted planning team at the building or district level. This represents a new but still not final level of commitment.

The objective of the planning team should be to get to the point where volunteers, or willing assignees, are ready in every way to teach a full course, or at least two learning units of 2 or more weeks each. Evaluation of the first unit and planning for the third can continue while the second is being taught, thus avoiding a jerky stop-and-go process that demoralizes implementers. The work of the planning team will continue and even intensify during the earliest units, but some of the responsibility begins to shift to implementers, where it will remain.

Whether elected or assigned, a new or existing group, the planning team should also be representative of various interests by including teachers and administrators, particularly the principal. Nonstaff members may or may not be included. Some or all members of the study group should be on the team or should make sure the planning team is thoroughly familiar with information so far obtained (the data base, for example) and any actions taken. Guidance from expert developers and implementers is most valuable during the planning stage to expedite matters, to promote success, and to forestall failure.

Responsibilities and time lines for the team should be agreed on, and adequate time and resources provided for their work. Regular reports should be made to concerned staff and regular feedback obtained from them during planning. Remenber, the planning process, like the needs assessment, can become excessive and drain so much energy that little is left for implementation. This need not be the case, however, if planners recognize that mastery learning is already well developed and researched and needs only adaptation to local circumstances. Loucks-Horsley and Hergert (1985) note that developing your own program can cost 20 times as much as adapting an existing one.

BEGINNING TO ROLL: FORMALIZING A PLAN

By now we hope you have already decided to use group-based mastery learning and to begin with interested volunteers, to start small, and to assess and adjust the program as it develops and grows. There are still some "thinking big" issues to consider, however, in identifying organizational constraints and possibilities for change. As more than one instructional developer can tell you, just as you may encounter resistance from individuals, so, too, can you get flak from the school or district organization and even from the state (see Champlin, 1987).

Both Westerberg (see Westerberg & Stevick, 1985), a Missouri secondary school principal, and Hoben (1981), a Michigan district superintendent, address the importance of up-front and continuous organizational planning and problem solving. Westerberg found that organizational readiness and support are crucial to successful implementation of mastery ideas at the school level. Readiness refers to "the abilities, plans and expectations that a teacher must have by the first day of implementation. Support centers on the information, encouragement and assistance that [are] essential for a teacher to effectively implement change" (Westerberg & Stevick, 1985, p. 24).

The Hoben Model

To provide support and readiness, Hoben has developed a very useful strategic planning model, like that of large corporations. This model is designed to avoid reactive crisis management, reduce adversary relationships, be cost effective, and expedite outcome performance. Specifically, the model encourages the planning team to begin identifying organizational constraints and possibilities by asking the following questions:

- Where are we?
- Where do we want to be in 5 years? One year?
- Is the change necessary? Is it worthwhile?
- What resources do we have? Do we need?
- What is our entry point?
- What plans must be in place to begin successful implementation?

Where Are We?   To answer this question, the planning team needs to ask another: In relation to what?

The planning team, already representing a variety of school or district interests, has at hand a variety of resources—existing local goals, a data base, the statement of philosophical commitment, and a brief on mastery learning from the study group. In reviewing these and other materials, team members should begin to discern gaps between where they are and where they want to be and to formulate tentative long-range, encompassing goals that might remove these gaps; these are for later discussion and agreement by the larger group. This tentative goal formulation should be done *before* the actual needs assessment because starting with the data tends to place mastery learning almost exclusively in a *remedial* posture. Starting with goals helps planners to focus on the *preventive* use of mastery learning to forestall learning failure (Block, 1985).

Now the planning team can turn to needs assessment. Since needs assessments frequently become catchalls, absorbing a great deal of time and energy and leading nowhere, we recommend that you conduct a more focused assessment that takes your desired outcomes into account. Since these outcomes generally concern excellence and equity in student learning, the heart of your needs assessment will be student learning data.

The planning team should use whatever tests or other achievement results already exist for purposes of this student learning needs assessment. If you already know the subject area, grade level, and approximate size of the group with which you will begin implementation, focus your assessment accordingly. Ask of these data questions like these: How much growth occurs from pretest to posttest, on the average and by subgroup? What kind of differences are there by level or track, if these exist? Do students do less well in reading than in math? If norm-referenced tests are used, do students achieve, exceed, or fall behind "normal" growth from year to year? How do they compare to other schools in the district, state, or nation? Does student achievement tend to level off or even decline after third or fourth grade?

In the interests of promoting student learning equity, the planning team should also be sure to disaggregate the student learning data to the extent possible by ethnic and gender identification and by family income level, using free-lunch status of the student for this last if more accurate measures are not available. Ask of these disaggregated data questions such as these: What percentage of students reach acceptable levels of mastery? Are there ethnic, sex, or income-level differences? Do black and white or middle- and lower-income students enter school at similar levels and get farther apart the longer they stay in school? Do female and minority students avoid or disproportionately flunk out of math and science courses? Do compensatory education students ever catch up with their peers? Are special education students tested, and if so, are the results reported?

The planning team might want to collect other types of student information as well. This information, as well as processes for gathering, presenting, and using it collegially for school improvement, appears in

Blum and Butler's (1985b) Profile. Figure 3.1 shows the contents of the Profile.

For purposes of planning staff development, you may also need to get a general sense of instructional approaches teachers currently use. Building-based teams usually know this already.

Where Do We Want to Be?   No program of significant scope has a chance of success unless the people affected by it have both sensed and internalized a need for change. Without intending to be exclusive, the approach most likely to be successful is one in which a discrepancy is created by establishing a picture of what might be (optimum) as reflected in the literature and contrasting it with actual practice. With few exceptions, the gap between optimum and actual will be significant enough to create a need for action and will present a golden opportunity to use a sound problem-solving procedure in which the entire staff can be expected to participate. This is an opportune moment to stimulate involvement by enabling all to be positive contributors. Need sensing within the organization should be continuous, accompanied by attempts to gather and employ the best data. Response to a perceived need should be neither clandestine nor revolutionary but rather studied and evolutionary, always reckoning with the variability and idiosyncrasies of those who would effect and be affected by the change (Champlin, 1983, p. 34).

Now that the planning team knows the kind of achievement that is possible with mastery learning and where you are in terms of student achievement, it is time to think about formalizing the fairly long-range achievement goals initially drawn in the consideration of "Where are we?" These goals are still tentative and should be adjusted up or down later, individually or collectively, by implementers. It is nevertheless important to think of them from the beginning. Mastery learning, cooperative learning, effective schools, and effective instruction—all are means to desired student achievement outcomes, not ends in themselves. Nothing helps a school group more to stay together, stay focused, and stay on task than common achievement goals.

Interim goals may also be proposed by the team. These goals should be reasonable, possible to accomplish with "stretching." If students are at the 30% mastery level, you should not set your sights on 90% attainment in the first year. Student achievement goals are meant to be reviewed at least annually and reset, as appropriate, by a collective staff process.

There is much disagreement, however, on how achievement goals should be established and stated, mostly centering around the "minimums become maximums" argument. A rule of thumb in mastery learning is to determine what would constitute A-level work in a course or subject, determine where students are in relation to that level of work, and then

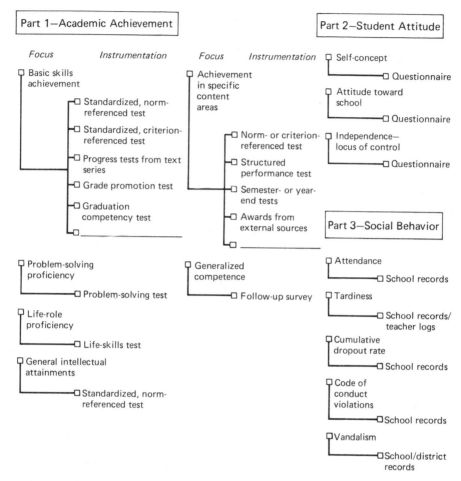

Figure 3.1. Blum and Butler's Profile (Blum and Butler, 1985b, p. 55)

decide how many (what percentage of) students should be at that A-level at the end of the school year. If this concept is in place, there is nothing wrong with expressing it in numbers, for example: $x\%$ of students will demonstrate mastery of $x\%$ of math objectives in fourth grade. Concise goal statements lend clarity and purpose to teacher planning and discussion, to student self-management, and to parent support.

The planning team may also choose other desirable student outcomes as goals, such as improved attendance, a decrease in referrals, better self-concept of academic ability, and various other affective or behavioral goals. We suggest, however, that such goals be few in number and clearly subordinate to and supportive of the main one of student achievement; most such outcomes are highly related to successful academic performance in any case. When there are too many goals, they all assume less importance. Staff members may feel they can pick and choose among lesser priorities and ignore the rest. The most common example of this is the staff that chooses to emphasize discipline and forget its relationship to the quality of instruction. There are cases, to be sure, where staff must get a handle on discipline before they have the mind-set to improve instruction, but this should be commonly understood as a beginning step on the way to bigger things. Another popular choice is making parent support a high priority long before the staff has decided what is is they themselves will be doing.

Implementation goals are also an appropriate focus at this point for the planning team, even in voluntary programs. How many teachers, departments, or buildings should be implementing mastery learning in the first, second, fifth year? If it begins in math, when should reading be included? And so on. Even though these goals may be disregarded by individual teachers, department heads, or building and district leaders, they serve a useful function. In particular, they remind everyone that the extent of anticipated implementation affects the extent of planning required.

Is It Worthwhile?   Sometimes in life we sense clear gaps between where we are and where we want to be, but we realize that closing this gap will be so costly—personally, socially, economically, and spiritually—that we conclude it is not worthwhile. So it is with schools and school districts. The planning team must now wrestle with the question of worth for itself.

To assist the planning team to step back and do this soul searching, let us look at answers that developed in a school community that decided it was worth doing:

> Those intent on implementing mastery must be aware that it requires an obvious, extra effort beyond that required to maintain an existing program. That extra effort is often a constant test of one's professional dedication, management skills, technical understanding and proficiencies and—last but not least—a severe test of willingness to reexamine one's own attitude and belief system.
>
> For those in the entry phase of mastery implementation, the answer to the question, "Is it worth the extra effort?" should be based on the following:
>
> • It is worth the extra effort *only if* you have reached an honest point of unhappiness with what your schools are doing compared with *what is really possible*. Your unhappiness should peak at a point of dissatisfaction which produces a strong personal commitment to do

everything possible to develop more efficient and more effective school programs.

- It is worth the extra effort *only if* you have the personal drive and dedication to stay with it, see it through, and make it "go." You must understand the [mastery learning] implementation is evolutionary and not revolutionary. The difficulty with which long-established belief systems about education are attacked and changed is a serious problem. There is no guarantee of smooth progress or orderly development, primarily because of the multiple complexities of dealing with the frailties of human nature in yourself and your colleagues.

- It is worth the extra effort *only if* you are tired of "fluff" and "catch programs" which seem periodically to sprout and then fade away just as quickly. The development of [mastery learning] requires your willingness to dig in and see a program develop from a sound philosophical understanding based upon sound operational understandings, supported through a vigorous program of staff development wherein participants can acquire *new* skills. This development must reflect your determined willingness to challenge and revise your own belief system whenever necessary.

- It is worth the extra effort *only if* you believe that educational leadership requires activism, involvement, and ownership. These are not automatic by-products of AASA membership or participation in a professional group such as the Network for Outcome-based Schools.

- It is worth the extra effort *only if* you believe that professionalism is not possible unless practice reflects the *best available data*. To operate on a lesser basis reduces our work to that of being a craftsman or a semiskilled practitioner.

- It is worth the extra effort *only if* you believe that schools should be organized around *how children learn* and not around time-honored arrangements. This dedication should be intense and should motivate you to make sharper, keener, professional decisions consistent with and reflecting sound data.

- It is worth the extra effort *only if* you are increasingly impatient with those who say "It won't work," "It's a fad," "It didn't work there," "I would like to know about the research," *ad infinitum*. Progress is never made by reluctant participants, nor is it stimulated by negative "killer phrases" such as these. The dedication to create and develop sound programs requires risk taking, the creation of a high silhouette, and a willingness to stand apart and above the reluctant.

- It is worth the extra effort *only if* you believe that education doesn't have unlimited chances for success in the eyes of a public that has grown ever more doubtful about us. This is not necessarily a message of gloom and doom; only a reminder that we are overdue in using the vast understanding at our disposal to create more efficient and more effective schools. (Champlin, 1981, pp. 4–5)

What Resources Do We Have or Need?   Once the planning team has decided that it is worthwhile to implement mastery learning, questions of resources become central. As before, we encourage the team to take stock of where you are by asking what resources you already have before trying to figure out what other resources you will need. In our experience, most schools usually have all the resources—human and otherwise—that they need to teach for mastery. The problem is identifying, tuning, and orchestrating them as necessary.

The following list includes questions that can facilitate brainstorming on resource matters and lead to a greater understanding of available and needed resources. Your planning team will have additional questions on local strengths and weaknesses.

- Is there common prep time for staff to plan work together?
- What kind of staff development time is available? Funds? Trainers and resource people, on-site or elsewhere? What related staff development has already occurred?
- Can release time be arranged for teachers to help, observe, or coach each other in the classroom?
- Is there an established curriculum? Does it have objectives already? Are tests or other procedures available to measure attainment of these objectives?
- What is the general skill and interest level of teachers who are expected to implement mastery learning? Are they already accustomed to lesson plans, to teaching to objectives, to error analysis, to use of data to plan and evaluate instruction, to whole class instruction, and so on? What is your current estimate of areas where they might want assistance?
- Do you expect the principal to be supportive? In what ways might the principal encourage, support, and assist in implementation? What is the general skill and interest level of the principal?
- Do you expect the board of education or central administration to be supportive? In what ways might they support, encourage, and assist in implementation?
- Are there school or district policies or procedures that would interfere with planned mastery learning implementation? (For example, grading policies may mean that report cards cannot reflect mastery, or a merit pay plan may be so divisive that staff will refuse joint planning and effort.) Which of these policies or procedures, if any, need to be changed?

Let us illustrate the kinds of resource issues the planning team might explore by using several examples. Consider, first, the example of school or district policies that prevent grading for mastery. A major incentive for students is the report card grade. You want to be able to say to them that reaching a predefined level of mastery on stated objectives means an automatic A for them, regardless of their participation or behavior in class or any extra instruction or time they required to achieve that mastery. However, current policy requires grading on an entirely different basis. Do you wait through the interminable committee process for changing that policy before beginning to implement mastery learning? A better alternative is to circulate written lists of objectives to students and their parents and to certify mastery of those objectives at the end of the course or year, as an adjunct to the report card. This does not interfere with policy or with other teachers' continuing observance of policy. If the need for a new grading policy becomes apparent to all, down the road, it is much easier at that time to accomplish the appropriate change. This is true of other needs that will surface and become salient to staffs, at which time they can be resolved most expeditiously.

To some extent the same is true of curriculum, although the size and level of beginning implementation have obvious importance here. On the one hand, over the long haul, you don't want to waste mastery learning on trivialized curriculum with disconnected, discrete low-level skills. On the other hand, a staff that lacks confidence in its ability to teach and in students' ability to learn is not in the best position to develop significant new curriculum before beginning implementation. The best approach seems to be like the one in the Philadelphia mastery learning program (see Conner et al., 1986). Curriculum materials are placed in loose-leaf notebooks for staff; sections can easily be added, removed, or replaced as program development requires.

You may be fortunate in already having a well-regarded local curriculum, developed and field-tested with staff involvement, with carefully sequenced learning objectives, planned initial, corrective, and enrichment instructional strategies and materials, and congruent tests. This was a major advantage in getting Baltimore County's mastery learning program off to an early start (see Kozlovsky, 1986). In such a case, mastery learning can be applied to the existing curriculum with only minor adjustments, such as adding mastery expectations.

To go the other extreme, there may be no established curriculum, no agreement on what is important, not even a common set of texts or materials across the same subject in a grade level. This situation clearly calls for a longer lead time and additional time for implementers to develop the beginnings of a curriculum. This might mean getting agreement on a set of objectives for the semester or year, gathering instructional materials, and jointly developing or identifying congruent mastery test items, a few at a time. It does not necessarily mean starting from the ground floor to develop a total curriculum for all grade levels in the school or district and the immediate scrapping of the district's regular testing program. Mastery learning is an instructional approach that can fit well into a setting without interfering with other classes and without disturbing existing articulation from grade to grade. Many teachers use student growth between locally developed formative and summative tests as their measure of success, without regard to any ill-fitting standardized testing program in use in the district.

What Is Our Entry Point?   Now that the planning team has decided to implement mastery learning and has assembled, or is assembling, the necessary resources, the next question becomes when and where to marshal these resources. Staff interest or pressing local priorities may be the deciding factor in where to begin. If there is a principal, school staff, English department, or group of math teachers, for example, that has already expressed serious interest, the team's choice of entry point may have been made for you.

If that is not the case, here are some point-of-entry considerations. Mastery learning has been used successfully in all subjects at all levels, from kindergarten through graduate school. Often the choice is made to use it with older students in subjects where they have already experienced considerable failure. This is an appropriate use for mastery learning, but as Block (1985) notes, the effort to improve instruction through mastery learning has a greater effect in *preventing* rather than remediating learning failures. This applies particularly to students' first years in the primary grades, to the first in any sequence of courses, and to the first year in any new level of schooling. In their first year of middle school, high school, or even college, many students have temporarily improved affective entry levels and a renewed sense of hope.

It also makes sense to apply mastery learning to the core curriculum, to mastery of the subjects that make current and future knowledge and skill acquisition possible—most obviously, language arts and math. Both subjects should include higher-order thinking skills from the beginning, or at least as quickly as teachers gain confidence in the use of mastery learning; math may also require supportive language development. It is our impression that many otherwise ineffective schools do moderately well on imparting the ability to compute, but as one middle school teacher in such a school put it: "Kids can do all the basic operations, but they don't have the faintest idea of what to do with them. Some can't even read the problem statements."

The size of a beginning program, as well as the nature of commitment to its growth, have important implications for success, especially with a complex innovation like mastery learning. Overambitiousness, as in expecting all teachers of language arts in a large district or all the teachers in a school building to begin implementing mastery learning at the same time, may strain the organization and prove fatal. Similarly, expecting teachers to begin implementing mastery learning in two subjects at the same time would certainly strain the teachers and may also prove fatal. Undersizing, though, as in allowing single volunteers to struggle along without peer support, is shortsighted and not likely to lead to easy adoption of mastery learning by other teachers.

In general, an incremental approach that starts with small groups of interested teachers, an interested principal, and some central office support, that contains planned follow-up, and that provides interactive, cross-hierarchical commitment to expansion of successful programs seems the most productive approach to resolving the size issue. Based on Maryland's attempt to implement mastery learning in schools and districts statewide (Roberts, Kenney, & Kozlovsky, 1986), we recommend that the most successful implementation approach is the pilot district one. This approach begins with one to three schools involved, an active principal and at least three volunteer teachers per school, and central office commitment to expansion. Early success in this approach leads to greater administrative involvement and in most cases the use of first-wave teachers as turnkey trainers for subsequent waves of teachers. The next most successful approach is districtwide or schoolwide implementation in a single subject or grade level, again with at least three participating teachers at a school and with the goal of all teachers implementing mastery learning in subsequent years. This approach requires the most work from the most people and is successful to the extent that attention is paid to building the commitment of school-based staff. Implementation approaches to be avoided are those called "lighthouse" (single school, no central office commitment, informal broadcasting of success) and "capacity-building" (training only, volunteer teachers, no administrative commitment to follow-up). Both of the approaches tend to kill an implementation rather quickly, according to the Maryland experience.

In anticipating who your volunteers might be, remember that an acceptable definition of *volunteer* includes both the person who eagerly steps forward and the one who must be persuaded over time, as long as the second one has the clear right to refuse without penalty. In this sense you may need to find some of the second type to fill in gaps in your initial lineup, starting with no fewer than three teachers for best results. It is important also to include volunteers who have a measure of credibility with other teachers.

What Kind of Implementation Plan Do We Need?   The essence of mastery learning is advance planning. What do students need to master, from easiest to most difficult? What prerequisite and component skills are essential, and which are not? How shall we teach to each objective, check for mastery, provide feedback, and correct and enrich student learning? What materials and strategies shall we use? Are they available from the experience of others, or must they be developed? Where can time be found or help obtained? How shall we maintain records in a minimum of time? How shall we check and grade for final mastery?

In setting a time to begin and deciding what must be in place ahead of time, it is a good idea to keep two concepts in mind. The first is that the planning team wants to build in early successes, and you want to be able to announce and replicate those successes to provide a firm base for continuing the program and increasing the number of implementers. This tends to *expand* the list of things that should be in place before beginning. The second concept is that of "organic adaptation and monitoring" referred to earlier, which means that much of the work of development takes place *during* implementation. It is during the process of implementation that problems arise, are recognized, and are solved. It is during implementation that behaviors and beliefs change and collegiality develops. This second concept tends to *limit* the number of things that must be in place before beginning.

The point, of course, is to get into action as quickly as possible, without frittering away people's energy unnecessarily and without introducing multiple major changes simultaneously. Plan to have beginning implementers limited in number and have all essential preparations made, no more and no less. We have said earlier that teachers should be fairly confident that they are ready to teach the first two units. Have your plans made for supportive follow-up on these units, for assistance in developing further units, and for rapid response to needs as they develop.

All beginning implementation efforts should be considered as pilot (or field) tests if the intent is to broaden, refine, and eventually institutionalize the use of mastery learning. This means that consideration should be given in advance to the kinds of information that should flow back to the planning team, between participants, and to interested observers from the implementation process.

With a small beginning group in a single building, this information flow can be relatively informal and personal at first. However, if substantial board and administrative commitment are anticipated and implementation will begin, for example, across buildings, more "informational" planning is needed.

Fortunately, Pringle (1985) has described the development of an effective management plan for this kind of situation, with attention to evaluation and information flow and to a rationale for each plan element.

Since Pringle's planning statement is so complete, we refer you to it and simply list its central elements here.

1. Goals to be accomplished in specified time period
2. Subject areas to be included
3. Time periods for plans
4. Provision for special students
5. Grading and promotion procedures
6. Teacher involvement in verifying effectiveness
7. Interventions for non-masters
8. School customization of plan
9. Principal role in verifying effectiveness
10. Principal reporting procedures and time lines
11. Central office use of report and data
12. Reports to boards of education and community
13. Course design and materials acquisition
14. Assistance to be provided to principals and teachers
15. Course revision
16. Revision and update of management plans. (p. 159)

Preparing Staff Orientation

At this point the team should have been regularly reporting to the school or district staff about progress in planning and have received regular feedback from them. As a representative team, you have a good idea of the "fit" of mastery learning to school or district priorities, the concerns various groups have about it, and at least a general sense of what is needed in staff development. You are now ready to conduct orientations for the total staff(s), preferably mandated. This is to make sure that potential volunteers have a common understanding of mastery learning and can make an informed choice, knowing what their roles and responsibilities will be. It is also so that all others will understand and can follow what is happening in implementation. Too many staff development activities go aground because nonimplementing teachers, those with a "wait and see" attitude, were not kept informed and lost interest.

Naming a Staff Development Coordinator

Now the planning team will want to designate a coordinator. This can be an administrator or an instructional leader, internal or external, with precontracted responsibilities for maintaining communication and orchestrating all parts of the mastery learning program. In Baltimore County (Roberts & Kenney, 1986), external facilitators were most useful when they were program [mastery learning] advocates, provided quality information, training and assistance relevant to local needs to facilitate rich fidelity of implementation; and engaged in cross-hierarchical problem solving that helped to clarify program purpose, maintain harmony and contribute to instructional improvement. [They] supported local leadership teams and acknowledged success. (p. 29)

ROLLING: MANAGING THE IMPLEMENTATION

Orientation

You may wish to conduct orientations for the entire staff and visitors (central office staff, parents, community members) and to mandate staff attendance, while keeping implementation voluntary. This helps to generate a climate of interest and enthusiasm. Each main presentation, whether by successful implementers, developers, trainer-facilitators, or the planning team, should clearly describe what mastery learning is and why its use is being promoted, with emphasis on anticipated student achievement and consequent behavioral and affective outcomes. Following this should be reports by the planning team with a clear statement of the brief for mastery learning, including the local needs and priorities it addresses and a preview of some of the how-to's developed for local use.

This preview should stress that the mastery learning program will contain certain *process* concerns such as *staff collaboration* to reduce teacher workload and support successful implementation; the use of *pilot groups* to clarify essentials of new areas of focus, and *leadership or cadre development* to build expertise that will remain in the school or district (Connor et al., 1986). The preview should also stress that the program has certain *product* concerns, especially student achievement and the development of a more effective school or district through the manipulation of schooling variables under direct staff control. Lezotte and Bancroft (1986) provide a useful frame of reference for this discussion:

> The improvement effort itself is a shared vision of the school and has the commitment of the school community. Underlying a meaningful improvement effort is the realization and acceptance of five major points, namely:
>
> 1. A focus on the single school as a strategic unit for school improvement.
> 2. A recognition that change is a long-term process (3 to 5 years) and not an event.
> 3. A belief that change is possible without infusion of major resources or personnel.

4. An acceptance of the idea that effective schools and effective teaching research provide a useful base for school improvement planning and implementation.
5. A representative team of administrators, teachers, and parents is needed to provide the leadership and inspiration for planning and implementing the design of school improvement. (p. 16)

Getting Consensus and Commitment

When trying to change school norms in an effective schooling process, it is important to get preliminary consensus from a "critical mass" of all those who work in a building. In beginning mastery learning on an incremental basis, the building is still the unit of interest, but different kinds of commitment can be sought from various role groups. We have divided these into mastery learning implementers, nonimplementers, administrators, and others and will consider them separately.

Mastery Learning Implementers. Teachers who volunteer or agree to implement mastery learning first are the front line, the group that will make or break mastery learning in the first year or two. Their concerns must be your main concern for a while, their needs paramount, and their professionalism respected. From the beginning they should see themselves, and others should recognize them, as in the forefront of improving professional practice in the building.

Expectations for this group may be put into written form for clarity and as a kind of public commitment between participants. This should be a limited agreement, with provisions for teachers being able to convince themselves of mastery learning's efficacy within a generous time limit and under appropriate conditions. Loucks-Horsley and Hergert (1985) capture the essential points of such an agreement as follows:

- Giving the new program a fair trial, sticking with it for a specified amount of time.
- Refraining from making major adaptations especially "watering it down" too early. In the trial period, fidelity to the program that was decided upon is an important expectation. Only after becoming adept in the program and understanding how it works and can work better for students should teachers make changes to suit their individual situations.
- Putting in the extra time needed to practice new skills, prepare new materials, and so forth. (p. 41)

We would add to this an informal agreement for constructive interaction among the volunteers. It should be made clear that this is for implementers to help each other and to save time, not to constrain their own teaching.

Potential volunteers will want to know how their workloads will be affected, what they will be doing that is different, the kind of help that will be available, the time lines, and whether there will be tenure-related performance evaluation of their use of the new methods.

Nonimplementers.   Under optimal conditions, mastery learning implementation basically spreads from teacher to teacher within a school. The most important thing to be remembered about teachers not in the first wave is that they are the pool of future implementers. They are not expected to do anything new in the classroom, but they can be asked to commit themselves to keeping open minds, evaluating the mastery learning process and its results along with other staff, and refraining from negative comments. If interested, they may be asked for various kinds of support to engage them more closely with mastery learning; if hostile, they should be asked to observe a noninterference policy.

Others.   Orientation and consensus building should include parents and parent-community organizations. Particularly if they have not had representatives on the planning team, parents need the same basic information that teachers and administrators receive: what mastery learning is, why it will be used, anticipated effects for students, local needs, priorities and goals related to mastery learning, and preliminary how-to's from the planning team.

The key group of parents are those whose children will be in mastery learning classes. Home reinforcement and support of classroom mastery learning, particularly when students have to put in unequal amounts of learning or homework time, are extremely valuable. Parents of mastery learning students should receive honest, frequent, and specific information on student progress, get concrete advice and assistance on ways to help at home, and stay in close touch with teachers by phone, notes, or visits when possible. Parents who have time to provide direct support to the school should be welcomed. Reaching other parents and groups, clerical and record-keeping assistance, materials location and preparation, in-school and after-school tutoring, and library research are some possible tasks for volunteers.

Administrators.   Programs at the school level typically have been the responsibility of district-level or, especially, building-level administrators. As a consequence, administrators play a central role in successful staff development even when a group of teachers intends to begin implementing mastery learning on its own. Some exercise of "bureaucratic self-restraint" (Finn, 1984) is an appropriate response in this case for administrators: Offer support and then wait to be asked. Some very successful programs have been teacher-dominated (Louis et al., 1981; see also Conner et al., 1986). Some have produced desired student outcomes and gained wide teacher acceptance *before* attracting support from administration. Others have developed to the point of recognizing the need for and requesting administrative backup in order to be more successful or to expand.

Whether administrative commitment is sought at the beginning or well into the implementation of mastery learning, the commitment should relate to the goal of *shared* instructional leadership and management. Collaboration has been increasingly shown to be the most effective approach to adoption of complex innovations (Lieberman, 1986). At the commitment stage, common understanding of the contributory participation of each role group can smooth the way to more successful implementation. Some conflict can be expected, even welcomed, as a sign that people are trying to change their ways of thinking and behaving; however, a collaborative approach helps participants to focus on *issues* rather than role conflicts.

Shared instructional leadership and management will require an important set of administrative commitments that parallel those asked of teachers: putting in the time and effort to understand mastery learning principles and practice, giving it a fair trial, and helping to maintain fidelity during the trial period. Though the experience in Maryland and elsewhere (for instance, Denver; see Barber, 1982) suggests that administrative and supervisory staff should receive awareness training before any teachers are trained (Roberts et al., 1986), we recommend joint staff development including both practitioners and administrators. In our experience such staff development not only is cost-effective but also has the advantage of allowing both sides to see the skills and judgment required of the other. This helps to lay the basis for increasing collegiality and trust.

One benefit of joint administrator-teacher staff development is that teachers can ask their administrators face to face for commitments of certain affective and logistical support for the new practices.

- Administrators can help to provide time for staff development and planning by groups of implementers, especially if some curriculum development is going on at the same time. This may mean arranging common prep time and/or release time, or paid time outside school hours, if that is possible and necessary.
- They can help to secure resources, both human and material, to support planning, training, and implementation.
- They can help to provide "protected practice" time (Paskal, Leverenz, Ruchgy, & Brandi, 1986) by blocking any interference with teacher use of mastery learning, by refraining from including such use in regular performance evaluation for a long period of

time, and by providing friendly, encouraging feedback to the experimenters.

- Both building and central administrators can play a key role in facilitating data collection, in helping to set a pattern for data-based decision making, and in circulating success stories throughout the school or district, based on these data.

Perhaps even more important, joint staff development can avoid the kind of "compliance mentality" (Chrispeels & Meaney, 1985) that can adversely affect both teachers and middle managers. In the absence of joint staff development, both groups may feel the need to create or refer to checklists to make sure they have considered everything or put it in place. While checklists can be useful guidelines and can provide a sense of security to participants (see, for example, the checklist in Jones, 1983), line supervisors may use them incorrectly to monitor and enforce every detail. The unintended result may be abdication of personal responsibility by those supervised. During early implementation stages, reflection, thoughtful discussion, and joint problem solving are more productive of real change in behaviors and beliefs than an authoritarian approach.

Shared instructional leadership and management in the implementation of mastery learning nevertheless takes into account the well-known relationship between successful change and an active style of administrative leadership. Little (1982) noted that the principal's role in successful change includes stating and demonstrating expectations for professional work, rewarding it when it occurs, and defending the professionals who take risks to achieve those expectations. And researchers in Maryland have found that where better implementation of mastery learning occurred, "administrators were well informed, supportive and expressed clear expectations of fidelity and intensity" (Roberts & Kenney, 1986, p. 32).

At the same time, we believe it is *every* educator's responsibility to contribute to improved methods and outcomes and that change should not depend on or wait for the readiness of, for example, the principal alone. Like teachers, principals often need support and retraining from their districts to carry out new responsibilities, such as the management of change (Louis, 1986). Recognition that principals cannot all be expected to be "heroes" (Corbett & D'Amico, 1986) riding to the rescue of a school should come as a relief to many overburdened people.

To our mind, the kind of administrative leadership that mastery learning will primarily require is as much moral as technical. Champlin (1983) has captured the characteristics of such a leader:

1. a clear sense of purpose and direction;
2. a consistently high level of expectation and performance;

3. an extensive knowledge of the skills and processes associated with programming;
4. a dedication to effectively use the human resources of the district through collaborative activities that afford participants influence and opportunity; and
5. an understanding of the leader's role as gatekeeper, both expecting and allowing things to happen.

[Further, such leaders] provide opportunities to acquire new skills and then encourage their implementation in surroundings where growth and renewal replace the "right or wrong" syndrome associated with many innovative efforts. (p. 31)

In order to identify with important changes such as mastery learning, administrators need to present a high profile; they must be seen often around the school, in the classroom, and at staff meetings. Modeling of the desired new attitudes and behaviors and active involvement in problem solving build collegiality with other staff members and promote their respect and, most important, the conviction with which they try new practices (Bandura, 1977).

Are your administrators such effective leaders? Koehn (1983) has developed a lighthearted but trenchant way for the planning team to ask administrators to examine their skill levels for effective leadership in mastery learning by answering a series of questions. This checklist appears in Box 3.4.

Of course, administrators who respond with mostly A's have the necessary mastery leadership skills. For those who do not and are still interested in trying mastery learning, we recommend participation in an administrator training program that is supplemental to the joint administrator-staff one. Fitzpatrick has developed such a program (see Fitzpatrick & Charters, 1986) for use at the secondary level, but its basic ideas apply at the elementary level as well.

Participating administrators were given an overview of the research-based instructional principles included in the teachers' training program, and a discussion of their implications was held. The program director also suggested ways for administrators to support the teachers in their efforts to implement the recommended instructional strategies. These support strategies, drawn from the research on effective schools, included administrative support functions (Gersten & Carnine, 1981), the instructional leadership behaviors linked to the characteristics of effective schools (Russell & White, 1982), administrative behaviors related to instructional improvement (Bauchner & Loucks, 1982), and the leadership functions that facilitate the implementation and effectiveness of staff development programs (Gall et al., 1984).

BOX 3.4   A Checklist for Administrative Responsibilities

Responsibility 1: The Administrator as Staff Developer

The ability to conduct meaningful staff development activities is strongly emphasized as an administrative skill in the implementation of a Mastery Learning plan. Consider the following checklist as your opportunity to assess the skills of the administrative staff in your district. You might try the test first from the viewpoint of the administrative staff as a whole, then take it again using your own personal vantage point.

1. ____ A. Is able to demonstrate knowledge of the theory of Mastery Learning; or
   ____ B. Merely uses the jargon associated with Mastery Learning as discussed in popular literature.
2. ____ A. Applies principles of human relations and group dynamics in teacher training activities; or
   ____ B. Prefers to "lay it on" staff in shallow, meaningless programs.
3. ____ A. Understands the dynamics of school organization and plans accordingly, involving those who need to be involved; or
   ____ B. Goes off "half-cocked" and involves the wrong people in the process of staff development.
4. ____ A. Utilizes creative and individualized approaches to staff development and inservice; or
   ____ B. Depends upon "one-shot" lecture, large-group inservice programs.
5. ____ A. Puts his "money where his mouth is" in matters of staff development and inservice; or
   ____ B. The last thing considered in the budget is staff development.

Responsibility 2: The Administrator as Instructional Leader

In order to lead a Mastery Learning effort in an effective way, the administrator must possess refined skills in the analysis and appraisal of instruction. The administrator must be an instructional supervisor whose authority is based upon competence in the field of instruction, not on staff position. Again, check the items you feel are appropriate for the total administrative staff in general; then rate yourself as the points apply to you individually as an administrator.

1. ____ A. Can define the instructional program and the identified skills to be mastered by students; or
   ____ B. Has a vague notion of the exact skills which the program is designed to teach and hopes teachers are teaching them.
2. ____ A. Can help find time and resources so that individual students get feedback and corrective help when needed; or
   ____ B. Considers time a constant and insures that all students cover the same material—whether they need it or not.

3. _____ A. Can evaluate outcomes which insure that students are ready for the next learning task; or

_____ B. Permits students to engage in activities regardless of readiness.

4. _____ A. Is able to evaluate learning—not just teaching; or

_____ B. Evaluates the program only on the basis of teaching covered.

5. _____ A. Shares in the selection of material being utilized and coordinates such materials with the goals and objectives of the program; or

_____ B. Allows textbook companies to provide the curriculum for the school.

Responsibility 3: The Administrator as Climate Manager

The management of school climate is one of the most crucial factors in implementing Mastery Learning. Careful attention should be paid to insuring high levels of productivity as measured by both the satisfaction and achievement of staff and students. A basic premise of ML is the maintenance of a positive self-concept among learners. As an administrator, check the items that state your administrative staff's view and, then, your own.

1. _____ A. Is aware of and manages the "hidden curriculum" being implemented in the school; or

_____ B. Is oblivious to the "hidden curriculum" and allows it to run the school.

2. _____ A. Trusts the staff and gives the necessary autonomy to implement Mastery Learning effectively; or

_____ B. Second-guesses staff members as they attempt to learn and teach.

3. _____ A. Cares about the school, the staff, and the students; or

_____ B. Is an inaccessible, bureaucratic hardnose.

4. _____ A. Respects and provides for the human needs and concerns of the staff; or

_____ B. Administers from an "ivory tower."

5. _____ A. Knows that satisfaction and achievement are positively related to one another; or

_____ B. Subscribes to the principle of "You don't have to like it, you just have to do it."

6. _____ A. Is an active listener and judges both the intent and the content of the message being delivered; or

_____ B. Strives to "get the work out" from the top down.

Scoring Instructions

(Score administrative staff and yourself separately.)

1. Count number of "A" responses and indicate total: _____
2. Count number of "B" responses and indicate total: _____
3. If you have:

0–6 "A" responses   Don't try it, just hope you survive!

(continued)

7–12 "A" responses	You stand a chance. Do some more reading in the areas where you scored lowest.
12 or more "A"'s	Go for it. You probably have the skills to do the job.
More "B"'s than "A"'s	Better go back to the "drawing board" and brush up on your administrative theory!

Koehn, 1983.

Administrative strategies for strengthening the teachers' instructional improvement efforts included:

- Advocating the commitment to help students achieve a mastery level of performance
- Helping teachers overcome obstacles to implementing mastery learning strategies
- Monitoring instructional performance and providing feedback
- Understanding that teachers' initial efforts to implement recommended instructional strategies may be somewhat awkward at first
- Providing teachers with encouragement by recognizing their accomplishments
- Providing teachers with opportunities to share instructional ideas with each other by scheduling peer observations and collegial planning sessions (p. 34)

Staff Development

Staff development programs frequently emphasize discrete skills pertaining to particular areas of schooling. Although we do not want to overload teachers and administrators with too much information in a short time, we do believe it is essential that people understand their part within the larger processes of school improvement. Placing mastery learning implementation into the context of general school improvement can prove useful to staff members as they grapple with specific day-to-day problems. Some of the issues to consider then are time for staff development, "mutual adaptation," school improvement processes, belief systems, classroom actions, and closure.

Time for Staff Development.   Time for staff development has been a major problem with most approaches to innovation in education. So it is with mastery learning. For mastery learning to work, there must be a commitment to adequate staff development time on the part of the board, teachers, and administration. Successful mastery learning implementation schoolwide is a process that takes years, not months. Staff members need not only presentations on research findings and instructional principles but also assistance in applying these in the classroom—time for follow-up, staff collaboration, peer observation and feedback, and so on. Teachers may wish to use some prep time for staff collaboration but frequently release time, after-school, or weekend sessions are also necessary, especially when some curriculum development is also required.

This time should not come out of teachers' hides, as Champlin (1983) notes, but must be paid for. We are fully aware of the severe financial limitations many districts face these days but must nevertheless question their priorities if they have not budgeted some staff development time. The cost effectiveness of well-planned, research-based staff development that focuses on local curricula is evident from many major programs (see, for example, Fitzpatrick & Charters, 1986).

Mutual Adaptation.   Researchers have found that staffs with little involvement or influence in decision making tend to develop no feelings of ownership in new programs and participate, if at all, in only perfunctory ways. The "mutual adaptation" approach is especially useful for providing staffs with such involvement and influence. This approach is related to Levine's (1985a) organic adaptation and monitoring and has three parts (Berman & McLaughlin, 1978; McLaughlin, Pfeifer, Swanson-Owens, & Yee, 1986): modification of program design, changes in the institutional setting, and changes on the part of individual participants, all occurring at the same time. With an acceptance of this approach, participants can make the fine adjustments in programs, setting, and selves as they learn by doing, thereby promoting success.

Lezotte and Bancroft (1986) summarize some of the advantages of a mutually adaptive approach to staff development:

> It is satisfying for the faculty to know that not only will some changes be expected of them, but that there also will be changes in policies and the organizational structure to implement and support school improvement. A common goal elicits a common bond. Faculty begin to share and speak a common language relative to the characteristics of effective schools. Above all a single common purpose unites the school—the overarching goal of increasing the level and altering the distribution of achievement. (p. 16)

School Improvement Processes.   Effective teaching behaviors are not likely to be sustained unless they are nested in effective school processes. It takes a very supportive climate to keep people working near peak performance. A negative or unsupportive climate often has staff members isolated from each other or at loggerheads, unwilling to put in extra time and effort that will be unrecognized, unappreciated, or even sharply criticized by administrators or other staff members. Like students, teachers often prefer not to attract attention to themselves in such a setting, even if this means continuing to engage in unproductive behavior. Yet most teachers find themselves in just such unsupportive work environments, according to a survey commissioned by the National Education Association (1986).

In the areas of clear organizational goals and priorities, adequate resources to do the job, communication and cooperation among staff, and involvement of all employees in decision making, schools ranked the lowest when they were compared to other organizations. Only 13% of the respondents found in-service activities to be effective. However, the main conclusions of the report were encouraging:

> Not sweeping reforms, but incremental strategic change at the local level is needed ... simple, straightforward things that local districts can do tomorrow morning: improving the communication structure, educating administrators about the importance of shared decision making, and ensuring that teachers have the material resources and time to do their jobs. (Olson, 1986, p. 1)

Staff development activities should be aimed at group building, at creating bonds between participants so they can support, encourage, and help each other as implementation progresses. Conyers (1985) provides one of several useful lists of effective school group-building processes to be used during mastery learning staff development:

> Effective school processes exist where staff:
>
> **a.** cooperatively plan the school program by developing shared curriculum
> **b.** cooperatively plan the school program by establishing a discipline code
> **c.** cooperatively plan the school program by structuring opportunities
> **d.** obtain consensus about clearly defined total school goals
> **e.** assess and monitor attainment of total school goals
> **f.** reward the progress students make toward the school goals
> **g.** model behaviors that are consistent with the school goals (p. 20)

Additional useful references on effective school processes, with an emphasis on staff development, are *Creating Effective Schools: An Inservice Program for Enhancing School Learning Climate and Student Achievement* (Brookover et al., 1982), *Effective Schools and Classrooms: A Research-based Perspective* (Squires, Huitt, & Segars, 1983–1984), and *Building Effective Schools: Assessing, Planning, Implementing* (Chrispeels & Meaney, 1985).

Belief Systems.   Whether behavioral changes precede, follow, or coincide with attitudinal changes, there is no question about the importance of dealing with belief systems throughout training, implementation, and beyond.

This is the thread that runs through all of mastery learning. Without changes in the stereotypical thinking embedded in American education, which consigns a third or more of the nation's children to less than full education and participation in society, generation after generation, mastery learning cannot succeed. It can be implemented, but it cannot succeed unless belief systems change while professional practice changes. To us belief connotes knowledge *plus* conviction, even a passionate emotional commitment to bringing about the excellent and equitable education of the many rather than the few. We shall have more to say about the role of belief systems in mastery learning in our concluding chapter.

Classroom Actions.   Mastery learning has features that make it like and unlike more traditional nonmastery approaches to instruction. Indeed, mastery learning trainers used to joke about how often someone in their groups would say, "But that's just good teaching" or "I've always done it that way." The trainers' usual (unspoken) reaction was a mocking, "Sure you have!" However, closer examination often revealed that such a teacher was in fact using many of the methods of mastery learning, but using them inconsistently.

It becomes critical in staff development activities concerning mastery learning, therefore, to draw out similarities and differences, especially the latter, such as regular and systematic use of formative evaluation and corrective and enrichment strategies. This is the primary purpose of the classroom actions section of the staff development program. We will return to this issue in our discussion of staff development processes.

Closure.   Miles (1983) has suggested that the institutionalization of an innovation is harder than its implementation. For example, earlier we discussed beginning the implementation of mastery learning by working around, rather than changing, policies that do not allow mastery grading. We suggested using a process of mastery certification in addition to regular report cards. At some appropriate point during implementation, however, you will want to make mastery grading the standard operating procedure for all. This helps to weave curriculum objectives, mastery standards, and mastery expectations into the fabric of the school for future teachers and students.

We find the concept of closure useful in our programs to keep participants aware that institutionalization of mastery ideas is the goal of staff development. The disappearance of outside facilitators and special funding and the return of internal trainers to other full-time duties should be anticipated and plans made for continuance.

A variety of strategies can be used to promote institutionalization. Miles (1983, pp. 17–18), in particular, suggests three:

1. Mandated, stable use: "requiring the use of the innovation, and maintaining much stability in personnel and their use of the innovation"
2. Skillful, committed use: not requiring the innovation, but spending "much energy on assisting users and developing their commitment"
3. Vulnerable use: pivoting on the availability of funding and the nonmobility of key personnel

Of these, though we have seen the first work rather well (see Abrams, 1985), we prefer the second, the strategy of skillful, committed use. At the heart of this strategy seems to be the building of a maximum number of skillful implementers at each site, developing leadership skills at each site, putting group processes in place that will promote staff commitment and continuous renewal, and examining conformance or nonconformance of local policies and procedures to mastery ideas.

Institutionalization of mastery learning ideas is relatively easy to recognize. You will know that you are approaching institutionalization when three plateaus have been reached:

- Staff expects all students will be effective in school.
- Staff places emphasis on basic skills and academics.
- Students expect that their own constructive behaviors will lead to achievement.

As Sizer and Powell (1984) say:

> The heart of fine education is the constructive confrontation of able teachers and willing pupils—a joining that cannot be mass produced. It emerges from deft and sensible adaptation, school by school, even classroom by classroom, and from a commitment to learning [that] flourishes when students and teachers feel a strong sense of ownership of their particular schools. (p. 17)

When you have reached this point, the program may even die, but the ideas will live.

Staff Development Models

As noted earlier, the implementation of mastery learning programs requires that teachers and administrators learn about the similarities and differences between mastery learning and more conventional approaches to instruction. Typically, this learning will be conveyed through some type of mastery-oriented staff development process.

There are a variety of effective models for staff development. These models vary by grade level, by subject matter, and by philosophy of the staff developer. Any model selected should be appropriate for your particular site. No one model, regardless of any claim it may make to be the "best" mastery learning program, is likely to be appropriate for all teachers and administrators.

Two of the most copied staff development models are those of Denver and Philadelphia. The former model focuses primarily on elementary and secondary school students' intellectual development, the latter on their affective development as well.

In Boxes 3.5 and 3.6 we have listed the basic staff development units that form the core of each of these programs. In our experience, teachers

---

BOX 3.5   The Denver Model

 I. Orientation to the Mastery Learning Process
 II. Planning for Mastery Overview
    A. Planning and writing behavioral objectives
    B. Task analyzing the overall objectives
    C. Using the task analysis in planning a mastery unit
    D. Using practice theory in planning effective lessons
    E. Using transfer theory in planning effective lessons
    F. Lesson planning format
    G. Developing correctives
    H. Developing extension activities
 III. Teaching to Mastery Overview
    A. Orienting students to mastery learning
    B. Teaching mini-units to mastery
    C. Diagnosing student learning
    D. Prescribing appropriate instruction
    E. Grading and reporting
    F. Evaluating mastery program effectiveness
 IV. Managing a Mastery Classroom
    A. Using motivation theory
    B. Using reinforcement theory
    C. Signaling techniques
    D. Giving directions
    E. Using "sponge" activities
    F. Questioning techniques
    G. Cooperative learning techniques.

Barber, 1982, p. 14.

BOX 3.6   The Philadelphia Model

I. Presentation of the Mastery Learning Belief System
  A. Virtually all students can learn all important academic content to a level of excellence.
  B. The primary function of schools should be to define mastery goals and to help all students achieve them.
  C. Individual differences in students' motivation and rate of learning are a result of their past learning histories, and under favorable conditions these differences tend to disappear.
II. Preparation of Mastery Learning Units
  A. Select what is to be learned
  B. Develop parallel formative and summative tests
  C. Develop daily goal statements
  D. Plan learning alternatives (correctives and enrichments)
III. Implementation of Mastery Learning Units
  A. State goals
  B. Teach the lesson
  C. Conduct formative testing
  D. Provide immediate feedback
  E. Provide learning alternatives
  F. Conduct summative testing

Adapted from Conner et al., 1986, p. 11.

---

must be trained to master the ideas and practices contained in each of these units, unless they are already parts of current practice. Just as important, they must be trained to orchestrate the ideas and practices from one unit with not only those of the other units but also with their customary style of teaching. Since training procedures, as well as manuals for this training, are widely available and can be obtained by writing these programs' developers (see the Appendix), we shall not repeat all these procedures here. We will, though, indicate in general how these procedures are taught.

Both Denver's and Philadelphia's mastery learning programs offer teachers and administrators supportive services that include extended training, lesson observation, conferences about the lesson, lesson demonstration, and use of mastery learning materials. But each program offers these services in various ways.

Denver employs three delivery models, the most interesting of which is one in which interested principals serve as the primary building site staff developer. Barber (1982) describes these three delivery models as follows:

1. District project principals are trained in inservice content by the project manager and then they deliver the content to the teachers in the building. Workshops generally last an hour apiece and are held before or after school. Each has a topic and gives teachers opportunities to apply it. Principals also receive training in observing and conferencing with teachers.
2. The collaborative teacher-to-teacher training approach includes resource specialists released from full-time classroom assignments who train volunteers. Intensive five-day workshops are held, and the resource specialists then provide follow-up services to the volunteer teachers as they try out mastery learning in the classroom.
3. The resource specialists also train trainers, who then work with other staff members in their own buildings. The specialists also function as facilitators for this training. This approach provides a more flexible schedule for teachers who don't want to leave their classes for five days, or who don't have a principal who can train them. (p. 15)

Barber notes that use of all three delivery models helped to account for widespread dissemination to Denver schools, helped develop leadership skills and expand the roles of staff members, and gave them a strong sense of ownership, responsibility, and accomplishment. She also comments that the model using the building principals, in particular, dramatically increased the quality and quantity of instructional supervision teachers received.

Philadelphia's training models are similar except that they make little use of the building principal technique, suggesting once again that it is instructional leadership that is a key to mastery learning and that this leadership needs to be provided by someone but not necessarily the principal. Conner and colleagues (1986) describe the staff development aspect of Philadelphia's Mastery Learning Program (PMLP) as follows:

Most introductory training is done in groups of 30–50 teachers (3–5 teachers from each of 10–15 schools) who meet over a school year for about 18 hours of staff development. These teachers, who are preparing and implementing mastery units throughout the year with one class or subject area, are visited on-site several times per year by PMLP staff for support and coaching. Other introductory training takes place in on-site clusters, where a teacher who has successfully implemented the mastery approach provides training for interested members of his or her staff, with leadership training from the PMLP. A third model is school-based, with an entire faculty receiving training and implementing the approach in one or more subject areas. (p. 11)

Despite the general utility of the Denver and Philadelphia models, we are frequently asked about staff development models specific for secondary school teachers. There seems to be an abiding assumption among secondary educators that their staff development needs, especially in the areas of classroom management and subject matter specialization, are different from those of elementary educators.

Fitzpatrick (see Fitzpatrick & Charters, 1986) has developed and validated a most interesting secondary school scheme for staff development called the Time for Mastery Program. This scheme places great emphasis on not only mastery learning but also the classroom management of mastery learning at the secondary level, especially the management of classroom teaching and learning time. The program is designed to help high school teachers, who are pressed for content coverage, to find time to assist students to reach mastery or, as the authors put it, to minimize the time costs of mastery learning by maximizing the use of instructional time. The classroom management strategies taught were preventive rather than reactive. We have summarized some of them in Box 3.7.

According to Fitzpatrick and Charters, this program has helped teachers to achieve the following results:

- Increase the amount of time they spend in the crucial feedback and corrective phase of instruction from less than 1% to an average of 21% of classroom time
- Decrease off-task student behavior by half
- Cut noninstructional time lost to transitions by one-third
- Drop in-class review and homework-correcting time from 43% to 28%
- Cut in-class independent practice (seatwork) in half
- Spend more class time presenting new material and quizzes
- Maintain the scope and pace of the instruction

BOX 3.7   Some Elements of the Time for Mastery Program

- Establishing clear expectations and consequences for student academic and behavioral performance
- Eliminating or minimizing interruptions of instructional time
- Maintaining an academic focus
- Monitoring student behavior
- Planning for smooth transitions between instructional activities
- Holding students accountable
- Establishing a positive classroom climate

Adapted from Fitzpatrick and Charters, 1986, p. 27.

It also helped students, including honor students, according to the teachers' own analysis, do much better than the previous year's students on the same content.

Staff Development Processes

Mastery learning is a complex innovation, not a simple one. Joyce and Showers (1983) distinguish between new learning and skills that can be transferred from the training setting to the workplace as is (horizontal transfer) and new learning and skills that require adaptation to workplace conditions and additional learning on the job before they can be used to solve problems (vertical transfer). Clearly, mastery learning belongs in the second category. The researchers call the process of mastering vertical transfer gaining "executive control," which they define as follows:

> Understanding the purpose and rationale of the skill and knowing how to adapt it to students, apply it to subject matter, modify or create instructional materials attendant to its use, organize students to use it, and blend it with other instructional approaches to develop a smooth and powerful whole. (p. 8)

Mastery learning must be fitted to the needs, objectives, goals, and conditions of the classroom, including the teacher's own style, strengths, and weaknesses. This requires numerous skills, judgment, and continual decision making on the part of the teacher, decision making that is closely supported by the mastery learning process. Gaining executive control is an incremental process, the length and difficulty of which are dependent on many factors. Just one of the contextual factors, for example, might be variance in pupil readiness; the complexity of mastery learning increases when students lack many prerequisites. Diagnosis, plans to address prerequisites within or before new units of learning, deciding whether temporary mastery and nonmastery grouping or whole class review is the most appropriate corrective, and organizing the time for this—all are necessary. The old way was simply to ignore the mastery question, either by presenting the content "cold" and avoiding responsibility for outcomes or by consigning the less prepared students to lower levels of instruction (tracking). This is more familiarly called "teach the best, shoot the rest" by disapproving educators.

Variance in student readiness, of course, is common, even universal, and must be faced and solved. Some teachers, and some systems, will themselves be at higher levels of readiness for mastery learning; others will need ongoing support in order to master the whole galaxy of teaching, organizational, management, and other skills brought into play during initiation and refinement of mastery learning practice. The presence or absence of *essential* skills must be taken into account by staff developers and participants at various points. In fact, ongoing support and follow-up are *more* important than initial training (Loucks-Horsley & Hergert, 1985) if mastery learning is to reach its potential.

We are thus concerned here with mastery learning's special staff development requirements. We will recommend that the obvious way to ensure that teachers acquire the essential skills they need to teach for mastery is to use a mastery learning approach to staff development. Specifically, we recommend that your staff development program use the following elements of mastery learning: recognition of affective and cognitive entry levels of trainees; planning and initial instruction; feedback, correction, and enrichment; and using evaluation for improvement.

Affective Entry Levels.   Just as many students enter a new class unconvinced that they can learn new material or that the system will give them a fair shake, so too do many teachers—even those who have volunteered—enter mastery learning training as nonbelievers. The sorting and labeling process is endemic in schools and in teacher-training institutions; many teachers do not know or remember anything different. Their working lives have often been spent identifying various levels of ability and achievement, learning disabilities, background factors, behavior problems, and so on, and treating students "accordingly," with the best of intentions in most cases. They want all children to learn, and by now they have heard that this is possible, but many are far from convinced that they can achieve that happy state in their own classrooms, with the students they know. In negative climates they may even be afraid to try, afraid of harsh judgments from supervisors and even harsher judgments from peers. They are much more hardened in their entering attitudes and behaviors than students, having reached some equilibrium or set of coping skills in their professional lives.

Every teacher has seen one or more students suddenly catch fire and move ahead more rapidly than anyone thought possible. This is one of teaching's most rewarding and memorable moments and usually results from the student's sudden recognition of success: "I can do it!" Caring teachers applaud this recognition, bring it to parents' and other students' attention so *they* can applaud it, help the student to generate a whole string of successes to reinforce the original recognition, point out the value of sustained effort, and in the process help the student to redefine her or his self-concept of academic ability—a kind of renorming of the individual. Mastery learning staff development can take the same route by consciously *planning* for early success in some aspect of implementation and then reinforcing that success. This is the best way to overcome previous failure experiences, self-doubt, and system doubt.

There are a number of ways to plan for success in mastery learning. First, it is essential that trainees understand the theoretical base and the rationale for group-based mastery learning. Teachers (like most people) are sometimes impatient with this aspect of training, have little regard for research findings, and may prefer that "someone just show me what to do and I'll do it." There is no way they can "do it" more than once or twice, successfully, without decision making and judgment based on *knowledge*. If teachers do not fully understand the aptitude-time equation of mastery learning and the centrality of quality of instruction, they will not be able to plan and carry out the sequence of instructional behaviors that are known to result in extensive student mastery; they will fail. Administrators who do not understand these things will not know how best to support teachers' use of this sequence of behaviors or to help extend it to other staff. We recommend again here that teachers and administrators be jointly trained at this stage for common understandings that lay the base for collegiality.

Second, it is important that educators see credible evidence of the success of group-based mastery learning, preferably in settings similar to their own. Unfortunately, there is still a gap between research and practice, the historical reasons for which we will not repeat here. Educators simply do not believe most laboratory reports and are deeply suspicious even of the success of "real" schools. There is always a list of reasons why "it won't work here." They need to touch base with other practitioners and satisfy their curiosity about details—how this or that was done, how long it took, how people (teachers, students, and parents) feel about it, and so on. Observing a mastery learning program in action and making personal contact with other mastery learning practitioners are the best for trainees or for a small group of them who can report back to the others. If this is not possible, in these days of low budgets, other creative solutions can be found. These can include videotapes and vivid, careful descriptions of existing programs, even conference calls between trainees and successful practitioners elsewhere. Exposure to current good practice also answers some of the *personal* concerns all teachers have when they approach implementation: "How does it affect *me*?" (Loucks & Hall, 1979, describe the stages of concern that new implementers go through.)

Third, participants should experience some success in their early trials of mastery learning. People can and should be asked to suspend disbelief to some extent when they try mastery learning the first few times—but not indefinitely. Guskey (1985d) studied a large group of teachers trained in the use of mastery learning procedures, some of whom never implemented it, some who did but did not see improvement in their students' learning, and the largest group, those who did see improvement, who, in other words, were successful. The teachers who did see improvement became more positive about teaching and expressed greater personal responsibility for student learning. Guskey concluded that training, implementation, and evidence of improved student learning are all necessary conditions of change in teachers' attitudes and behaviors.

One effective way to produce such changes in teachers' attitudes and behavior has been proposed. Guskey (1985d) argues that mastery learning staff developers should

> organize and present changes required of teachers in small incremental steps, described clearly and explicitly with emphasis on efficiency and practicality. Further, they should begin with changes that are relatively modest but that can result in *demonstrable* student improvements in a fairly short period of time. (p. 59)

There are several ways to accomplish this incrementalism. One way involves testing. In the widely implemented Philadelphia mastery learning program (Conner et al., 1986), for example, teachers are initially encouraged to do summative tests after *each* unit of instruction, rather than combining several units for a test at the middle or end of a marking period. The purpose of this is to provide feedback more rapidly to both students and teachers on their success in learning and teaching. If learning improvements are not seen in the first few units, quite possible in a new program, other kinds of improvement may be noted, such as increased time on task, more student interest in learning, and the teacher's own increased understanding (Smith, 1985).

The choice of objectives is another way to accomplish mastery learning incrementally. If possible, the objectives for the first few units should not be those that have proved most difficult for students in the past and should have limited prerequisites or prerequisites that can be taught as part of the unit. Teachers will be encouraged to tackle the big ones when they are more confident of the process, of their own skills, and of student mastery of basics.

In sum, then, teachers should *understand* success (theory and rationale), *see* success (evidence from other projects or earlier on-site implementation), and *feel* success in improved student learning (implementation) near the beginning of any mastery learning program. Their successes in the classroom should be recognized, reinforced, and replicated so that they will be willing to expend the effort necessary to continue implementing and improving mastery learning practice.

However, it takes more than individual expertise and motivation to sustain lasting change, as year-to-year behavioral and outcome variance among subjects in the teacher-effects research clearly shows. The effective schools literature points to the need for a school environment that supports experimentation and improvement. As staff development proceeds, attention must also be paid to group building, not just with the first wave of implementers but with all interested staff. Middle managers (principals) and other instructional leaders, as well as trainers, play a key role here in creating new building norms and new expectations for staff behavior and student outcomes by modeling support for the first wave of implementers, assisting them as necessary, *publicly* recognizing any early successes, and refraining from interference and hostile or nonproductive criticism or evaluation. This represents a major step toward wider implementation and eventual institutionalization of mastery learning.

Cognitive Entry Levels.   Mastery learning is sometimes referred to as a scaffolding for instruction, a structure and approach that can eventually accommodate all the skills a teacher can muster and some that he or she does not yet have and will want to learn, at least as mastery learning progresses to the highest levels of implementation. For new implementers, however, it is important that as few disruptions as possible occur in their teaching as they begin mastery learning. In other words, they should use the teaching approaches with which they are most comfortable and familiar. The objectives of this teaching *do* change in mastery learning, however, to include mastery for all or nearly all students; this requires the addition of the feedback and corrective loop, which is about as much as many teachers can handle at the beginning. There is a question of balance here, however. Staff developers must be sensitive to the skills that teachers bring to mastery learning training and must discriminate between those that are essential to mastery learning and those that are merely nice to know. This is analogous to teachers discriminating between critical and noncritical prerequisites for students in a new learning unit. Philadelphia, for example (Conners et al., 1986), aims for simplicity by having pilot teachers identify steps in the process that can be left out without compromising quality.

   The cognitive part of staff development, therefore, should help teachers with skills essential to mastery learning implementation that are based on teachers' entry levels, needs identified before or during implementation, and teacher interest. This can be accomplished in a variety of ways.

   Consider the use of time, which is so integral to mastery learning programs. We have already mentioned Fitzpatrick's Time for Mastery Program (Fitzpatrick & Charters, 1986). This program provides mechanisms by which the feedback and corrective loop, which requires "extra" time amounts depending on student aptitudes, entry levels, and quality of initial instruction, can become a nonrestrictive part of the teacher's regular in-class instruction. Goodlad (1984), in his national study of schools, found that typically less than 2% of school time is spent on this important part of education. Yet this loop is central to the effectiveness of mastery learning and must not be done in a "Robin Hood" fashion, that is, by stealing time from the academically rich in order to give to the academically poor (Arlin, 1984).

The Time for Mastery program recognizes that many high schools particularly operate on the (unspoken) assumption that students, as presumed independent learners by this time, are responsible for mastery and teachers are responsible for content coverage. Of course, many high school students are *not* independent learners because they have not learned to learn in their previous schooling. The classroom management and organization skills included in the Time for Mastery training help to create conditions that support, but do not necessarily change, teachers' styles of instruction.

Another significant way to increase student engaged time, that is, to minimize the time costs of mastery learning by maximizing the use of instructional time, is student cooperative or team learning (Philadelphia's program is a good example). Like the classroom management and organizational skills taught in the Time for Mastery program, the use of cooperative learning in the classroom can support and reinforce the teacher's instruction without necessarily changing it. Team learning responds to the problem of how to keep the rest of the class on task while the teacher provides corrective or enrichment instruction to small groups or individuals. It is adaptable to all classrooms and can be used instead of or in addition to independent practice. It is useful for drill and practice *and* for mastering the most difficult material on high-level skills, a good setting for corrective and enrichment instruction from the teacher and tutoring from peers.

Cooperative learning is also an alternative to the endless (and boring) "teacher talk" that Goodlad (1984) and his colleagues found so prevalent in their "Study of Schooling." The cooperative classroom can variously be teacher-centered, group-centered, and student-centered at different times. Although this does not lessen the teacher's overall responsibility for student learning, it does provide some relief and variety to both the teacher's day and the student's.

Finally, cooperative learning responds to Block's (1984) contention that schooling should more often resemble play; there is a creative freshness and liveliness to most teamwork that teachers may begin the day with but find hard to maintain until 3 o'clock. Students feel the same connectedness and pleasure in the company of peers that Friday night card-playing buddies feel and become just as adept at anticipating, challenging, and supporting each other's moves as they learn to work together.

Another direct approach to maximizing instructional time is use of one of the effective instruction models—for example, active teaching (Good, Grouws, & Ebmeier, 1983), clinical supervision and mastery teaching

(Hunter, 1984), and direct instruction (Rosenshine, 1979). Generally, these techniques are designed to maintain active participation in learning by all students. In the mastery learning structure, such participation makes the initial whole class instruction phase more productive of learning, thereby cutting down the time needed for reinstruction. Barber (1985), for example, built on Hunter's mastery teaching model in her original development of the Denver approach. The model has subsequently been expanded to build on still more effective instructional techniques. Conyers (1985), in fact, now lists some 19 characteristics that Denver expects of teachers pursuing mastery in student learning. Teachers must learn how to do all of the following:

a. spend a large portion of their time on direct instruction
b. require on-task behavior of students
c. monitor and adjust to students' learning of materials
d. establish early and enforce quickly appropriate classroom conduct
e. start and end lessons on time
f. structure the lesson through the use of introduction, presentation, practice, and review
g. indicate clearly to students the aims of the lesson
h. remain on task (academic focus)
i. choose activities that are challenging and promote success
j. present lessons with enthusiasm
k. praise students and use appropriate student contributions
l. ask frequent questions of all students and mix the cognitive level of questions
m. give and check homework
n. schedule regular periods of time for students to work quietly
o. write clear, detailed lesson plans
p. focus lesson plans toward the school's stated goals and objectives
q. assess daily student progress
r. eliminate unproductive instruction procedures
s. [be] open to and available for counseling students (p. 20)

One word of caution is in order, however. These effective instructional techniques do tend to impinge more directly on teachers' style. They should be seen as part of mastery learning instruction, not a substitute for it.

Planning and Initial Instruction. Staff developers will need to develop objectives for mastery learning and mastery learning–related training that are clear and specific so that teachers know exactly what is expected of them. For example, they should know that they will have many options in fitting mastery learning to their classrooms but that fidelity is also a concern. Here is an example: Teachers can substitute their own procedures (such as examining writing samples or observing performance of a new skill) for paper-and-pencil tests in the formative or summative evaluation stages.

However, there must be clear mastery criteria that apply to all students, and the formative evaluation, whatever its form, must be systematic, frequent, and objective.

As with students, the list of staff development objectives should be shared with all participants at the beginning, along with information on how training and support for implementation will be organized, time lines, how they can get help, and so on. Changes suggested by trainees should be incorporated whenever possible.

Training should further include a variety of approaches, demonstrations, examples, guided practice, and frequent checks on understanding. This should include formative testing, either paper-and-pencil or observation, to determine mastery and any reinstruction needs and also to help the teachers remain serious about learning!

Finally, the training should include "overlearning." Just as students may need several opportunities to practice a new skill correctly, teachers may need the same opportunities to become more comfortable with some aspects of mastery learning during training. The consistent modeling of mastery learning practice by staff developers has the same effect in accustoming trainees to mastery learning ways.

Nevertheless, even with clear objectives, a variety of training approaches, and opportunities for overlearning, some staff members will still feel discomfort as they try out these new ways in the classroom. They will feel awkward, clumsy, and disoriented, the more they are used to smooth operation of their classroom; in other words, the better the teacher, the higher the discomfort level. They may also not get the best results the first few times as they and their students try out new ways of doing things.

We suspect that many of these teachers suffer from the fact that mastery learning classroom practices are built on the concept of the learning unit and that they involve a certain amount of diagnosis, reteaching, and retesting. Ryan (1985), in her review of research on teacher preparation, for example, found that most conventional curriculum planning is taught with a focus on daily lesson plans; very little is done on organizing curriculum into units or developing assignments and tests relevant to objectives, what Ryan calls "preactive" planning tasks. Pringle (1985) notes that from fourth grade up, teachers are less and less accustomed to diagnosis, reteaching, and retesting.

To deal with the distress we have followed a course suggested by Joyce and Showers (1983), who point out that helping teachers to anticipate this temporary discomfort allows them to tolerate it better, keep trying, and move on. In particular, we have helped teachers anticipate temporary discomfort by engaging in the process of cooperatively developing sample teaching-learning units that reflect their actual classroom curricular objectives. Roberts and Kenney (1986) point out that unless a mastery curriculum is already in place, new implementers of mastery learning will begin by planning their own mastery learning units in any case. We simply accelerate this natural process.

In the process of building these sample units, lines between staff development and curriculum development blur. Teachers are even more clearly now the subjects, not the objects, of staff development as they move into final preparations for initiating mastery learning. Their combined skills and experience put the meat on the bones of each unit. Moreover, joint development of these first (and subsequent) units saves teacher time, improves the product, and lays the base for the cooperative planning, implementation, and evaluation that will help to sustain mastery learning instruction. And although these units may be revised or even scrapped after field testing, they help to lay the base for instructional files that will save time and repetitive experimentation for future mastery learning implementers.

Unit development does not have to be a long, drawn-out affair. Gruener (1984), the district superintendent, describing the 5-year phase-in of mastery learning in all grades and subjects in Norristown, Pennsylvania, estimates that the following tasks could be carried out by three competent teachers in 2 or 3 weeks:

- Write twenty or so objectives for a grade level subject
- Sequence content that relates directly to each objective
- Construct two forms, A and B, of a criterion-referenced test that evaluates the objective
- Determine the percent of objectives considered as mastery (set mastery standard). (p. 39)

Our experience parallels Gruener's. Indeed, we have found that groups of teachers, working together, can often develop content-rich units for an entire year's worth of work in about a month. The first few units are the most time-consuming, but unit building is like driving a car: Once you get the hang of it, it starts to go faster and faster. We estimate that the first unit may take on the order of 80% more planning time than one might usually spend, but by the third or fourth unit only about 10% to 20% more.

Gruener noted that the greatest problem at the beginning was getting everyone to understand exactly what was wanted; the requirements shown were developed as a response to that problem. In other words, it was in the process of developing units that staff members began to make the transition from learning mastery learning to applying mastery learning in the classroom.

Feedback, Correction, and Enrichment.   The basic form that feedback, correction, and enrichment take in mastery learning staff development is follow-up activities. Early implementation efforts are the basis of formative evaluation; feedback, correction, and enrichment take place in observation, assistance, coaching, and collegial discussion and reflection. These tend to occur closer to the classroom than to the training sessions.

Joyce and Showers (1983), Little (1981), Stallings (1980), and Lortie (1985) are among the many researchers who emphasize the importance of collegial time following training. Sparks (1983) compared results from three training models: workshops only, workshops plus individual coaching from a trainer, and workshops plus peer observation. The greatest improvement in staff performance resulted from the third model because of the objective feedback and suggested modifications that teachers received from peers and also because teachers learned new ideas and strategies from each other for their own classrooms.

Observation feedback schemes, whether between peers, trainer and teacher, or administrator and teacher, can range from open-ended informal to elaborate, depending on purpose. Training should stress to all participants, along with their responsibilities in mastery learning, their right to take more time to learn, to be awkward, to make mistakes, and to fail during learning stages. Feedback and correction should be constructive, generally positive, and encouraging. Further instruction and assistance should be provided to those who need it, either by trainers or by teachers further along in the process. Regular district performance evaluation has no part in the feedback, correction, and enrichment stage and should not for a considerable amount of time, or until there is staff agreement on this point.

The whole feedback, correction, and enrichment part of staff development should be a set of cooperative learning experiences for everyone involved. A step at a time, mastery learning program and staff development have emphasized putting staff members in interdependent relationships with common goals, in order to build trust as well as collegiality. Asking teachers to assist, observe, coach, and comment on one another's mastery learning implementation in the classroom takes these relationships to a new and higher level. This is even more the case with administrators and trainers working with teachers in the classroom.

Many teachers say the best aspect of school improvement is the chance to talk and work closely with others on what is most important to them professionally. Others are more reluctant to join in; they should not be pushed but should be given opportunities to contribute independently to whatever project is at hand. Trust builds slowly and is easily damaged, but once collegiality is in place, you will wonder how you ever did without it!

Using Evaluation.   Staff development should include training in the use of formative and summative evaluation results and in related testing issues. Teachers may need training and support in developing instructionally referenced test items and procedures and using test data to support decision making in mastery learning. Levine (1985a) notes the importance of introducing techniques to minimize record-keeping burdens for mastery learning teachers by reducing the number of skills for which records must be maintained, avoiding seductive computerized schemes that promise to reduce record keeping but instead increase it, utilization of whole class progress charts rather than a proliferation of individual profiles, and provision of personnel to help collect and maintain data (p. 275).

Boxes 3.8 and 3.9, from Philadelphia's Mastery Learning Program (Conner et al., 1985), describe the comprehensive approach they have taken to formative evaluation.

Results of evaluation pinpoint strengths and weaknesses of individual students and also of the teachers' instruction, directly pointing the way to improvement. Evaluation keeps the mastery learning process going well, helping to identify problems before they become serious and making recognition and replication of successes possible. Three important staff recognitions should result from this part of the training:

1. Test data are of no use unless human beings look at them and discern the patterns in them (Levine, 1985).
2. Instructional leadership, whoever exercises it, should include regular examination of outcomes. If the outcomes indicate a uniformly high level of mastery, do not interfere in the process (Ryan, 1983).
3. The proper measure for evaluation of teaching is verified student learning outcomes.

KEEPING IT ROLLING: EVALUATION AND RENEWAL

As we have suggested earlier, the combination of feedback and correctives is one of the key aspects of the successful implementation of mastery

---

BOX 3.8   The Formative Process at the School Level

Steps	More Effective When . . .	Less Effective When . . .
1. Stating the belief system	Emphasis is on developing student ability. There is commitment to learning for all students.	Emphasis is on identifying the "best" students.

(continued)

Steps	**More Effective When** ...	**Less Effective When** ...
2. Setting goals and measuring a. Goal	There is a shared goal (between principal and staff members).	Goal is imposed.
	Goal is explicit and clear.	Goal is not explicit or clear.
	Goal is significant.	Goal is frivolous.
b. Measurement device	Test is criterion referenced (measures specific objectives).	Test is norm-referenced (separates students on curve).
	Criteria are objective.	Criteria are subjective.
	It is manageable.	Measure is difficult to score.
	It is valid and systematic.	
3. Collecting data a. Recording form	The year's work is divided into small units that can show interim progress.	The year's work is divided into large units that cannot show interim progress. (The information is available only once or twice yearly and does not provide a way to take action that year).
		It is complicated and in an overwhelming form.
	The fewest possible entries are made.	Many entries are needed.
b. Collection	There is regular, periodic collection.	Data is collected only once or twice yearly.
	There is a definite, explicit procedure as to who gets information.	It is unclear who gets forms.
	Forms are promptly returned to teachers.	There is a delay in returning forms to teachers.
4. Acting on test information a. Data analysis	Data are analyzed promptly.	Data are collected but not analyzed.
	Adequate pacing is considered.	Mastery, but not pacing, is considered.
	The percentage of students mastering each test is considered.	Coverage of material, but not mastery, is considered.

	Particular students having trouble are considered. Proper placement is considered.	Individual students are not considered.
	Positive and negative aspects are both considered.	Only negative (or positive) aspects are considered.
b. Feedback	Feedback is current, specific, and objective. There is a balance of positive and negative aspects.	It is general. It is not current. It is evaluative.
	It is direct[ed] to individual teachers.	It is punitive.
	The focus is kept on students.	Teachers feel blamed.
	In faculty meetings: It is specific, but no teacher is identified— balanced. It is visible, clear, and current.	*In faculty meetings:* Individual teachers are singled out in front of peers. It is difficult to understand or not current.
c. Support	It is goal-directed; the focus is on students who aren't making it rather than on teachers.	No help is provided to the teachers.
	Actual support is provided.	Teachers see the process as blaming or checking up on them.
	Resources are redirected when needed.	Teachers are told when they are wrong, but no help is provided.
d. Follow-up	The principal indicates at the initial conference that there will be follow-up.	It is done by surprise.
	It is informal and casual at first. It is supportive.	It is formal and impersonal. It is threatening.

Conner et al., 1985, fig. 3.

BOX 3.9   Essential Features of the Formative Testing Process

Stating the belief system	Virtually all students can learn what schools teach to a level of excellence. The primary role of schools is to define learning goals and ensure that all students master them.		

	Classroom	**School**	**District**
Setting goals and measuring	Goals relate to unit content. Two tests are given per unit (formative and end-of-unit).	Goals relate to schoolwide achievement. Tests are criterion-reference and aligned with school curriculum.	Goals relate to district achievement. Tests are criterion-referenced and aligned with district curriculum.
Data collecting	Administer formative test after instruction.	Collect test data (by class) periodically throughout the year.	Collect test data (by school) periodically throughout the year.
Acting on test information	Teacher provides feedback and enrichment or reteaching based on results of formative test.	Principal (or delegate) analyzes test results, meets with teachers, engages resources to solve problems, and follows up on solutions.	Superintendent (or delegate) analyzes test results, meets with principals, engages resources to solve problems, and follows up on solutions.

Conner et al., 1985, p. 67.

---

learning in classrooms. It should come as no surprise, then, that some form of feedback and correctives is also one of the key elements of successful implementation of mastery learning in districts and schools. In general, we would argue that whatever the unit of *intended* improvement (student, teacher, classroom, or school), *actual* improvement is more likely when valid, meaningful data are systematically collected and subsequently used to inform and guide improvement efforts in some desirable direction or toward some specified goal. In this discussion we shall use the terms *evaluation* and *renewal* in place of the more traditional, classroom-based terms *feedback* and *correctives*.

That the collection and use of information and evidence are vital to the success of mastery learning has been suggested by several authors. Barber (1986), for example, states quite emphatically that mastery learning is "goal based and data driven" (p. 2). Similarly, Pringle (1982) asserts:

> The verification of learning outcomes is the most important part of [a mastery learning] system. Several factors enter into the success or failure of student learning, such as the materials used in teaching, the teaching itself, the [goals] specified for each grade or course, the [standards] set by the district to define mastery, and the tests used to measure learning. *Only by taking measures to verify learning can a school district collect information upon which to base decisions regarding any one of these factors....* [As a consequence,] districts that develop [mastery learning] programs do not just produce a course of study that states [goals]. They implement the course of study in the classrooms, work to achieve the [goals], and find out each year whether they did or not. (p. 15)

Champlin (1983) draws parallels between the role of student evaluation in mastery learning classrooms and the role of faculty and staff evaluation in mastery learning districts and schools.

> Evaluation is one aspect of renewal through which one seeks to measure achievement against clearly stated goals and objectives. Unfortunately, evaluation too often suggests judgments in terms of right/wrong or good/bad. The fear of being considered wrong or bad often serves to prohibit unrestrained and enthusiastic staff involvement.
>
> The term self-renewal implies moving on from one's previous experiences and using them as a basis for planned intervention and improvement. *The spirit of renewal is enabling and not punitive in any sense.* We need to engender this spirit in our organizations if we are to gain any confidence from workers as they consider either the costs or security afforded in taking risks.
>
> Feedback and reinforcement are essential in every stage of program development, but they are particularly important as one strives to renew. Both are given and received in an atmosphere of mutual trust and respect. (p. 40)

Based on this discussion, a series of generalizations concerning the role of evaluation and renewal in maintaining, refining, and institutionalizing mastery learning programs within districts and schools can be offered.

First, evaluation, like instructional leadership and management, is a shared responsibility, although there may be some specialized functions within the general responsibility. Teaching peers, internal or external trainers and coaches, building administrators, R&D departments, central administration, students, and parents can all be sources, collectors, and users of evaluation data in the improvement process.

Second, not only do the current approaches to, or designs for, program and personnel evaluation need to be modified, but so do the motives for conducting such evaluations. House (1984) contends that large numbers of program evaluations are conducted for primarily political reasons, that is, to show that a program "works" because the "powers that be" want it to work. Far fewer evaluations are conducted to find out whether the program really works, whether how well it works is worth the time and effort invested, and how it can work better. We need to shift our motive from one of showing to one of knowing (and ultimately acting on that knowledge).

Similar motives exist in the area of personnel evaluation. Calls for systematic evaluation of deans and department chairs in institutions of higher learning are most frequently signs that something is amiss. The faculty needs to "get the goods" on the person in question in order to convince the administration that their perceptions are accurate and that something (negative) should be done to the targeted dean or department chair. Much of the current interest in staff evaluation in public schools can be traced to feelings on the part of legislators, the public, or both that some teachers and principals simply are not doing their jobs or at least not doing them very well. We need to "get the goods" on these people so we can "rid the public schools of them." For example, the question on the tongues of many school administrators as they examine a proposed teacher evaluation system is "Will it stand up in court?"

A better way to promote organizational health, it seems to us, is to conduct evaluations in an atmosphere of mutual trust and respect. The aim must be to improve the skills and working environments of staff members, not to sort and discard them (Bridges, 1986). A healthy organizational climate supports this aim, with expectations of good and improving performance from everyone.

Third, evaluation must be seen as an ongoing process, rather than a one-time thing. As part of this process, in addition to "harder" data such as test scores, the opinions of people likely to be holding various perspectives should be solicited. In combination, ongoing evaluation based on a wide variety of data permits a more complete understanding of the status and direction of a program, the sources of particular problems, and clues to what might be done to ameliorate these problems. Such evaluation is requisite for improvement efforts to be on target and, ultimately, successful. A number of checklists, observation instruments, and questionnaires have been developed to aid in the successful implementation of mastery learning in districts and schools.

Checklists.   Perhaps the most complete checklist pertaining to the evalua-tion of mastery learning programs has been developed by Jones (1983). This composite checklist includes questions pertaining to some 38 elements of successful mastery learning programs. These elements include concerns for objectives, learning units, teaching, testing, and recording student progress. Jones, Friedman, Tinzmann, and Cox (1985) have also developed more detailed checklists or methods of analysis for the organization of the learning unit, the delineation of objectives, and the development of sound paper-and-pencil tests.

The checklists developed by Jones and her colleagues focus attention on the need for a careful examination of the quality of the instructional support materials developed within the context of mastery learning. It must be pointed out, however, that these checklists have a heavy "pro-duct" orientation. Concerns for the process by which the materials are developed and disseminated are equally, if not more, important. In this regard, Conyers (1985) has developed a series of "assessment worksheets." These worksheets ask staff members to rate on a 5-point scale the extent to which certain characteristics are present in particular situations. A series of "process" indicators is available to the staff members as they contemplate and make their ratings. An example of an "assessment worksheet" con-cerning the extent to which "staff members cooperatively develop shared curriculum" appears in Figure 3.2.

Questionnaires.   Prior to collecting observational data, Guskey (1984, 1985c) suggests that several additional teacher qualities are worth monitoring during the implementation phase of mastery learning. The first is the responsibility teachers assume for their students' learning. As has been mentioned, and as Guskey's (1984) data suggest, teachers implement-ing mastery learning with some success assume greater responsibility for the learning of their students. The second is the explanations teachers give for their increased effectiveness. Teachers implementing mastery learning should indicate that their increased effectiveness stems from what they "do," not what they "are." Once again, Guskey's (1985d) data suggest that teachers do shift in this area.

Monitoring of such changes in teachers' beliefs and perceptions plays an important part in understanding the concepts of evaluation and renewal. Fortunately, Guskey has developed a set of instruments that makes such monitoring relatively easy.

Observation Instruments.   Observation of mastery learning "in action" provides extremely useful evaluation data. At present, approaches to observing and recording classroom occurrences and events differ in the amount of structure the observation or recording instruments impose on

Assessment Worksheet for:

Staff members cooperatively develop shared curriculum.

	1	2	3	4	5

Directions: Rate the degree the above characteristic is true for the situation being rated. Circle the number indicating the degree this characteristic is present in your school. To assist in your decision, check the evidence below.

1 — Does not apply/cannot assess
2 — Not a characteristic
3 — Somewhat a characteristic
4 — Usually a characteristic
5 — Definitely a characteristic

Evidence Used: Check those found.

_____   1. Meet within grade/department and across grade levels/departments to plan for consistent approaches to achieving school goals.

_____   2. Communicate effectively with other staff members within grade/department and across grade levels/departments.

_____   3. Participate on committees for curriculum study and material selection.

_____   4. Contribute suggestions and time to various school improvement projects.

_____   5. Share responsibilities for outcomes of school projects.

_____   6. Emphasize school goals in classroom.

_____   7. Share ideas among staff members.

_____   8. Talk to others about effective teaching practices often.

_____   9. Work together to discuss, plan for, design, conduct, analyze, evaluate, and experiment with the business of teaching.

_____ 10. Other evidence _____

Figure 3.2. Sample assessment worksheet (Conyers, 1985)

the observer. Smith (1984) employs a system with minimum structure. Smith records the lesson aim or objective, lists "commendations" and "recommendations," and prepares a summary. Within these four general categories Smith makes copious notes during the observation, which he then shares with teachers during a conference held the same day.

An example of a highly structured observation instrument is the

Instructional Functions Time Allocation Instrument (IFTAI) developed by Fitzpatrick and Charters (1986). Based largely on the work of Rosenshine (1983), the IFTAI includes over a dozen "instructional events" in its left-hand column. The remaining columns on the instrument correspond to 1-minute time intervals. Each event noted by the observer during any single minute is coded in the appropriate column by circling the appropriate "letter code." Every minute, then, observers move from column to column to record their observations of the various instructional functions. A portion of the IFTAI is shown in Figure 3.3.

Differences in the degree of structure of observation instruments are not trivial. In fact, instruments that differ greatly in the amount of structure they impose on observers typically provide quite different data. While relatively unstructured instruments provide rich data sets for discussion with individual teachers, attempts to aggregate such data are frustrating and, typically, unsuccessful. Thus if one's concerns are with particular teachers, the use of relatively unstructured instruments is recommended.

The strength of more structured instruments lies in the potential aggregation of data. Since the categories to be observed and coded as well as the times during which observations are to be coded are specified, aggregation of data across groups of teachers is possible and desirable.

Since our emphasis is on the improvement of entire programs *and* the improvement of personnel, we would advocate a balance between the use of more and less structured instruments. Initially, we would favor the more structured. Such instruments, by their very design, would communicate to the teachers the instructional functions that should be accomplished if they are to be successful in their classrooms. Norms can then be prepared so that the distribution of teachers in terms of the various functions can be observed and examined.

At this point in time we would shift to the use of a less structured instrument, especially for teachers in the "tail end" of the distribution who need some peer support and assistance or additional training. Such instruments portray the events observed in the classroom in such a way that maximum individual feedback and correctives (or in the words of Smith, 1984, "commendations" and "recommendations") are possible.

Before leaving the issue of classroom observation, we must raise one more point. So far in the discussion the emphasis in classroom observation has been on teachers—what they say and do. It is possible that more information would be available if we focused on the students rather than the teachers. Observing students' reactions and responses to various classroom events may provide a wealth of data concerning the appropriateness and meaningfulness of various classroom activities and teacher explanations. "Clarity" and "difficulty of assignments" may, like beauty,

Classroom Observation Instrument

Event	1:00	2:00	3:00	4:00	5:00	6:00	7:00	8:00	9:00	10:00	11:00	12:00	13:00	14:00	15:00
Transition	T	T	T	T		T	T	T	T		T	T	T	T	—
Nonacademic Interaction	N	N	N	N		N	N	N	N		N	N	N	N	
Number of students off-task					—					—					
Review	R	R	R	R		R	R	R	R		R	R	R	R	
Collect Homework	H	H	H	H		H	H	H	H		H	H	H	H	
Quiz	Q	Q	Q	Q		Q	Q	Q	Q		Q	Q	Q	Q	
Development	D	D	D	D		D	D	D	D		D	D	D	D	
Practice	P	P	P	P		P	P	P	P		P	P	P	P	
Formative Assessment	A	A	A	A		A	A	A	A		A	A	A	A	
Feedback	F	F	F	F		F	F	F	F		F	F	F	F	
Reteaching															
t = teacher led	Rt	Rt	Rt	Rt		Rt	Rt	Rt	Rt		Rt	Rt	Rt	Rt	
m = materials	Rm	Rm	Rm	Rm		Rm	Rm	Rm	Rm		Rm	Rm	Rm	Rm	
p = peer tutor or aide	Rp	Rp	Rp	Rp		Rp	Rp	Rp	Rp		Rp	Rp	Rp	Rp	
Enrichment															
t = teacher led	Et	Et	Et	Et		Et	Et	Et	Et		Et	Et	Et	Et	
m = materials	Em	Em	Em	Em		Em	Em	Em	Em		Em	Em	Em	Em	
Independent Practice	I+	I+	I+	I+		I+	I+	I+	I+		I+	I+	I+	I+	
Other	O	O	O	O		O	O	O	O		O	O	O	O	

Figure 3.3. Instructional Functions Time Allocation Instrument (Fitzpatrick & Charters, 1986)

Event	16:00	17:00	18:00	19:00	20:00	21:00	22:00	23:00	24:00	25:00	26:00	27:00	28:00	29:00	30:00
Transition	T	T	T	T		T	T	T	T		T	T	T	T	
Nonacademic Interaction	N	N	N	N		N	N	N	N		N	N	N	N	
Number of students off-task					—					—					—
Review	R	R	R	R		R	R	R	R		R	R	R	R	
Collect Homework	H	H	H	H		H	H	H	H		H	H	H	H	
Quiz	Q	Q	Q	Q		Q	Q	Q	Q		Q	Q	Q	Q	
Development	D	D	D	D		D	D	D	D		D	D	D	D	
Practice	P	P	P	P		P	P	P	P		P	P	P	P	
Formative Assessment	A	A	A	A		A	A	A	A		A	A	A	A	
Feedback	F	F	F	F		F	F	F	F		F	F	F	F	
Reteaching															
t = teacher led	Rt	Rt	Rt	Rt		Rt	Rt	Rt	Rt		Rt	Rt	Rt	Rt	
m = materials	Rm	Rm	Rm	Rm		Rm	Rm	Rm	Rm		Rm	Rm	Rm	Rm	
p = peer tutor or aide	Rp	Rp	Rp	Rp		Rp	Rp	Rp	Rp		Rp	Rp	Rp	Rp	
Enrichment															
t = teacher led	Et	Et	Et	Et		Et	Et	Et	Et		Et	Et	Et	Et	
m = materials	Em	Em	Em	Em		Em	Em	Em	Em		Em	Em	Em	Em	
Independent Practice	I+	I+	I+	I+		I+	I+	I+	I+		I+	I+	I+	I+	
Other	O	O	O	O		O	O	O	O		O	O	O	O	

131

reside more in the eye of the beholder than in any objective criteria and standards that may purport to measure them. Asking questions of students or observing their attentiveness, compliance, and effort may be our keys to understanding the quality of instruction provided to students in our classrooms.

Long-Term Evaluation and Institutionalization

Meaningful changes simply take time. Educators intent on implementing mastery learning should prepare for the impending change by collecting some baseline data or information on where they are just prior to implementation. Several years of baseline data are even better, since they permit a more accurate and reliable estimate of the starting point.

The baseline data show where educators are; the goals of mastery learning provide an estimate of where they believe they should be in terms of level and distribution of student learning. The challenge of mastery learning is quite simple: to reduce the distance between where a district or school is and where informed sources suggest that the district or school should be.

As a consequence, longitudinal data should be collected so that changes can be observed and examined. An example of the dramatic effect of longitudinal data can be seen in Abrams (1985).

As you begin to move closer to your goals, the distribution of achievement changes in all significant subgroups of the student population must be carefully studied longitudinally as it was in the earlier needs assessment. If there were initial achievement disparities between groups, it is not enough that all groups maintain equal growth over time. As Levin (1987) points out, the gap must be closed, using preventive as well as remedial measures. Individual growth may vary widely, occur in spurts, and so on; extreme variance in growth between groups must be investigated and corrected. As in classroom mastery learning, equal treatment and equal opportunity to learn are no longer the issues; equal outcomes, or bringing every student to at least a school-determined mastery standard, is the goal.

Disproportionate time or "treatment" needed by individuals *and* groups tends to diminish under fully implemented mastery learning conditions and so should be considered as finite needs. As a consequence, establishing time lines for closing the gap is useful in some cases. Levin proposes an all-out effort by the end of sixth grade so that no student goes unprepared into secondary school. Others (such as Efthim, 1984) suggest that no gap should be allowed to exist beyond first grade since differences in school-important skill levels are generally slight between entering groups of students. In any case, at all grade levels where mastery learning is used, the objective should be for each student to have the prerequisites for the next stage of learning, as teachers have determined those requirements.

A key function of the central administration and the R&D department, if any, is the maintenance, analysis, and reporting of these kinds of data. They are typically beyond the capacity of most individual schools to provide. The collection of data and the use of such data to inform decisions of what *is*, what *should be*, and what *could be* lie at the heart of mastery learning at all levels—student, classroom, school, and district.

Looking Forward

Building and central administrators have two other major roles in institutionalizing the practice of mastery learning after determination of its success. One of these is continuous examination of policies and procedures that hinder or enhance the use of mastery learning and associated instructional innovation, working closely with staff to make necessary changes at the appropriate time. For example, practices that were at first exceptional, such as certifying or grading for mastery, become routine and necessary, part of the everyday business of the school. When teachers at a grade level have reached consensus on a set of goals or objectives for the year, that becomes part of the school's curriculum and is placed in teachers' handbooks. Materials and test selection and development support what teachers are doing. Contradictory practices are not introduced, nor are committees established to work at cross-purposes. Within the framework of explicit school or district goals and with full staff participation, it becomes easier to expand successful practices and discard unsuccessful ones.

We suggest the use of a "data screen" such as Champlin (1983) describes to inform decision making. This is especially useful under reform or special funding pressure and can help to avoid unintended outcomes. Which of these would help you achieve your goals, and which would not? A lengthened school day may be exactly what your district needs—or it may obliterate joint staff planning and development time. A merit pay plan may arouse healthy competition among teachers to get the best results—or it may destroy the fragile beginnings of staff cooperation and coordination. Resources for planning enrichment might be most welcome with money for the gifted and talented—but do you really want to take the most advanced students out of their classes? Do you really want compensatory education students to miss the daily classroom reading program? Is there a better way? Federal and state initiatives have had an enormous, largely beneficial impact, but they must be bent to the purposes of the school or district for maximum value. A proactive stance on the part of the administration is required.

A second major way for administrators to consolidate gains is the broadcasting and celebration of effort and successes in the system in professionally meaningful ways, beyond the pennants and flags. A classroom or school that has moved students to high mastery levels deserves visits, observation, and serious discussions in methods with other staffs and with "top brass" and board of education members. Mastery teachers deserve professional recognition at faculty and district meetings; mastery principals should not get the silent treatment at district principals' meetings; top administrators who advocate and advance mastery instruction should not be treated as pariahs by the superintendent. An administration that says one thing and does another—calls for higher mastery and ignores it when it happens—diminishes respect for itself and its authority, as well as its ability to advance system goals.

A success in any part of the system should be treated as a success for the whole system, an advance toward shared goals, and an opportunity for everyone to move forward. Building on the legitimate successes of people in the system supports renewal, the process of resting on laurels only briefly and then reaching higher.

We are so far from the limits of learning in most schools that we cannot yet tell what those limits may be. We have no argument with, in fact we applaud, those schools and districts whose first priority is making sure that no child falls through the cracks on current basics. That is the first and probably the hardest step toward what Block (1985) has called "equalence," or equal excellence. Such a school or district will probably find a strong correlation between upward growth on norm-referenced and criterion-referenced (curriculum-sensitive) test results over time. This can be used to encourage each other and students to attempt more difficult material, concepts, and applications with the use of Bloom's taxonomy and to avoid the temptation to confine instruction on problem-solving and higher-order thinking skills to only the most advanced students. These are *universal* needs.

Excellence should not be a mask for a subtle return to elitism in education. Equity should never be satisfaction with a low level of learning, equally distributed. The evidence that these are not mutually contradictory concepts is in and growing stronger. It seems appropriate to end this discussion with the words of the late Ron Edmonds (1978):

> We can, whenever and wherever we choose, successfully teach all children whose schooling is of interest to us. We already know more than we need to do that. Whether or not we do it must finally depend on how we feel about the fact that we haven't so far. (p. 35)

CHAPTER 4

How Do I Implement Mastery Learning in My Classroom?

How do you recognize a mastery learning classroom? For several years, researchers have contended that it is impossible to distinguish one from any other classroom on a daily basis. They are right! The unique features of mastery learning classrooms are not necessarily evident to the human senses of sight and sound. For example, mastery learning teachers ask classroom questions, just like other teachers. And mastery teachers help students correct errors and misunderstandings, just like other teachers. The differences reside in the nature of their work, not personality, daily classroom behaviors, or teaching activities. Mastery teachers constantly work toward the *accomplishment* of a series of critical *tasks*. Their awareness and accomplishment of these tasks is what differentiates their classrooms.

We shall describe these tasks in this chapter. For each task we shall raise a series of critical questions or issues and propose some alternative answers. The appropriate choices from among these alternatives will depend on your particular situation.

OVERVIEW

Teachers intent on implementing mastery learning in their schools and classrooms face four primary instructional tasks: (1) defining mastery, (2) planning for mastery, (3) teaching for mastery, and (4) grading for mastery.

In considering these tasks, two important points must be made. First, if mastery learning is to be successful, all four tasks must be accomplished. Mastery learning is a gestalt, a unified whole that is more than the sum of its parts. Simply defining mastery by identifying objectives, matching tests with those objectives, and setting performance standards to indicate mastery will not guarantee success, nor will simply teaching for mastery in a systematic fashion (for example, review, develop, provide for guided practice, and provide for individual practice). The completion and alignment of all four major tasks—defining mastery, planning for mastery, teaching for mastery, and grading for mastery—is necessary.

Second, that the tasks are accomplished at all is far more important than how they are accomplished. Each task serves an important function within the context of mastery learning (Anderson, 1981). A summary of these functions is presented in Table 4.1.

Before we discuss various approaches to accomplishing these tasks, however, one caveat is in order. Recall that mastery learning attempts to operate within many of the constraints currently imposed by schools (Bloom, 1968; Block & Anderson, 1975; Anderson & Block, 1985). Since one of these constraints is that the curriculum is parsed into sets or sequences of what typically are referred to as "courses," we intend to focus our discussion on the course as the primary unit of analysis and improvement.

A course is a body of knowledge, skills, strategies, activities, or experiences within a given subject area taught at a certain level (for example, third or fourth grade, level I or II, introductory or advanced) within a finite period of time (term, semester, year). Third-grade social studies, Algebra II, and advanced physics are all courses.

Although courses exist at all grade levels and in all subject areas, their structure is different. Some courses emphasize a *body of knowledge* to be acquired. This body is typically present in one or more textbooks, reference books, or other written material. For the purpose of discussion

TABLE 4.1. MAJOR TASKS AND THEIR PRIMARY FUNCTIONS

Tasks	Functions
Defining mastery	Makes learning expectations explicit
Planning for mastery	Enables teachers to be proactive
	Requires teachers to decide on the content and objectives to include in a course or year within the time available
	Ensures that the course or year is organized and structured for excellence in learning
Teaching for mastery	Ensures that virtually all students learn well, swiftly, and confidently
Grading for mastery	Links the reward structure of schools to excellence in learning

we shall refer to these courses as *content-oriented*. Elementary science courses and high school history courses tend to be examples of content-oriented courses.

Other courses emphasize a *set of general skills and strategies* that students should acquire. These skills and strategies are typically independent of any specific content. Whatever content is included in the course is intended primarily as a means to an end, the end being acquisition of the skills and strategies. For the purpose of discussion we shall refer to these courses as *process-oriented*. For example, elementary reading courses and high school vocational education courses tend to be examples of process-oriented courses. One of the goals of elementary reading courses may be for students to learn to predict likely consequences or outcomes of a series of events (what will happen next and why). Virtually any story on almost any topic or subject, fiction or nonfiction, can provide the content for that goal to be achieved. Similarly, in a high school auto mechanics course, students may be expected to learn to diagnose problems in the operation of automobiles. Almost any automobile of any make, model, or year can provide the content for that goal.

Still other courses emphasize a *set of activities or experiences* to which students should be exposed. In these courses the activities and experiences take precedence over any type of learning outcome (be it acquisition of content or objectives). Rather, participation in the activity or experience is seen as an end in itself. For the purpose of discussion we shall refer to such courses as *activity-oriented*. Elementary art courses and high school English courses tend to be activity-oriented courses. In the former courses, for example, students draw and paint just to draw and paint. The content of the picture tends to be general, often the choice of the student. There are no criteria used to judge the skill or quality of the drawing or painting. Comments such as "Very nice, Billy" and "Interesting picture, Rhonda" echo throughout the room quite independent of the picture or painting being observed. Similarly, in the latter courses, sophomores read Shakespeare's *Macbeth* simply because every sophomore should have the experience. Frequently, discussions of plot and character are held. Sometimes students are encouraged to memorize various passages of significance. But such activities are clearly subordinate to the main purpose for which *Macbeth* was chosen.

We shall focus primarily on content-oriented and process-oriented courses in most of the following discussion. Only periodically we will allude to activity-oriented courses, because generally the orientation of such courses must be changed if mastery learning is to be workable and effective.

Also, in the ensuing discussion, we shall emphasize intellectual mastery rather than emotional or psychomotor mastery. This emphasis is not intended to downplay the importance of these other two "domains of learning," nor is it intended to indicate the inapplicability of mastery learning to them. In fact, mastery learning ideas can be and have been used in fostering emotional and psychomotor development (Blakemore, 1985; Block & Cantlay, 1979). Emotional development, in particular, is a key component of major long-term mastery programs in Philadelphia (Connor et al., 1986) and Johnson City, New York (Mamary, 1986).

Our emphasis on intellectual mastery corresponds to the current state of affairs. Although the back-to-basics movement has given way somewhat to calls for broader graduation requirements, schooling today is still quite focused on academic achievement.

DEFINING MASTERY

In many respects the task of defining mastery is the key to the overall effectiveness of mastery learning. In defining mastery, for example, teachers must answer the following questions: What is worth learning and worth learning well? How must students demonstrate that they have, in fact, learned well? What do we mean when we say that something has been mastered? Program failure is virtually guaranteed if mastery is defined in any of the following ways:

- Mastery is defined in terms of rather trivial goals and objectives. A large number of objectives in such programs will fall into the general area of factual recall. Students will be expected to memorize large sets of unrelated material, most of which are easily accessible to them via reference books. The net result will be trivial learning.
- Mastery tests or assignments are unrelated or misaligned with expected student learning outcomes. Such is often the case when national or state-developed standardized tests are used to assess student mastery of locally derived curricular goals and objectives. Such is also the case when students are taught basic facts about particular events or phenomena but are tested on their abilities to apply those facts in new situations or settings, analyze their interrelationships, or evaluate their utility under varying circumstances. Unfortunately, in their efforts to correct the misalignment, some mastery educators accept the tests as given and alter the goals and objectives to conform to the tests. This foolishly allows the tests to drive the curriculum and instruction (Spady, 1982). In a sound mastery learning program, the goals and objectives do the driving. The tests and other assignments are simply intended to provide

evidence concerning whether these goals and objectives have been mastered.

- Mastery is determined by students' attainment of minimal performance standards on tests or other assignments. Many standards currently in place require that students know little more than nothing at all to be certified as having "mastered" some body of knowledge. The standards set by the Nedelsky (1954) procedure and, to a slightly lesser extent, the Angoff (1971) method are good examples. Such procedures have as their aim the differentiation of students with absolutely *no* knowledge or skill from the rest. Mastery learning performance standards, by contrast, are intended to differentiate students who have *excellent* knowledge or skill from those who have not.

Having seen how mastery should *not* be defined, let us now turn to how it should. To do this we shall return to the three basic questions associated with defining mastery.

What Is Worth Learning and Worth Learning Well?

Since goals and objectives drive mastery learning curriculum and instruction, the identification and specification of goals to include as *desired end points* for the course is critical. For future reference, these goals shall be referred to as course-level goals.

Several sources can be used to aid in the determination of course-level goals. For content-oriented courses the index of the textbook provides one such source (Block & Anderson, 1975). To use this source, simply read through the index and note the entries associated with the most page numbers or subentries. These entries become the basic building blocks for the derivation of course-level goals. Since these entries are typically in the form of major content categories, they must be transformed into goal statements. This transformation is aided by selecting a verb or verb phrase that indicates how the students are expected to "think about," "operate on," or "cognitively process" the content being learned. To complete the transformation, both the verb and content category are embedded within a sentence that begins, "The students should ..."

Several category systems, or taxonomies, have been developed to aid educators in determining appropriate verbs to include in their goal statements. The most famous of these is by Bloom (1956). The six levels of Bloom's taxonomy, brief descriptions of each level, and verbs indicative of the thinking required at each level are displayed in Box 4.1. Also in the box is a sample question for each level that might be asked about the children's story of Goldilocks.

BOX 4.1   Key Words for Bloom's Taxonomy of Cognitive Processes

6. *Evaluation*: Judging material, ideas, and problems based on established criteria.

debate	defend	evaluate
judge	recommend	select

Was Goldilocks good or bad? Why do you think so?

5. *Synthesis*: Producing a solution using original, creative thinking.

compose	create	formulate
design	imagine	predict

How might the story have been different if Goldilocks had visited the "three fishes"?

4. *Analysis*: Breaking down the given material into its constituent parts and seeing relationships.

analyze	categorize	classify
distinguish	separate	survey

What parts of the story couldn't have really happened?

3. *Application*: Using what has been learned to solve a new problem.

apply	choose	compute
construct	demonstrate	report

If Goldilocks came to your house, what might she have tried to use?

2. *Comprehension*: Showing that the meaning of the material has been understood.

explain	illustrate	interpret
match	rephrase	tell how

Why did Goldilocks like the things that belonged to the little bear?

1. *Knowledge*: Remembering what has been learned through recall or recognition.

define	identify	list
find	name	state

What are some of the things Goldilocks did?

School District of Philadelphia, 1986, adapted from Bloom, 1956.

To illustrate the procedure for determining appropriate course-level goals, consider the portion of the index of a U.S. history textbook shown in Box 4.2. Not unexpectedly, the U.S. Constitution emerges as an important topic; it is referred to on a number of pages and includes several

---

BOX 4.2   Excerpt from Index of a U.S. History Textbook

- Conscription Act (1863), 313
- Conservation, 494–495, 758
- Consortium (def.), 513
- *Constellation,* 133, *illus.* 131
- Constitution, U.S., 102–119; adoption, 80; Bill of Rights, 117; compared with Articles of Confederation, 105; no provision for political parties, 121; provisions for amending, 115, 116; ratification, 111, 113, 114; sectional interpretations, 283; "three-fifths clause," 202; writing of, 110. *See also* Reference Section.
- Constitution, U.S., amendments: Ninth Amendment, 117; Twelfth Amendment, 138; Thirteenth Amendment, 317, 318, 340; Fourteenth Amendment, 342; Sixteenth Amendment, 424; Seventeenth Amendment, 424; Twentieth Amendment, 568. *See also* Reference Section.
- Constitutions, state, 87, 215
- Constitutional Convention (1787). *See* Philadelphia Convention.
- Continental Congress, first (1774), 47, 52
- Continental Congress, second (1775), 55, 60, 87
- Continental currency, 97

Current, DeConde, & Dante, 1967.

---

subentries. Other major topics in the textbook are agriculture and farming; the American Revolution; business, industry, and labor; cities; the Civil War; colonies and the colonial period; education; foreign affairs and trade; immigration; Negroes and slavery; political parties; population growth and shifts; the Supreme Court; transportation; and World Wars I and II.

Once these topics have been identified, each must be transformed into a goal statement. With respect to the U.S. Constitution, for example, several transformations are possible. The students should be able to *interpret properly* various portions of the Constitution. The students should *understand the significance* of the Constitution in U.S. history as well as in their current lives. The students should be able to *determine the constitutionality* of various situations by citing relevant portions of the Constitution. These goals would seem appropriate for inclusion in a high school U.S. history course. Similar goal statements can be written for each of the other important topics reflected in the textbook's index.

For courses that are more process-oriented, a different approach is in order. Sets of related skills or strategies pertaining to a larger, superordinate skill or strategy are identified. These larger, superordinate skills or strategies form the basis for course-level goals. Quite often these superordinate skills and strategies are, in fact, stated as course-level goals.

If not, some transformation into appropriate goal statements may be necessary.

Consider, for example, the set of 12 general skills or strategies taken from an elementary reading course and displayed in Box 4.3. They can be organized around four major course-level goals:

1. Students should increase their vocabularies. (skills 1–4)
2. Students should read with understanding. (skills 5–7)
3. Students should make proper inferences about what they read. (skills 8–11)
4. Students should understand the nature, structure, and function of language. (skill 12)

A third approach to determining relevant and appropriate course-level goals is particularly useful for activity-oriented courses, educators developing new courses, and those who are dissatisfied with the way in which existing courses are currently functioning. Anderson and Jones (1981) have identified three general categories of "content elements," which, they contend, transcend subject matter and age level. These content elements are *information, concepts, and procedures.*

According to Anderson and Jones:

> Information can be defined as sentences or phrases which society (or its designate, such as curriculum guides, teachers, or school boards) believes to be important or interesting in their own right. Two levels of information can be identified: facts and generalizations. Briefly, facts are sentences or phrases which pertain to a particular person, object, event,

---

BOX 4.3   Objectives of an Elementary Reading Course

1. Understanding prefixes, roots, and suffixes
2. Using dictionaries and glossaries
3. Using context clues to determine word meaning
4. Understanding synonyms and antonyms
5. Remembering details of stories
6. Paraphrasing portions of readings
7. Differentiating fact from opinion
8. Drawing conclusions
9. Determining main idea and supporting details
10. Predicting likely consequences, events, and outcomes
11. Expressing and defending opinions
12. Understanding the nature, structure, and function of language

or experience. Generalizations are sentences or phrases which pertain to a category of persons, objects, events, or experiences.

Concepts can be defined as categories of objects, events, experiences, or ideas which give meaning to symbols (e.g., words, numerals, pictures). All members of the concept must share a thing or things in common. The thing(s) they share are termed the "critical attributes" or "defining features" of the concept.

Procedures can be defined as sequences of mental or physical activities that can be used to solve problems, gather information, or achieve some desired goal. Two types of procedures are of interest in most school settings. *Linear procedures* are those in which the sequence of activities is performed in order. That is, regardless of what the outcome of the first activity is, the second activity is performed based on that outcome. *Branching procedures* are those in which one or more of the activities involve decision-making. That is, depending on the outcome of the first activity, the person may need to perform either the second or the third activity. Single step procedures are frequently termed *rules*. (p. 127)

Educators who are interested in applying this approach to identifying course-level goals would be wise to convene a small study group to aid in the process. Each member of the study group identifies what he or she believes to be the most important information, concepts, and procedures to include in the course. Next the study group meets to compare thoughts. Facts, generalizations, concepts, and procedures identified by all members become strong candidates for inclusion in the course. Other facts, generalizations, concepts, and procedures are discussed, and decisions as to their inclusion or exclusion are made either by consensus or by majority rule.

Consider, for example, the set of concepts, information, and procedures, derived from a brainstorming session pertaining to an elementary mathematics course, shown in Box 4.4. At this point in the process, the result is a grocery list of facts, generalizations, concepts, and procedures. To derive appropriate course-level goals, clusters of interrelated content elements are formed. Then a label describing each set is attached to the set. These labels should be broad enough to describe all included content elements but narrow enough to allow one set to be differentiated from another.

Continuing with the elementary arithmetic example, the concepts of whole numbers, fractions, and decimals can be placed under the umbrella of a larger concept, numeration, or the structure of numbers. The concepts of multiplication, factor, and product and the procedure involved in multiplying whole numbers can be placed under the umbrella of the whole-number multiplication algorithm. In a similar way, sets of content elements can be clustered under the labels "number facts," "measurement concepts

---

BOX 4.4   A Content Analysis of an Elementary Mathematics Course

Information

1. Metric units of measurement, their relationships, and their English equivalents
2. Multiplication facts
3. Division facts

Concepts

Whole numbers, fractions, decimals, shapes, solids, vertices, faces, edges, lines, line segments, perimeter, capacity, units of measure, mass, area, volume, symmetry, multiplication, factor, product, division, quotient, remainder

Procedures

1. Finding perimeter, area, and volume
2. Comparing and ordering numbers (decimals and fractions)
3. Multiplying numbers (whole numbers)
4. Dividing numbers (whole numbers)
5. Solving problems

---

and formulas," "geometric figures and terminology," and "whole-number division algorithm."

Once the clusters of concept elements have been formed and labeled, they must be transformed into course-level goals by supplying appropriate verbs and the perfunctory "The student should ..." In the elementary mathematics example, then, six course-level goals would be stated, as presented in Box 4.5.

Regardless of which approach is used to determine course-level goals, several criteria should be considered. First, educators must begin the process with a full awareness that there are no "right" or "wrong" goals in any absolute sense. In many respects, goals are simply the expressed values of subject matter specialists, curriculum experts, and/or classroom teachers concerning what students should learn. Quite clearly, goals should reflect current knowledge in the discipline, the philosophy of the school, and, in certain instances, the community's values. However, once proposed course-level goals have passed through these "screens," their inclusion in the course depends largely on pragmatic issues such as available time, available materials, and the pedagogical expertise and value orientation of the teacher vis-à-vis those goals.

Second, the goals should be important. At first blush this criterion seems obvious, but it is surprising how many goals are pursued simply

---

BOX 4.5   Course-Level Goals for an Elementary Mathematics Course

1. The student should understand the nature and structure of the number system.
2. The student should memorize the multiplication and division facts.
3. The student should understand basic measurement concepts and formulas.
4. The student should identify geometric figures and understand associated terminology.
5. The student should know how to multiply whole numbers.
6. The student should know how to divide whole numbers.

---

because, like Mount Everest, they are there, in textbooks. Csikszentmihalyi and McCormack (1986) speak succinctly on this point.

> [Students] don't need just information; they need *meaningful* information. They don't need just knowledge; they need knowledge that makes sense and inspires belief. They need knowledge that helps them understand why learning and living are worthwhile. (p. 419)

Third, the number of goals set for each course should depend on the complexity of the goals and the time during which students are enrolled in the course. Nine-week courses in written composition, for example, may only have two or three course-level goals.

Fourth, few goal statements, if any, should be written at the knowledge level of Bloom's taxonomy. Although this level may be quite appropriate for specific objectives, general course-level goals should be written at the comprehension, application, analysis, synthesis, and evaluation levels.

Fifth, goals of sequentially adjacent courses should be considered before the final determination of the goals for any given course should be made. One obvious purpose of comparing these goals is to avoid unnecessary duplication. In addition, the most appropriate and useful relationships of the goals across grade levels within subject areas can be established. For example, goals that are introduced at one grade level but whose mastery is not expected until the next level can be noted. Teachers at both grade levels gain a better understanding of their role in facilitating student mastery of these goals. Similarly, goals that require a large amount of knowledge or a number of skills before they can be mastered can be placed in courses later in the sequence. Finally, goals that may have "slipped through the cracks" in the curriculum for a given subject can be identified and placed properly.

Last, goals of courses in other, related subject areas should be examined before the final determination of the goals for any given course is made. This examination will allow the specification of school-level goals (through an inductive process similar to that used in the Anderson and Jones approach mentioned earlier) and the identification of goals that have a multidisciplinary emphasis. For these goals, cross-discipline planning will likely be advantageous.

What Do We Mean by Mastery?

In simplest terms, mastery means that a student has learned something— some piece of knowledge or skill: to name the capitals of the 50 states, to recognize a noun in a sentence, to write a business letter, to conduct an experiment for determining the relationship between pressure and volume, to solve quadratic equations, to critique the plot of a novel.

One of the earliest educators to use the term *mastery* was Morrison (1926). Morrison defined mastery in the following way:

> When a student has fully acquired a piece of learning, he has mastered it. Half-learning, or learning rather well, or being on the way to learning are none of them mastery. Mastery implies completeness; the thing is done; the student has arrived, as far as that particular learning is concerned. There is no question of how well the student has mastered it; he has either mastered or he has not mastered. It is as absurd to speak of degrees in mastery as to speak of degrees in the attainment of the second floor of a building or degrees in being on the other side of the stream, or of degrees of completeness whatever. (p. 35)

One important point inherent in Morrison's definition, but often overlooked by educators, is that the term *mastery* applies to a "piece of learning" or "that particular learning," not to learning in any general sense. Morrison writes:

> While it is idle to speak of mastering a given field of knowledge, it is not only entirely possible to master important units within that field, but no less attainment constitutes learning in the educational sense at all. (p. 37)

Hence the most important aspects or elements of a particular course or subject matter must be identified before we can talk of mastery at all. For example, one cannot master social studies. One can, however, master the names of the capitals and leading exports of various countries and the rights and responsibilities of citizens in a democracy. One can also master the skill of map reading and the ability to differentiate monarchies from democracies.

Critics of mastery learning have contended that such an absolute definition of mastery is too severe in that it doesn't permit the recognition of the degrees or stages of mastery they see in so many excellent learners. In an effort to clarify the meaning of the term *mastery* further, Anderson and Block (1977) contrasted it with *competency* and *proficiency*.

> Competency, as we see it, is a two-dimensional construct.... The first dimension is, in fact, mastery.... Mastery can be thought of as the intellectual component of competency.... However, competency also consists of the attainment of self-confidence or the sense of being able to cope. This attainment of self-confidence is the emotional or affective component of competency. While mastery may provide the foundation for the development of learner self-confidence, and hence competency, mastery and competency are related concepts, not synonymous.
>
> While mastery refers to the *effectiveness* of the learning process in producing the desired learning product, proficiency refers to the *efficiency* of the use of the learning product once it has been acquired. ... We believe that proficiency follows mastery; that is, an individual must master something before he can become proficient. One speculation is that learners become proficient through practice of a previously mastered learning outcome. Thus, in one respect, proficiency resembles what some psychologists have termed "overlearning" [and others have termed "automaticity"], while mastery represents what we may call "original learning." (p. 165)

Thus, while we recognize no degrees in mastery of specific learning outcomes, we do recognize degrees in competency and in proficiency as they pertain to these specific learning outcomes. Students may become increasingly competent and increasingly proficient as they continue to explore and make use of knowledge and skills they have initially mastered. Indeed, we see mastery as the key to both competency and proficiency (Anderson & Block, 1977).

Critics have also suggested that mastery implies that "all students get A's." Such a criticism is clearly not valid. Because of the nature of courses and learning units within courses, students may vary in the number of specific learning outcomes mastered during any given course. As Morrison (1926) indicates, that student "may continue to other masteries, and there will be all sorts of degrees in the number of masteries he attains" (p. 35). Variations in the "number of masteries" can be considered in assigning course grades to students, as we shall see later in this chapter. Thus students within mastery learning do not all receive grades of A. They do all have the *opportunity* to receive them should their performances warrant.

Now that we have considered what mastery does and does not mean, we must concern ourselves with ways in which we can employ this meaning in practice. What does mastery mean operationally or pragmatically? How do we know that a student has, in fact, mastered some piece of knowledge or some particular skill?

To answer this question, we need to do two things. First, we need to identify a set of questions, exercises, or problems that a person having mastered a course-level goal would be able to answer, perform, or solve. Second, based on those answers, performances, or solutions, we need to make a determination that the student has or has not achieved mastery. It is to these issues that we now turn.

Identifying Questions, Exercises, and Problems

Several years ago one of the authors pondered aloud to an audience of classroom teachers whether it was necessary ever again to write an exercise requiring students to find the main idea of a paragraph or short passage. He suggested that it was quite likely that every possible exercise for every possible grade level had already been written for finding the main idea. Moreover, he noted that these exercises appeared in some nationally normed test, some state proficiency examination, some set of textbook or workbook exercises, some compendium of test items (such as those housed at the Instructional Objectives Exchange in California), or some yellowing, dog-eared handout prepared by some teacher in rural America.

Although his observations were greeted with some laughter, their point is both serious and important in the context of this chapter. Educators hoping to identify appropriate questions, exercises, and problems for their course-level goals have two alternatives. They can write or prepare their own questions, exercises, and problems for each goal, or they can select from the large number of available questions, exercises, and problems the most appropriate ones for each goal.

Those who choose the first alternative are fortunate to have an excellent set of resources available to them. Over the past several years, something of a technology for preparing appropriate questions, exercises, and problems has emerged on the educational scene. Two books capture this technology well: *A Technology for Test-Item Writing* by Roid and Haladyna (1982) and *Modern Educational Measurement* by Popham (1983). Although a detailed discussion of both of these books is well beyond the scope of this book, a summary of their general approach seems both appropriate and worthwhile.

The approach contains four steps. It begins with a clear statement of each goal or objective for which questions, exercises, or problems are to be prepared. Next a specific blueprint for translating the goal or objective into appropriate questions, exercises, or problems is developed. Depending on the specific technique used, this blueprint is referred to as an item form (Hively, Patterson, & Page, 1968), a mapping sentence (Guttman, 1969), or an item specification (Popham, 1983). In order to choose the most appropriate type of blueprint to use in preparing the questions, exercises, or problems, the nature or type of goal or objective should be considered. For example, the blueprints for knowledge goals tend to differ from those for skill goals, and the blueprints for conceptual goals tend to differ from those for procedural goals.

Once the blueprint has been developed, sets of sample questions, exercises, or problems are prepared. If the blueprint can be translated into a computer program, the questions, exercises, or problems can be generated by computer. If not, a group of teachers working from the same blueprint can generate similar questions for each goal or objective. In this way, not all the effort in producing a set of questions, exercises, or problems falls on a single teacher.

Finally, the sample questions, exercises, or problems are reviewed. Two general categories of review exist: logical and empirical. Logical reviews are based on an analysis of the *nature* of the questions, exercises, and problems themselves. Empirical reviews are based on an analysis of the *responses* students actually make or give to them. Quite obviously, the two reviews are sequentially related, with logical preceding empirical. But both types of reviews are important in producing the best actual questions, exercises, and problems for use in assessing student mastery of the important course-level goals.

As can be seen, such a systematic approach will likely result in questions, exercises, or problems that are of high quality and are technically sound (that is, it will provide valid and reliable information pertaining to student learning). It is equally clear, however, that the approach requires substantial amounts of time and effort. In view of the present existence of large numbers of questions, exercises, and problems for virtually all important course-level goals, the expenditure of such time and effort may be premature and somewhat unnecessary.

Consequently, an alternative approach to the identification of appropriate questions, exercises, and problems is suggested for large-scale use in mastery learning. This approach involves the selection of sets of existing questions, exercises, and problems. To use it, teachers should initially prepare a folder for each course-level goal. On the outside of the folder a clear statement of the goal should appear. Available tests (such as chapter tests, teacher-made tests, and practice tests) and worksheets should then be perused for potentially useful questions, exercises, and problems. Obviously, groups of teachers working together on this task will likely identify greater numbers of questions, exercises, and problems. As such questions, exercises, and problems are found, they (or copies of them) can be pasted on 3- by-5-inch file cards and placed in the appropriate folder. Eventually these file cards can be organized and put into a metal file box or typed into a word processor or computer.

This activity creates the equivalent of what have been termed "item banks" for each course-level goal—a "large collection of distinguishable test items" (Arter & Estes, 1985, p. i):

> *Large* means that the number of items available is greater than the number to be used in any one test. *Collection* implies that the items, whether developed by the user or someone else, are kept together in some retrievable form. *Distinguishable* means that the items carry some information that permits the test constructor to select precisely those items he or she wants to use for each test.

In *Item Banking for Local Test Development: Practitioner's Handbook,* Arter and Estes (1985) discuss the development and possible uses of item banks by teachers. A companion volume, *A Guide to Item Banking in Education* (1984), contains a listing of 41 existing item banks as well as information concerning the subject areas they include and how to access them. These banks cover subject areas ranging from reading, mathematics, and language arts to life skills, health, science, and social studies.

Once sufficient numbers of questions, exercises, and problems have been found, the review process begins. A logical review is conducted first. To facilitate such a review, a set of review criteria should be prepared to serve as a guide. Questions, exercises, and problems failing to pass the logical review are removed from the folder. Box 4.6 presents an example of a set of review criteria.

One of the major advantages of this item-banking rather than self-construction approach is the large numbers of questions, exercises, and problems that are generated. As a consequence, these questions, exercises, and problems can be used for several purposes in mastery learning.

BOX 4.6   Sample Criteria for Conducting a Logical Review

1. Do the questions, exercises, or problems "match" the goal?
2. Do the questions, exercises, or problems appear to be written at an appropriate level of difficulty given the students and the instruction they will receive?
3. As a set, do the questions, exercises, or problems represent a good cross section of all of the questions, exercises, or problems that could be asked pertaining to the goal? (That is, is it a comprehensive set of questions, exercises, or problems?)
4. Are the questions, exercises, or problems clearly stated?
5. Have clues as to the correct answers, responses, or solutions been avoided?
6. Are the scoring keys or procedures and criteria clearly stated?

Some can be used as teaching examples and illustrations. Others can be used as in-class or homework assignments. Still others can be used in preparing the very important unit, or formative, tests. Finally, others can be used in preparing the summative tests. And as the questions, exercises, and problems are used, teachers can note student successes as well as difficulties. These notes provide a useful global empirical review by which problematic or undesirable questions, exercises, and problems can be eliminated from their respective folders.

Determining Mastery

The purpose of the questions, exercises, and problems is to elicit responses from the students that will permit teachers to decide whether mastery has been achieved. Unfortunately, we currently have no way of directly examining the student's mind to see if, in fact, the desired learning has "sunk in."

In order to help teachers make this decision, therefore, mastery performance standards are set. These standards include the number or percentage of correct answers, performances, or solutions that will be accepted as indicative of mastery. In light of our discussion of mastery, these performance standards should be set on a goal-by-goal basis.

We would argue that these standard should not be set in a capricious fashion. Rather, they should be arbitrated (Block, 1978b); competing standards should be openly discussed and choices made by consensus or majority rule. The proper setting of standards requires, then, that informed, professional judgments be made by teachers or other educators.

Fortunately, several such "informed judgment" approaches exist (Popham, 1983). These approaches nicely combine educator logic with available empirical evidence.

The "known group" approach suggests that we consider the test performances of students perceived by their teachers as definitely having mastered the course goals. Teachers identify those students and examine their performance on all course summative tests. The average score of these students on each test is accepted as being indicative of mastery.

The "comparative group" approach suggests that we compare the test performances of students perceived by their teachers to have definitely mastered the major goals with those who have definitely not; the test performances of students about whom the teachers are unsure are not considered. The test score distributions of the "masters" are compared with of the "nonmasters" on all summative tests. The point at which the distributions first overlap on each test is accepted as the mastery performance standard.

The third approach is usually referred to as the "educational consequences" approach. Using this approach, standards are set in such a way as to maximize the likelihood of student success in future educational experiences and coursework. For example, those performing above the standard in earlier courses should perform far better in later courses than those scoring below the standard. Since most educators are either unwilling or unable to invest in longitudinal examination of their students, they must rely on extant research evidence to set standards using this approach. Although little research has been conducted in this area, the results of the available research are nonetheless consistent (Block, 1972; Chan, 1981).

Regardless of the approach used, mastery performance standards must be set sufficiently high to ensure that the desired learning has been attained but not so high as to be perceived by the students to be unattainable or unnecessary to achieve. We must strive for mastery, not perfection. This means that for the more common paper-and-pencil tests such as multiple-choice, true-false, matching, and short-answer completion, standards somewhere between 85% and 95% correct are likely to be useful first approximations. However, many assessment procedures do not lend themselves to the computation of a percent correct score. In these cases we would suggest that examples of excellent performance or products (those above the standard) and substandard performance or products be used as models against which to compare individual student's performances or products. Those resembling the excellent models rather than the substandard ones would be considered "mastery" performances or products.

In either case we believe that standards become increasingly meaningful as they approximate Block's (1972) characteristics of an ideal performance standard.

1. Such standards would be derived from the same values that guide the choice of course-level goals; that is, they would not be value-free standards.
2. They would be derived in such a manner as to allow the teacher to defend the superiority of the standards vis-à-vis other possible standards *logically* or *empirically*.
3. They would be absolute standards in three senses: They would divide students into masters and nonmasters; they would evaluate student learning only on the basis of individual learning and not in relation to the learning of others in the class; and they would be the sole standards used to judge a student's learning.
4. They would be attainable with reasonable amounts of resources, both human and nonhuman, and time.
5. They would be representative of *mastery*, and not proficiency or competency.

To this list we would add one more characteristic. All initial attempts at setting mastery performance standards should be viewed as tentative. Based on data collected from students, modifications based on applications of either the "known group" approach or the "comparison group" approach would seem both appropriate and essential.

PLANNING FOR MASTERY

The role of planning in everyday life is quite apparent in the number and variety of sayings about it: "To fail to plan is to plan to fail." "Plans are nothing; planning is everything." "The best-laid plans of mice and men often go awry." The importance of planning in teaching is equally apparent.

Yinger (1980) has suggested that at the beginning of the year teachers are faced with what he terms the "general teaching dilemma." In essence, teachers are told: "Here are the organizational constraints, this is your classroom, these are the students you are going to teach; now what are you going to do?" In response to this dilemma, teachers make a series of plans, to cover different lengths of time. According to Yinger, teachers plan at at least five different levels: yearly, term, learning unit, weekly, and daily.

Burns (1984) has also suggested that teachers are required to make decisions at several levels. Four of these levels require some preactive planning: course or grading period, learning unit, lesson, and lesson segment (for example, plans for the lecture portion of the lesson and for the seatwork portion of the lesson). The fifth level—episodes—requires interactive planning "on the spot" or "in flight." As Burns comments: "It is important to note that this type of decision-making is not thoughtless behavior, but decisions appear to be based more on feeling and intuition rather than the deliberate reasoning process that characterize preactive [or planned] teaching behavior" (p. 99).

In combination, then, Yinger and Burns have identified three general levels of teacher planning, although Yinger's levels are more temporal while Burns's are more functional. The three levels are short-term planning (daily, lesson, and lesson segment), intermediate-term planning (weekly and learning unit), and long-term planning (yearly, term, course, and grading period).

In planning for mastery, teachers address questions pertaining primarily to long- and intermediate-term planning. How should the entire course or year be organized and structured? How should the available time be allocated to particular topics or units? What general strategies or methods should be employed to teach for mastery? What provisions should be made for students who fail to attain mastery within the allocated time and those who attain mastery earlier than anticipated or desired?

This emphasis on longer-term planning is not meant to undermine the importance of short-term planning but to highlight the centrality of the learning unit and not the learning lesson in mastery learning (Anderson, 1985a). Learning units are longer-term yet concrete entities that lie somewhere between teachers' immediate concerns for "what to do tomorrow" and the abstract, hoped-for outcomes of months or years of instruction. They represent milestones at which progress toward the course-level goals can be noted and corrections made when progress is unsatisfactory. Perhaps most important, they provide a larger context within which individual lessons, particular pieces of knowledge, or specific objectives acquire meaning and purpose.

The learning unit has historically been central in mastery learning. Morrison (1926), in particular, contrasted what he called "unit learning" with what he referred to as "lesson learning."

> The whole process of education, of adjustments to the objective conditions of life, is made up of unit learnings each of which must be mastered or else no adaption is made. These unit learnings . . . can all of them be evidenced by symptoms or signs revealed in the learner's behavior. . . . It follows that the course material which we find in the curriculum is valuable in education only as it is analyzed into significant units of learning which generate adaptations in the pupil and in that way contribute to his adjustment. It is meaningless to prescribe a course in arithmetic or English or grammar or French, and let it go at that. The issue is not learning any of these but rather the mastery of certain significant units in arithmetic or English or grammar or French. (p. 36)

"Lesson learning," in contrast, focuses on the daily activities and tasks of teachers and students.

> Instead of definitely listing the units to be mastered, and guiding and constraining the pupil into a genuine mastery of each as shown by tests focused on each, and then, if you will, counting the units mastered, the pupil has been required to [fix in memory] and recite upon a number of pages, solve a certain number of problems, and translate a certain number of exercises. In the common parlance of the schoolroom, a pupil is said to do "good work" or "poor work," meaning that he prepares his assignments efficiently and industriously or poorly and negligently, as the case may be. (p. 40)

In 1920 Morrison conducted a series of studies in several subject areas (foreign language, mathematics, science, and spelling). The purpose of these studies was to investigate the relationship of success in daily lessons with what he referred to as "actual achievement in certain courses" (in our terminology, tests based on course-level goals). In all studies, daily performance was *unrelated* to unit performance. Apparently, good lessons did not automatically produce good longer-term achievement.

Many years after Morrison, Bloom (1968) also recommended the formation of learning units as a "useful operating procedure" in mastery learning.

> One useful operating procedure is to break a course or subject into smaller units of learning. Such a learning unit may correspond to a chapter in a textbook, a well-defined content portion of a course, or a particular time unit of the course.... We have attempted to analyze each unit into a number of elements ranging from specific terms or facts, more complex and abstract ideas such as concepts and principles, and relatively complex processes such as application of principles and analysis of complex theoretical statements. (p. 9)

Mastery learning has been criticized, however, for its failure to attend to lesson-level concerns. Jones and her colleagues (1985), for example, state that "early proponents [of mastery learning] do not provide adequate guidelines for developing and implementing day-to-day instruction and assessment" (p. 91). Such guidelines, while useful and perhaps necessary, are, though, clearly outside the major focus of mastery learning as envisioned by Morrison, Bloom, and the authors of this volume. To return to the opening discussion of this section, educators who are concerned with effective lessons and those concerned with mastery learning are simply operating within different teacher planning and decision-making frameworks, namely, short-term versus intermediate- and long-term. Besides, a number of educators and researchers have attended to concerns for the structure and format of more effective lessons. Some of these educators, such as Jones herself and Reid (1985), have been affiliated with mastery learning for several years. Others such as Good and Grouws (1979) and Hunter (1984), however, arrived at their recommendations based primarily on research results and practical experiences quite independent of any awareness or endorsement of mastery learning. Consequently, it seems wise to consider concerns for the development of more effective lessons to be independent of concerns for the development of more effective mastery learning programs.

Designing Learning Units

Some general guidelines for the development of learning units currently exist (Anderson & Block, 1977, 1985; Block & Anderson, 1975; Guskey, 1985c). The units should be organized around a subset of the course-level goals. They should also be sequenced in such a way that the mastery of one unit will facilitate mastery of subsequent units. And they should be sequenced so that mastery of subsequent units will reinforce and extend into competency and proficiency the mastery of earlier units. The sequence of learning units provides the across-unit structure of the course.

Each unit should further include the specific content or objectives associated with mastery of the unit goals. The content can be described in terms of the important terms, facts, concepts, principles, and procedures (Block & Anderson, 1975), the important concepts, information, and procedures (Anderson & Jones, 1981), or the primary declarative knowledge (knowing *that* . . .), procedural knowledge (knowing *how* . . .), and cognitive strategies (Anderson, 1980). If desired, verbs indicating the various "mental operations" or "levels of cognitive processing" students are to perform on the content can be specified, thereby creating what educators refer to as instructional objectives. As defined by Block and Anderson (1975), "an instructional objective simply specifies some content to be learned and something the student is expected to be able to do with this content" (p. 10). Whereas the sequence of learning units provides the across-unit structure of the course, the content, processes, and instructional objectives included in each unit provide the within-unit structure.

Each unit should, moreover, be "long enough to allow sufficient time for students to learn an interrelated set of facts, concepts, principles, skills, and appreciations" but short enough "to permit the close monitoring of each student's learning as the units and course unfold" (Anderson & Block, 1985, p. 3223). Concerns for the amount of time to be spent on each learning unit help educators resolve the persistent dilemma between what *should* be included in a course and what *can* be included given the time available. Specific recommendations concerning the actual length of learning units include 1 to 2 weeks (Bloom, 1968), 10 to 14 days (Block & Anderson, 1975), or 2 to 3 weeks (Anderson & Block, 1977). In actual practice, the length of learning units has ranged from 4 days (Keller, 1968) to 2½ weeks (Chandler, 1973).

For each unit a parallel set of diagnostic progress tests or "formative" tests should be constructed in order "to determine whether or not the student has mastered the unit and what, if anything, the student must still do to master it" (Bloom, 1968, p. 9). These tests should be "brief so that [they do] not take up inordinate amounts of instructional time," while at the same time providing sufficient "information or feedback to both the students and [the teacher] regarding *where* the student might, if necessary, start . . . restudying and review of particular material" (Block & Anderson, 1975, p. 30). Since some students will likely fail to demonstrate mastery the first time a unit test is given, alternate forms of the unit tests should be developed; hence the importance and utility of item banks.

For each unit a set of instructional materials, presentations, and activities should also be prepared. These materials, presentations, and activities are keyed to specific course-level goals (Anderson & Block, 1985). They are separated into two general instructional plans: the "original instructional plan" and the "supplementary instructional plan." As we noted in Chapter 1, the former plan is intended basically to introduce students to the unit goals and help them master them. The latter one has two intents. One is to help students who have not mastered particular goals, as evidenced by their formative test performance. The materials, presentations, and activities included in this portion of the supplementary plan are commonly called *correctives* (Block & Anderson, 1975). The other intent is to challenge students who have mastered these goals. The materials, presentations, and activities in this portion of the supplementary plan are commonly called *enrichments*.

Let us now turn to a more detailed, somewhat prescriptive examination of these issues. Specifically, we shall address the issues of (1) identifying the goals, associated content and objectives, and appropriate sequence of learning units; (2) determining appropriate time allocations for each learning unit; (3) preparing unit formative tests; (4) preparing the original instructional plan; and (5) preparing the supplementary instructional plan of correctives and enrichments.

Unit Goals, Content, and Sequence

Since not all of the course-level goals can be pursued at the same time, some sequencing is necessary. In content-oriented courses the *sequence of goals* tends to correspond to the sequence of major topics. That is, the topics are arranged in some order, and the goals associated with those topics are sequenced almost by default.

In the U.S. history example some of the topic sequences are obvious. The unit on agriculture and farming should precede the unit on business, industry, and labor. Similarly, the unit on Negroes and slavery should precede the Civil War but should follow the unit on the American Revolution. Other topic sequences require more thought. For example, where should the unit on political parties or the unit on education be placed? Since these units tend to transcend any specific historical period (indeed, stability and change across historical periods seems relevant to their discussion), their placement in the course is somewhat arbitrary. But once the units have been properly sequenced, the goals have been sequenced by definition.

Clues to the specific content and objectives to include within each learning unit come from two sources. The first is the subentries in the index. In the U.S. history example several subentries appear under the major entry "Constitution, U.S.": the writing of the Constitution, the process by which it was adopted, the fact that there is no provision in it for political parties, the provisions for amending it, the Bill of Rights, several important amendments, and several others. All these subentries are candidates for inclusion in the learning unit dealing with the U.S. Constitution.

A second source is the way in which most textbooks are written and presented. A variety of subheadings, text-embedded questions, summaries, graphic displays, highlighting (boldface, italics), and colors of ink are used by authors and publishers to draw attention to important aspects of each chapter. Again, using the U.S. Constitution example, the bulk of the textual material pertaining to this topic appears in a single chapter of 19 pages titled "The Making of the Constitution." Several subheadings appear in this chapter: "Vital decisions were made by only a few men," "Opponents were willing to compromise," and "A government with checks and balances was formed." Similarly, charts titled "How the Constitution overcame weaknesses under the Articles of Confederation," "The structure and powers of the government," and "Amending the Constitution of the United States" are featured. Several small sets of review questions are embedded in the chapter itself. These questions ask "What new powers were given to the central government by the Constitution?" and "Why was the Bill of Rights added to the Constitution?" Finally, a summary and a somewhat longer set of questions conclude the chapter.

From the entries in the index and the wide variety of clues inherent in the textbook's organization and printing, key content elements (facts, generalizations, concepts, and procedures) associated with each unit goal are easily identified. Once identified, these content elements can be transformed into instructional objectives, if desired, and listed on one or more sheets of paper for placement in the folder pertaining to the appropriate course-level goal.

In more process-oriented courses a different approach is often taken to the identification of unit goals and the proper sequence of learning units. Often the same goal is pursued for several units. Consider, once again, the elementary reading example. The goals of students increasing their vocabularies, reading with understanding, making proper inferences, and understanding the nature, structure, and function of language are truly course-level goals. Many days, weeks, months, and perhaps years are spent by both teachers and students in their pursuit. As a consequence, the units are organized around different types of reading materials or stories. In elementary reading courses, then, it is not surprising to see units labeled "Stories of Families," "It's a Big, Wide, Wonderful World," and "Monsters, Monsters, Monsters!" As a consequence, the particular sequence of units likely matters very little (although it makes sense to place units containing easier stories earlier in the course than units containing harder ones).

An alternative approach to organizing and sequencing units, more appropriate for use in mastery learning, is to consider the function of the stories rather than their difficulty. Thus stories are analyzed in terms of their relationship with each of the general skills and strategies. Which stories, for example, are particularly useful in helping students draw conclusions or differentiate facts from opinion? Which stories are sufficiently difficult that students will have to use dictionaries or context clues to decipher meanings of words? In this approach the general skills and strategies form the basis for placing stories in units. Units will be organized around drawing conclusions, determining main ideas and supporting details, predicting likely consequences and outcomes, and expressing and defending opinions. The specific readings included in these units will be selected primarily because they are useful teaching examples for achieving these unit goals.

The sequencing of units in this approach is facilitated by the use of a careful task analysis and a subsequent examination of the required prerequisite skills and abilities necessary to master the goals of each successive unit (Gagné, 1968; Resnick, 1976). Such analyses are performed for each unit by asking the question "What do students have to be able to do before they can master the goals of this unit?" For example, do students need to remember details before they can learn to determine the main idea? If so, the unit on details would precede the unit on the main idea. Do students need to be able to draw conclusions before they are able to express and defend opinions? If so, the unit on drawing conclusions would precede the unit on expression of opinions.

In some respects task analysis is a never-ending process. Given any set of unit-level goals, the prerequisites for these goals are first identified. However, these prerequisites themselves may, in the larger scheme of things, be goals of other units. If so, decisions of sequencing units can be made. At the same time, however, additional task analyses must be performed on these newly identified unit-level goals. A likely stopping point in the process is reached when all identified prerequisites are known or suspected to be included in one or more previous courses.

As a result of a general task analysis, units can generally be placed near the beginning, middle, or end of a course. Most often, greater refinement in the placement of units is unnecessary.

In the elementary mathematics example, six course-level goals were identified. Each of these goals easily becomes a unit goal. If the length of each unit becomes problematic (approximately 6 weeks per unit in a 36-week school year), smaller units can be devised by focusing on subgoals associated with each goal. Consider, for example, the goal that students should understand the nature and structure of the number system. At least two subgoals can be delineated. First, students should be able to compare and order numbers. Second, students should determine numerical equivalencies. Each of these subgoals can serve as the basis of a shorter unit (lasting approximately 3 weeks).

Consider, as a second example, the goal that students should know how to multiply whole numbers. Subgoals often conform to the length of the numbers being multiplied. Thus one unit pertains to two- and three-digit numbers and the other pertains to four- and five-digit numbers. This approach to determining subgoals is unsatisfactory in mastery learning. The course-level goal states, in essence, that students will master the whole number multiplication algorithm. The algorithm contains a sequence of steps to be performed in a given order. Some of the steps require that students make decisions (such as to regroup or not). We would argue that students who are able to multiply correctly every pair of three-digit numbers they encounter have mastered the algorithm. Requiring them to multiply pairs of four-digit, five-digit, or six-digit numbers adds nothing to our understanding of their mastery of the algorithm and greatly increases the chances that computational errors will occur. Thus careless computational mistakes rather than a lack of mastery of the algorithm will likely yield incorrect answers. If a large enough number of computational mistakes occur (placing the students below the mastery performance standard), teachers will infer incorrectly that students have not mastered the algorithm.

Thus rather than form subgoals based on the inclusion of "bigger numbers," subgoals of computation and application may be far more appropriate. One unit will be devoted to teaching the algorithm and providing numerical exercises on which students can develop their mastery of it. The other unit will focus on the application of the algorithm to a variety of problems (involving areas of rectangles, annual salaries, and the like).

Once the unit goals have been identified, concerns shift to the sequencing and structuring of the units. In process-oriented courses, task analyses can be used to help determine the order in which units appear in the course. The sequence of some of the units is readily apparent. Units pertaining to the memorization of multiplication and division facts should probably appear before units pertaining to the multiplication and division algorithms. Similarly, the unit emphasizing mastery of the multiplication algorithm should probably precede the unit focusing on the applications of that algorithm to various problem situations and settings.

Decisions as to the specific content elements or instructional objectives to include in each unit can be aided by reexamining the results of the content analysis displayed in Box 4.4, on page 144. To place each content element or instructional objective into the appropriate unit, a question similar to that asked by those conducting task analyses is posed. "Which of the concepts, information, and procedures I have identified will likely help me teach and my students achieve the unit goal?" In response to this question, identified concepts, information, and procedures are placed in one or more units. Thus, for example, the concepts of units for measure, perimeter, area, and volume; information pertaining to metric units of measurement; and the procedures used to calculate perimeters and areas of two-dimensional figures and the volume of three-dimensional figures will likely appear in the unit(s) pertaining to the goal of understanding basic measurement concepts and formulas. It should be noted that the concepts of perimeter, area, and volume and the procedures used to calculate them could also be included in the unit(s) pertaining to the goal of identifying geometric figures and understanding associated terminology. The fact that the same content can be associated with different goals indicates the complexity of the structure of knowledge, not the limitations of mastery learning.

Estimating Time Allocations

Since the advent of formal schooling, the number of hours, days, months, and years devoted to the education of children has changed very little. Students are expected (or required) to attend school for about 6 hours a day, 180 days a year, for 12 years. Unfortunately, over the past century or two the amount of knowledge and the number of skills that can be transmitted within that fixed and finite amount of time have increased dramatically.

As a somewhat silly example, consider a U.S. history course for high school students in the 1890s. The relevant content for that course would begin with the period of discovery and colonization and end, perhaps, with the government's attempt to intrude into the business sector and the increased role of the populists in politics. Next, consider a U.S. history course for high school students in the 1990s. Most courses will still begin with a discussion of discovery and colonization. However, such courses now include discussion of several wars, depressions and recessions, isolationism, foreign affairs, the "advent of technology," and the "politics of power."

How is it possible to include more content in a course that meets for the same amount of time? In many ways, the answer to this question—that it is not possible—points to a very basic need for mastery learning. When the time available exceeds the content to be taught or the processes to be acquired, the need for carefully selecting what to teach, test, and emphasize does not exist. In fact, teachers are faced with the opposite problem, namely, finding something to do or learn to fill up the available time. When the amount of content to be covered or processes to be developed exceeds the time available, however, the need for decisions concerning inclusion and exclusion becomes apparent.

It is precisely the dramatic increase in the amount of knowledge available, the number of skills that could be acquired, the number of stories that could be read, and the diversity of opinions that currently exist that makes mastery learning so essential. Choices need to be made, and someone will make them of necessity.

For each course, then, the goals identified and the units developed represent views of what *should* be under ideal conditions and circumstances. We now must raise the difficult question as to whether what should be *can* be; is it *feasible* under present conditions to address all the identified goals and complete all the designated learning units? To address this question properly, two basic issues must be considered. The first is Carroll's (1963) "Model of School Learning," specifically the concept of "time needed to learn"; the second is Dahloff's (1971) concept of "steering group."

In virtually every discussion of mastery learning (including this one; see Chapter 1), some discussion of the Carroll model appears. In essence, the point made is that if students are provided with sufficient amounts of time and encouraged to spend that time actively involved in learning, virtually all students will learn (save the small percentage who suffer from major genetic, biological, or constitutional deficiencies). To understand Carroll's model, then, we need to know two estimates: the amount of time students need in order to learn well and the amount of time students actually spend trying to learn. Unfortunately, as Anderson (1985c) points out, much current research has focused exclusively on the second estimate (time spent rather than time needed), and as a consequence most current practice has emphasized the need for students to spend more time on learning.

Some estimate of the amount of time needed to master unit goals plus their associated content and objectives is imperative for the success of mastery learning programs. If such an estimate is unavailable, concerns for time spent (or the more familiar synonyms of time on task, academically engaged time, or academic learning time) are in vain. Some students can be highly engaged in learning for an entire 50-minute period but need 75 minutes to master what is being taught. These students likely will not learn. Other students can work for only 20 minutes and master what is being taught. These students needed only 20 minutes or less to learn.

While students differ in the amounts of time they need to spend in order to learn, teachers must make decisions as to how much time they can reasonably allocate to any given goal or unit in light of their students and the number of goals or units to be completed. Stated simply, teachers need to know when to move on from lesson to lesson or unit to unit.

Dahloff has suggested that teachers rely in making these "in-flight" decisions on the reactions of a small number of students, so-called steering groups. When the reactions of these students indicated they were having difficulty understanding the material presented, teachers would take additional time to explain it. Quite obviously, this decision slowed the pace at which the entire class moved from lesson to lesson or unit to unit. If, however, their reactions indicated they understood the material presented, teachers would move on to new material, goals, or units, with a resultant increase in pace.

How do you identify an appropriate steering group? We would recommend that you seek students whose average achievement test performances are much higher than that identified by Dahloff (20th percentile) or the 30th to 35th percentile apparently used in some mastery learning implementations (see Arlin, 1982). We would suggest that the median of the steering group be set around the 75th percentile; that is, look for students just below those in the top quarter of the class.

We recommend the use of a higher-achieving steering group for several reasons. First, the pace of instruction must remain fairly brisk if the boredom experienced by many of the faster students in any classroom is to be lessened. We feel there is a tendency for many mastery learning teachers to move too slowly through their units and courses. Many of these teachers have indicated to us that they are uncomfortable administering the units tests until they are quite sure *all* of their students have mastered the material. We believe this reasoning, although humanitarian, is an inefficient use of the power of mastery learning. Second, many students tend to move at whatever pace is expected of them. Increasing the pace will likely have a positive effect on students who simply "do enough to get by." Third, corrective instruction is available for those for whom the pace may be initially too fast. The gain in knowledge and skills made possible by the corrective instruction will result in students who are able to move at a more rapid pace as the course progresses.

The concepts of "time needed" and "steering group," then, provide useful ways of thinking about the amount of time to allocate to any individual goal or unit. In mastery learning, teachers are asked to visualize their steering groups in advance and, based on their understanding of the nature of such groups of students in the past, estimate the amount of time they would need to cover the content and objectives in each unit and to master the unit goals. We have found that a simple form can be used to obtain these estimates, an example of which is displayed in Table 4.2.

To complete the form, the teacher first considers each content, process, or instructional objective included in the first unit. He or she then asks how many lessons (in elementary school) or class periods (in secondary school) will the students in the steering group need to master

TABLE 4.2. ESTIMATED TIME ALLOCATIONS FOR LEARNING UNITS

	Class Periods/Lessons
Unit _____	
Goal 1 _____	
Content/Objective 1 _____	
Content/Objective 2 _____	
Content/Objective 3 _____	
Content/Objective 4 _____	
Content/Objective 5 _____	
Content/Objective 6 _____	
Content/Objective 7 _____	
Content/Objective 8 _____	
Content/Objective 9 _____	
Content/Objective 10 _____	
Goal 2 _____	
Content/Objective 1 _____	
Content/Objective 2 _____	
Content/Objective 3 _____	
Content/Objective 4 _____	
Content/Objective 5 _____	
Content/Objective 6 _____	
Content/Objective 7 _____	
Content/Objective 8 _____	
Content/Objective 9 _____	
Content/Objective 10 _____	
Goal 3 _____	
Content/Objective 1 _____	
Content/Objective 2 _____	
Content/Objective 3 _____	
Content/Objective 4 _____	
Content/Objective 5 _____	
Content/Objective 6 _____	
Content/Objective 7 _____	
Content/Objective 8 _____	
Content/Objective 9 _____	
Content/Objective 10 _____	

this content, process, or instructional objective. The answer to this question goes in the far right column of the form, across from the row indicating the number and brief description of the appropriate content, process, or instructional objective. The same procedure is then used for each content, process, or instructional objective in the first unit. The result looks something like that presented in Table 4.3. As you can see, approximately 21 class periods are needed for steering-group students to master the three goals included in the unit on the U.S. Constitution. If we add one class period for the unit test and three class periods for the review of the test and the provision of additional corrective instruction as

TABLE 4.3. ESTIMATED TIME ALLOCATIONS FOR A UNIT IN U.S. HISTORY

	Class Periods/Lessons
Unit 4	
Goal 1. The students should understand the development of the U.S. Constitution.	
1. The Constitutional Convention	1
2. The Virginia Plan, the New Jersey Plan, and the Great Compromise	1
3. Federalists and Antifederalists	½
4. Comparison with Articles of Confederation	1½
5. Process of ratification	1
Goal 2. The students should be able to interpret properly various portions of the Constitution.	
1. Separation of powers; "checks and balances"	2
2. Article 1—Legislative	3
3. Article 2—Executive	1½
4. Article 3—Judicial	1
5. Article 4—Relations of the States	1
6. Articles 5, 6, and 7	1
7. Bill of Rights	1½
8. Selected amendments	1
Goal 3. The students should understand the significance of the Constitution in their lives.	
1. Constitution as "living document"	1
2. Current issue 1—school prayer	1
3. Current issue 2—school desegregation	1
4. Current issue 3—abortion	1

necessary, this single unit would require 5 weeks of instruction. At this rate, approximately 7 units would fit in a 36-week course.

The importance of estimated time allocations and the dilemma confronting classroom teachers are apparent in this example. First, as we noted earlier, some 16 units were tentatively identified. If our time estimates are fairly accurate, which seven units should be included in the course? Second, if we wish to include more than seven units, which goals or content, processes, or objectives in a unit should be eliminated? Third, if nothing can be deleted (that is, if all goals, objectives, or content elements must be maintained), can we upgrade our steering group and revise the time estimates?

Carroll's model suggests that the more goals, objectives, processes, and content taught during a finite amount of time to a fairly heterogeneous class of students, the fewer the students who will actually master them. Thus in many ways teachers facing the constraints imposed by 50- to 60-minute class periods and 36-week courses face the choice between content covered and student mastery, a potentially unpleasant choice (see Arlin,

1982). Quite clearly, some balance between concerns for what must be taught, on the one hand, and the welfare of the students, on the other, must be achieved if courses are to be both meaningful and feasible. The use of preplanned time estimates permits such a balance to be achieved.

Unit Formative Tests

Once reasonable learning units have been identified, attention turns to the preparation of unit formative tests. As has been mentioned, these tests are intended to provide teachers with information on how well students have mastered the unit goals and what goals, objectives, and content elements are causing difficulty for groups of students or individuals. Because of this dual purpose such tests have been termed *diagnostic progress tests* (although the order of the purposes suggests that we should refer to them as progress diagnostic ones).

In preparing these tests, several factors should be kept in mind. First, the questions, exercises, or problems should be selected from those compiled for each goal during the process of defining mastery. This will help your test have a high degree of *curricular validity* (Popham, 1983). Second, the tests should require no longer than one class period (and probably less) to complete. We already have a time problem without devoting large amounts of instructional time to testing. Third, questions, exercises, or problems should be available for each goal in the unit. Whether questions, exercises, or problems are included for each objective or content element, specific process, or objective will depend on practical grounds, such as constraints on length and time. Fourth, the larger the number of questions, exercises, or problems per goal, content element, process, or objective, the more *reliable* your test is likely to be.

In preparing the formative tests, then, several steps should be followed. First, estimate the total number of items (questions, exercises, and problems) that can be reasonably included on the test. Second, in view of the number of unit goals, determine the number of items to include for each goal. If some goals are more important than others, more items can be included for them. Third, search through the collection (item bank) of questions, exercises, and problems and select the number necessary. Fourth, in arranging the items on the test, consider first the format of the items (true-false, multiple-choice, matching, short-answer, or short-essay) and then the goal associated with the items. Generally, items are arranged on tests by format; that is, all multiple-choice items are placed together, then all short-answer completion items, and so on. Within a particular format, all items pertaining to a single goal are then clustered together. Within multiple-choice items, for example, items pertaining to goal 1 are placed first, then items pertaining to goal 2, and so on. Quite obviously, if all items are of the same format, the arrangement is purely by goal.

Fifth, prepare test directions. We suggests directions similar to those proposed by Block & Anderson (1975).

> This diagnostic-progress test is intended to give us feedback regarding how successfully you have learned the important material presented thus far in this course. *You will not be graded on the basis of your test results.* [At the same time, however, you will be expected to spend additional time working on the material your responses to this test indicate you have not learned successfully.]
>
> Select [or write] the one best answer for each question. Kindly mark your answer on the separate answer sheet. You will notice that you are required to enter your answer twice on the answer sheet. *You will keep one half of the answer sheet and I will collect the other.* (p.32)

Directions of this type tell the students that the primary purpose of the test is to find out how well they are learning. They also emphasize that the test results will not be used for grading purposes. Finally, they indicate that the test results will be used to identify specific weaknesses or learning deficiencies that students will be expected to remedy in order to achieve mastery. This third purpose is particularly important to help compensate for students' possible lack of motivation to do well on the test because it will not be graded.

Sixth, prepare answer sheets and scoring keys. For "standard" paper-and-pencil tests, Block and Anderson (1975) have suggested the use of "double answer sheets." An example is shown in Box 4.7. The answer sheets are identical except for the bottom portion. The bottom portion of the left-hand column contains spaces for the teacher to assign a score for each goal and, based on this score and the mastery performance standard, indicate whether the student has mastered (M) or not yet mastered (NYM) that goal. The bottom portion of the right-hand column indicates the relationship of the test items and the three goals.

The answer sheet can be torn in half, with the left-hand column returned to the teacher and the right-hand column kept by the student. In this way the student can review his or her answers by reviewing the test or by comparing answers with other students. The information at the bottom of the left-hand column permits students to tie in their responses to individual items and sets of items in the unit goals.

As just noted, the teacher scores the left-hand column and completes the bottom portion. She or he then prepares a class summary of student performances on the test. An example is shown in Table 4.4. Note that this summary provides two primary sources of information. The percentage of students responding correctly to each test item is given in the right-hand column, and the percentage of students attaining or surpassing the mastery performance standard for each unit is given at the bottom of the table.

The information in Table 4.4 is a continuation of the U.S. history

---

BOX 4.7   A Unit Diagnostic-progress Test Answer Sheet

Name _____   Name _____

Date _____   Date _____

Directions: Circle the letter of the   Directions: Circle the letter of the
correct answer or supply the correct   correct answer or supply the correct
answer in the appropriate space.   answer in the appropriate space.

1. a   b   c   d   1. a   b   c   d

2. a   b   c   d   2. a   b   c   d

3. a   b   c   d   3. a   b   c   d
        .   .
        .   .
        .   .
25. a   b   c   d   25. a   b   c   d

26. _____   26. _____

27. _____   27. _____

28. _____   28. _____
        .   .
        .   .
        .   .
40. _____   40. _____

_____   _____

Goal 1 Score   Goal 1 = Items 1–10;

  M   NYM

Goal 2 Score   Goal 2 = Items 11–25;
                                                               Items 26–32.
  M   NYM

Goal 3 Score   Goal 3 = Items 33–40.

  M   NYM

_____   _____

---

example in Table 4.3. In looking at it we see that between two-thirds and four-fifths of the students mastered each of the three unit goals. We also see that the primary problem area associated with goal 1 seems to be the comparison of the Constitution with the Articles of Confederation. Of the three items

TABLE 4.4. A CLASS SUMMARY FOR A UNIT TEST

Item	Objective/Content Element	% Correct
1	Constitutional Convention	93
2	Virginia Plan, N. J. Plan, Great Compromise	86
3	Virginia Plan, N. J. Plan, Great Compromise	98
4	Federalists and Antifederalists	76
5	Federalists and Antifederalists	79
6	Comparison with Articles of Confederation	52
7	Comparison with Articles of Confederation	75
8	Comparison with Articles of Confederation	43
9	Process of ratification	91
10	Process of ratification	79
11	Separation of powers; checks and balances	83
12	Separation of powers; checks and balances	68
13	Article 1—Legislative	38
14	Article 1—Legislative	58
15	Article 1—Legislative	53
16	Article 2—Executive	90
17	Article 2—Executive	84
18	Article 3—Judicial	76
19	Article 3—Judicial	85
20	Article 4—Relations of the States	87
21	Articles 5, 6, and 7	61
22	Articles 5, 6, and 7	44
23	Articles 5, 6, and 7	68
24	Bill of Rights	89
25	Bill of Rights	84
26	Separation of powers; checks and balances	71
27	Article 1—Legislative	64
28	Article 2—Executive	85
29	Article 3—Judicial	82
30	Selected Amendments	90
31	Selected Amendments	90
32	Selected Amendments	82
33	Constitution as "living document"	94
34	Constitution as "living document"	82
35	Current Issue 1—school prayer	96
36	Current Issue 1—school prayer	75
37	Current Issue 2—school desegregation	83
38	Current Issue 2—school desegregation	87
39	Current Issue 3—abortion	53
40	Current Issue 3—abortion	68
Goal 1	Understand development of Constitution (Items 1–10)	79
Goal 2	Interpret portions of Constitution (Items 11–32)	68
Goal 3	Understand significance in their lives (Items 33–40)	75

testing students' understanding of this comparison, two were answered correctly by only 43% and 52% of the students. The third item was answered correctly by 75% of the students, and all of the other items associated with goal 1 were answered correctly by 76% or more of the students.

Continuing with our analysis, we see two potential problem areas associated with goal 2: Article 1—Legislative and Articles 5, 6, and 7. Finally, the primary problem area associated with goal 2 is Current issue 3—abortion. As we shall see in a forthcoming section of this chapter, these four problem areas are strong candidates for group reteaching.

Quite obviously, the approach just described pertains only to hand-scored paper-and-pencil tests that require students to select or provide short responses. We are aware that computers are being used increasingly to score tests and report student scores on them and that other types of assessments are used to check progress and diagnose deficiencies.

With respect to computer scoring, we would suggest that the approach we outlined form the basis for a computer program that would combine data in the proper ways and display data in appropriate, understandable, and usable formats. Some useful efforts along this line may be found in *CMI 3000* (School District No. 12, 1984). Clearly, it makes no sense to do by hand what a computer can do.

With respect to the use of other types of assessments, a number of reporting possibilities are available. For example, if the form of assessment is an essay, we would suggest simply making notations on the essay itself and then preparing a summary of the comments as they pertain to the primary course-level goals on a separate sheet. If the form of assessment is some product or performance, we would suggest the use of appropriate rating scales or checklists. For further information, see Chapter 5 of Roid and Haladyna (1982).

Preparing the Original Instructional Plan

Most of the time spent in classrooms can be divided into two parts: a teaching portion and a work portion. During the teaching portion information is presented to students, and they are expected to pay attention and to absorb as much of it as possible. Researchers label the different ways in which information can be presented during the teaching portion as lecture, recitation, discussion, tutoring, audiovisual, and surrogate (a term encompassing all nonhuman methods of presentation, such as computers).

The teaching portion is typically multifaceted. It can contain a review of old information as well as the presentation of new. It can contain information about the information to be presented, as is the case when overviews, advance organizers, or instructional objectives are presented. It can serve to create an emotional readiness on the part of the learner, a desire to learn. It can be targeted toward helping students overcome difficulties and misunderstandings. It can be well or poorly organized, concise or rambling. It can be directed to the whole class, a small group, or an individual student.

Despite differences in the source of the information (human, machine), the format in which it is presented (whole class lecture, small group discussion, individual tutoring), and its aims (to review, introduce, facilitate mastery, correct errors), there is little doubt as to the presence of teaching portions in most classrooms. Equally prevalent, if not more so in certain classrooms, are the work portions. During these portions students are given assignments to complete during the class period. If these assignments are not completed, they are to be completed out of school, thus becoming homework.

Assignments can be many and varied. They may be sentences in textbooks or questions written on chalkboards that students are to copy and complete or answer. They may be worksheets distributed to students on which they are to fill in blanks or work through problems. They may be projects to be worked on for several days and ultimately completed at some later due date. Examples of projects are entries in science fairs, contour maps in geography, book reports in English, and chests of drawers in woodworking.

Assignments serve many functions in the typical classroom. They can give students practice in the knowledge and skills recently presented during the teaching portion. They can also permit students and teachers to check on the extent to which students understand or are able to apply them. Both functions are clearly instructional.

Assignments can also serve a managerial function. They give students something to do to keep them busy during the work portion of the class period. The extreme length of some assignments is likely the result of their management, not instructional, function. Because of this management function, students quickly learn that the reward for completing one assignment is the receipt of another.

As is true in the choice of any labels, the labels "teaching portion" and "work portion" may be subject to misinterpretation or misappropriation. Such is more likely to occur when the definitions emphasize only what the labels *mean*. To reduce the likelihood of misunderstanding, two points of clarification must be made. Both points emphasize what the labels *do not* mean.

First, the use of the phrase *work portion* does not exclude the possibility that some teaching is occurring. Indeed, actual teaching may or may not take place during the work portion. If teaching does occur, however, it is more likely to be directed toward individuals or small groups of students (rather than the whole class) and focused on the work the students are to be doing (for example, reviewing the safety rules with a student working on a lathe in a woodworking shop).

Second, the phrase *teaching portion* is not meant to imply passivity and blank stares on the part of students. Nor is *work portion* meant to imply drudgery. Rather, as Block (1985) has indicated, elements of play can be built into both the teaching and work portions of classroom life so that activities can be more elective, desirable, and fun.

In the ensuing discussion, however, we will not emphasize the teaching that occurs in the work portion or the opportunities for play that exist in both portions. At the same time, however, we will illustrate both of these concepts as they are appropriate.

Suffice it to say that teachers must plan for both the teaching and work portions of the lessons or class periods within each learning unit. Furthermore, they must do so in ways that attend to four potential instructional problems.

> The first problem is how to get students to attend to the source or sources of the instructional stimuli in the first place. We would call this the *attentional* problem. The second is how to get students to attend to the important stimuli presented by this source or sources. This might be termed the *presentational problem*. A third problem is how to get students to interact mentally with the instructional stimuli. We would label this the *involvement* problem. The fourth problem is how to encourage students to continue to interact mentally with the stimuli until the desired learning [has occurred]. This might be called the *encouragement* problem. (Anderson & Block, 1977, p. 169)

Let us examine possible solutions to these problems within the context of the teaching portions and work portions of classroom life.

Planning the Teaching Portions.   Quite clearly, the attentional problem must be solved first. Students must attend to the relevant source of information if they are learn anything at all from it. If the source of information is a movie projector, the attentional problem is partly solved by dimming the lights. Another part of the solution, however, involves ensuring that all students are seated in such a way that they can see the screen. If the source of information is the teacher, various routines (both verbal and physical) can be employed. Examples of such routines include the Cub Scout practice of having everyone raise their right hands with two fingers extended, the command "Eyes to the front!" and the simple request "May I have your attention, please?"

In some classrooms the attentional problem is solved when the teacher enters the classroom. Solutions to the presentation problem are more complex. Two issues are involved in identifying appropriate solutions to this problem. First, the presentation must be directly linked to the content, processes, or instructional objective of the lesson or class period. Second, the presentation must be made as clearly as possible. Fortunately, research has provided some advice on both of these issues.

"Teaching to the objective" commonly requires (1) informing students of the purpose or objective of the lesson, (2) telling or showing what is to be learned in as clear a manner as possible, (3) using strategies or tricks to facilitate memory (mnemonic devices, visual images), (4) relating new learning to what has already been learned, (5) providing opportunities for students to "try out" their learning in a safe, secure environment, (6) providing opportunities for them to "try their wings," and (7) reminding them once more of the purpose of all this activity and effort (Anderson, Evertson, & Emmer, 1980; Good & Grouws, 1979; Hunter, 1984).

But different kinds of objectives will require special teaching tricks. Anderson and Jones (1981), in particular, outline the specific steps needed to teach three types of objectives: informational, conceptual, and procedural.

For informational objectives, five steps are useful. One is to present the fact or generalization students are expected to learn. A second is to remind students of familiar facts and generalizations associated with the new fact or generalization. A third is to present memory strategies that aid the students in retaining the fact or generalization for longer periods of time. Examples of such strategies are rehearsal (for example, reciting the facts or generalizations, taking selective, verbatim notes), organization (sorting facts and generalizations into categories or classifications), and comprehension monitoring (self-checking on basic knowledge and understanding by asking questions such as "What is this about?" or "Do I understand what this means?") (Weinstein & Mayer, 1986). A fourth is to provide overt opportunities for repetition or recitation. Typically, some form of rapid-fire question-and-answer session is involved here. The fifth pertains to informational objectives that emphasize generalizations. In this case one or more examples or illustrations of the generalization should be provided. An example of the application of these steps in teaching students the Pythagorean theorem is displayed in Box 4.8.

For conceptual objectives, four specific steps are useful. One is the presentation of the critical attributes of the concept (that is, the features or dimensions that make the concept unique and that all examples or instances of that concept share). The next step involves presenting the relationship of the new concept with previously learned ones. Often this step involves engaging in a series of comparisons and contrasts. Another step involves presenting examples of the concept. The final one (and a step

---

BOX 4.8   Teaching Informational Objectives

General Steps	Illustration
1. Present the fact or generalization.	1. A very important theorem in mathematics is called the Pythagorean Theorem. The Pythagorean Theorem says that the square of the hypotenuse is equal to the sum of the squares of the other two sides.
2. Activate relevant prior knowledge and indicate the relationship between the new information and the prior knowledge.	2. Recall finding the *perimeters of triangles*. Suggest a situation in which it might not be possible to calculate the perimeter because the hypotenuse cannot be measured directly. Ask, "What would you do?"
3. Present memory strategies that aid student in retaining fact/generalization; e.g., stories and visual aids (especially diagrams of relationships and text outlines) as well as instructions to involve student in information processing (paraphrase, visualize, infer, summarize, apply, etc.).	3. Perhaps a pun on the theorem would do. Tell story of three pregnant Indian women who lived in tepees with different animal skins as floors. Punch line: The son of the squaw of the hippopotamus is equal to the sons of the squaws of the other two hides. (Admittedly a bad pun, but very effective.)
4. Provide opportunities for repetition and/or recitation.	4. (a) Have students look at various triangles with lengths of sides given. Ask: "Which triangles illustrate the Pythagorean Theorem?" (b) Have students practice telling each other the "pun" story ending with a correct statement of the Pythagorean Theorem.
5. If informational objective is a generalization, present example or illustration of the generalization.	5. Draw a right triangle 3 in. $\times$ 4 in. $\times$ 5 in. Demonstrate that $$5^2 = 3^2 + 4^2$$ Draw several other right triangles; demonstrate that theorem holds.

Anderson & Jones, 1981, p. 129.

too often overlooked) involves presenting nonexamples of the concept. Explanations as to which illustrations are and are not examples of the concept also are useful. The application of these steps to the teaching of the concept "mineral" is shown in Box 4.9. Other excellent examples can be found in Carroll (1964).

Four specific steps also are useful in teaching procedural objectives.

BOX 4.9   Teaching Conceptual Objectives

General Steps

1. Present the critical attributes of the concept.

2. Present relationships with familiar, related concepts.

3. Present examples and show *how* examples illustrate the critical features. This may be done by teacher explanation or by eliciting responses from students.

4. Present non-examples and explain why they are non-examples.

Illustration

1. A mineral is something that has four important features.
   - (a) A mineral is found in nature.
   - (b) A mineral is made up of a substance that was never alive.
   - (c) A mineral has the same chemical makeup wherever it is found.
   - (d) The atoms of a mineral are arranged in a regular pattern, and form solid units called crystals.

2. A few days ago, we learned about rocks and gems. Today, we're going to learn about things that are something like rocks and gems but are somewhat different. (Discuss similarities and differences among rocks, gems and minerals.)

3. Diamonds, gold, copper, iodine

4. Man-made diamonds (violate feature a). Coal, petroleum (violate feature b). Sand (violates feature c). Calcium found in milk (violates feature d).

Anderson & Jones, 1981, p. 130.

One is to present the stages that make up the procedure, defining key terms and concepts in each stage that students need to understand if the procedure is to be correctly applied. The second is to demonstrate how to use the procedure to find answers, complete exercises, or solve problems. In this demonstration teachers should be intent on "thinking aloud" as they work through the procedure or "showing their work" (for example, "At this point in the process, we have eliminated two of the alternative hypotheses with which we began our examination of this phenomenon"). The third is to present a variety of problems or situations to which the procedure might be applied. Problems or situations to which the procedure *does not* apply but which may cause some confusion for the students may also be presented at this step. The last step is to provide opportunities for supervised practice of the application of the procedures. Diagrams, other visual aids, or checklists can be used to emphasize and illustrate the major steps involved while students practice one or two applications. The application of these steps to the procedure of finding the main idea is given in Box 4.10.

In applying these specific approaches to the teaching of informational, conceptual, and procedural objectives, two points must be emphasized. First, the order in which the steps are performed is not fixed. The objective

---

BOX 4.10.   Teaching Procedural Objectives

General Steps

1. Define the key concept(s) and present the steps that make up the procedure.

2. Present applications of the procedure to use on three problems or situations indicating "answers" that follow from the successful application of each step.

Illustration

1. Explain what a main idea is. Explain that finding one is a process. This is best done in the form of a flow chart....

2. Begin with a paragraph whose main idea is stated in the first sentence. Move to paragraphs whose main idea is stated in a sentence other than the first. With these paragraphs, go through each step of the procedure showing that the main idea is *not* in the first sentence. Finally, end with paragraphs whose main idea must be inferred from the entire set of sentences. Again, go through the entire procedure, showing that the main idea is not stated in any of the sentences in the paragraph.

3. Present a set of problems or situations to which the procedure does apply.

3. Identify several paragraphs which possess three characteristics: (a) age-appropriate vocabulary, (b) age-appropriate sentence structure, (c) age-appropriate paragraph length. Some of the paragraphs should have the main idea explicit in the first sentence, some should have the main idea explicit in the last paragraph, and some should have an implicit main idea. Some of the paragraphs should be written without a main idea.

4. Present opportunities for supervised practice of procedures. Use diagrams, other visual aids, or checklists to illustrate the key concepts and steps in a procedural objective.

4. Present worksheet on which two or three paragraphs are presented. Make sure directions clearly indicate what students are to do. Have students work on each paragraph under supervision: (a) Work on paragraph, then put on board; (b) Work in small group; and (c) Work and check with answers on board.

Anderson & Jones, 1981, p. 131.

may be taught "top-down," "bottom-up," or in some other order. In teaching a conceptual objective, for example, a teacher may begin by presenting examples and nonexamples and move students to induce the defining attributes. Another teacher may begin by comparing and contrasting the new concept with previously learned concepts, then present the defining attributes, and finally present examples and nonexamples. Although the order is not fixed, some sequences of steps may be problematic. Presenting nonexamples prior to presenting examples is one important instance.

Second, not all steps are necessary for teaching all objectives. Steps may be omitted if available evidence about student learning indicates that they are not needed. Again, when teaching a conceptual objective, a teacher may find, after comparing and contrasting the new concept with previously learned concepts, that students have determined the defining attributes for themselves. In this case the teaching of the concept may end with a few examples and nonexamples.

Thus the steps in these approaches to teaching these particular types of objectives are not to be followed slavishly. Rather, decisions as to the order in which the steps are followed and possible omission of one or more steps must be made by knowledgeable teachers based on their monitoring of student reactions to the instructional presentation.

The steps in the foregoing discussion emphasize *what* teachers can do to improve the quality of their presentation in terms of specific content elements or instructional objectives. An equally important part of improving the quality of teacher presentation concerns *how* the presentation is made. Research on this issue typically falls in the category of teaching clarity or clarity of instruction.

From this research, several factors have been identified that detract from or reduce the clarity of presentation. One is the inclusion of "vagueness" terms in the presentation—terms such as *might, some, maybe, things,* and *as you know* (because the students might not know). Another is referred to as a "maze." Mazes are "false starts or halts in speech, redundantly spoken words, or tangles of words" (Brophy & Good, 1986, p. 355). Still another is "discontinuity." Students refer to teachers who practice discontinuity as "going off on tangents." More technically, discontinuity occurs when "the teacher interrupts the flow of the lesson by interjecting irrelevant content or by mentioning relevant content at inappropriate times" (Brophy & Good, 1986, p. 355; see also Hunter, 1984). The final one is the continual use of "distracting speech mannerisms" (*uh, well, um*). Although most of us are guilty of a few such mannerisms, distraction occurs when students pay more attention to counting the number of *uhs* than to the material being presented.

This research also provides hints that enhance the clarity of presentations (Rosenshine & Stephens, 1986). Teachers wishing to improve their clarity should begin by clarifying the goals and main points of the presentation. They should then organize and present the information in a step-by-step fashion. For complex material, outlines are useful. Finally, the presentation should include a variety of illustrations and concrete examples, even to the point of redundancy when necessary. Providing models or demonstrations also helps make the presentation more concrete and hence more palatable for the students.

In many ways clarity, like beauty, is a subjective concept, not an absolute. Consequently, it must be checked rather than assumed. This checking can be done in a number of ways (Rosenshine & Stephens, 1986). For example, teachers can ask students questions that go beyond the typical "OK?" "Do you understand?" and "Are there any questions?" Useful questions focus on particular aspects or elements of the presentation (for example, "Now before we go on, who can tell me when commas should *not* be used?"). In checking for understanding, teachers also can have students summarize the main points in their own words. Finally, teachers can have themselves rated on the "Clear Teacher Checklist" developed by educators in Phi Delta Kappa's Center on Evaluation, Development, and Research. This checklist, shown in Box 4.11, is intended for completion by students. It provides a rich source of feedback to teachers concerning the extent to which their presentations are clear "all of the time," "most of the time," "some of the time," or "never" to the students in their classes. We suggest that the checklist be used by mastery learning teachers on a regular basis (perhaps once or twice a unit).

Whatever method is used to check understanding, two important points should be noted. First, teachers need to be fairly sure that students understand one point or lesson before moving to another. Second, when teachers find that several students are having difficulty understanding, the lesson plan should be abandoned, at least temporarily. Some form of additional explanation, perhaps through the use of additional examples and illustrations or by having one or more students provide the explanation for the others, is required if students are to develop the level of understanding necessary to move on.

As will be seen, the distinctions among the presentational problem, involvement problem, and encouragement problem are not nearly so clear in planning the teaching portions as in planning the work portions. By teaching to objectives and improving teaching clarity, for example, the teacher can address concerns for both presenting the information to be learned and involving students in its learning. Indeed, suggestions concerning relating new learning to prior learning, presenting memory strategies, providing opportunities for repetition and supervised practice, and checking for understanding all acknowledge that an audience exists when a presentation is made. That audience must be involved in processing the information presented if learning is to occur.

Similarly, by using during the teaching portion of lessons or class periods such devices as enthusiasm, pacing, and questioning techniques and strategies (including the level of questions, the time teachers wait for answers, and their reactions to these answers), the teacher can address concerns of not only involving students in their learning but of encouraging them to stay involved, too. Teacher enthusiasm is particularly involving and encouraging (Brophy & Good, 1986).

Planning the Work Portion.   As a result of planning for mastery, teachers should now have a compilation of assignments for every course-level goal. The first step in planning the work portions for a particular unit is to pull out the folders pertaining to each course-level goal in that unit. Next, for each goal, recollect the number of lessons or class periods to be spent on that goal prior to the administration of the unit test. For the purpose of discussion, let us suppose that the number is 5. Within that time period,

BOX 4.11   Clear Teacher Checklist

As your teacher I hope I am clear. In order to improve my ability to be clear I need your help. Below are 28 statements that describe what clear teachers do. Read each statement and place a check mark in the column that tells how often I perform the behavior that is described. In that way I'll know what I do well and what I need to improve.

(Put a check √ in one column after each statement.)

As our teacher, you:

	All of the time	Most of the time	Some of the time	Never	Doesn't apply to our class
1. Explain things simply.					
2. Give explanations we understand.					
3. Teach at a pace that is not too fast and not too slow.					
4. Stay with a topic until we understand.					
5. Try to find out when we don't understand and then you repeat things.					
6. Teach things step by step.					
7. Describe the work to be done and how to do it.					
8. Ask if we know what to do and how to do it.					
9. Repeat things when we don't understand.					
10. Explain something and then work an example.					
11. Explain something and then stop so we can ask questions.					
12. Prepare us for what we will be doing next.					
13. Give specific details when teaching.					
14. Repeat things that are hard to understand.					
15. Work examples and explain them.					
16. Give us a chance to think about what's being taught.					
17. Explain something and then stop so we can think about it.					
18. Show us how to do the work.					
19. Explain the assignment and the materials we need to do it.					
20. Stress difficult points.					
21. Show examples of how to do classwork and homework.					
22. Give us enough time for practice.					
23. Answer our questions.					

24. Ask questions to find out if we understand.
25. Go over difficult homework problems.
26. Show us how to remember things.
27. Explain how to do assignments by using examples.
28. Show us the difference between things.

Based substantially on research findings contained in Kennedy et al., 1978.

now decide on the number of assignments to be given to the students. If there is to be one assignment per day, there would be five assignments for the hypothetical unit. If there are to be multiple assignments per day, more than five assignments would be necessary. And if there is to be one assignment every 2 or 3 days, only two assignments may be necessary.

Once the number of necessary assignments has been determined, search through the collection of assignments in the folder. Select assignments that seem the most appropriate. Several factors should be considered.

First, for which content, process, or objective are assignments definitely needed? An assignment may not be necessary for certain content, processes, or objectives (for example, memorization-type objectives). Nor is it possible, in view of the fairly rigid time constraints, to give assignments for every content, process, or objective. Consequently, choose the most advantageous in terms of student learning. In general, objectives indicating that students should understand concepts (for instance, "Circle the nouns in the paragraph below"), apply procedures ("Use the Pythagorean theorem to solve these problems"), or engage in higher levels of thinking ("Write the assumptions made by the writers of the following passages") will require one or more assignments. Questions, exercises, and problems pertaining to several objectives can often be embedded in a larger assignment. If several objectives are included in a single assignment, the relationship between the parts of the assignment and the specific objectives should be made clear.

Second, is the purpose of each assignment in terms of the unit goal and associated content, processes, or objectives clear? Answers to this question go a long way toward solving the *attentional problem*. If any assignment's purpose is unclear, students may become more interested in completing it than in understanding what it is about. Linda M. Anderson (1984), for example, begins an article on student seatwork by quoting a 6-year-old who, after completing a particular assignment, said, "There! I didn't understand that, but I got it done." Students who do not see the purpose of an assignment and are not interested in "getting it done" may see the assignment as being busywork and avoid it as long as possible.

Third, are the directions for completing the assignments clear? Answers to this question help address the *presentational problem*. Directions often do not appear on assignments handed to students because teachers want to give them orally. A little written redundancy may be useful, however, particularly for students who were inattentive when the oral directions were given. Also useful may be the inclusion of at least one example in these written directions (that is, a sample answer to a question, a completed sample exercise, or a solution to a sample problem).

Fourth, how much "holding power" do the assignments have (Kounin & Sherman, 1979)? Selecting assignments with holding power is one way of solving the *involvement problem*. Such assignments by their very nature keep students working and on task. They encourage students to make or do things, to be interested or intrigued, and to experience success. When assignments have little holding power, the involvement problem must be solved by teachers themselves. Teachers must circulate among students, checking their work and maintaining close physical proximity.

Fifth, how much assistance will students likely need to complete the assignments successfully? Answers to this question are related to the solution of the *encouragement problem*. Here teachers should check on the assignment's length, difficulty, and variety. Moreover, this check should be made relative to the level and amount of information and the kinds of questions, exercises, and problems presented during the teaching portion of the lesson or class period. In general, the *longer* and *more difficult* the assignment and the *less varied* its questions, exercises, and problems (Kounin, 1970), the greater the need for teachers or other individuals to provide encouragement to the students.

One final point must be made concerning the nature of the assignments given to students during the work portion of the lesson or class period. The vast majority of these assignments ask students to complete them all alone at school or at home. Despite the large amount of data collected in support of cooperative learning (Johnson & Johnson, 1983), team-assisted learning (Slavin, 1983), or peer work groups (Stodolsky, 1984), little in the way of group work on assignments is permitted, let alone encouraged, in most classrooms. The extensive use of individual seatwork overlooks the value of peer pressure or peer concern in helping to solve both the involvement and encouragement problems.

In summary, then, the selection and use of assignments provides the basis for the work portions of lessons and class periods. In selecting assignments, teachers must be attuned to their utility in terms of the content, processes, and instructional objectives of the unit and, ultimately, the unit and course-level goals. At the same time, however, teachers must be concerned with the extent to which their choice of assignments begins to solve the four fundamental problems confronting teachers as they try to improve the quality of their teaching: the attentional problem, the presentational problem, the involvement problem, and the encouragement problem. To the extent that the choice of assignments does not promote or even mitigates solution of these problems, teachers must take a more active role during the work portion of the lesson or class period.

The history of schooling in this country is one of large pendulum swings from emphasis on the teaching portion of classroom life to the work portion. Prior to the 1960s the emphasis tended to be on the teaching portion. Homework was typically given, so the work portion was somewhat invisible. Research studies comparing the effectiveness of lecture methods of teaching with discussion methods of teaching were in abundance. Such studies either ignored the work portion or considered what took place during the work portion to be an error in their research design. During the 1960s the emphasis shifted dramatically to the work portion. Upon entering the classrooms, students were expected to pick up their self-instructional learning packages or modules and get to work. Any teaching done by the teacher occurred during the work portion, which tended to last for the entire class period (save a few opening comments or directions).

Recent research argues for a balance between these two critical portions of classroom life (as well as some attention to the play portions; see Block & King, 1987). Evertson, Emmer, and Brophy (1980), for example, found that the most effective mathematics teachers spent about 23 minutes per class period in the teaching portion (approximately 40%), compared to only 11 minutes per class period (approximately 20%) for the least effective teachers. Similarly, findings by Good, Grouws, and Ebmeier (1983) suggest that at least 50% of class time should be spent on the work portion.

Preparing Supplementary Instructional Plans

Supplementary instructional plans are essentially contingency plans. Ideally, if the original instructional plans were perfectly designed and implemented, supplementary ones would be unnecessary. Unfortunately, original instructional plans are not perfect (although some plans are less imperfect than others). Likewise, the implementation of the plans is sometimes flawed (although again, as we shall see later in this chapter, some methods of implementation are less flawed than others).

Part of this imperfection stems from the nature of classroom teaching. Unlike tutors, classroom teachers work with groups of children. Even when they are engaged in individual tutoring or working with small groups (as in a reading circle), they have responsibility for the activities and actions of the rest of the students in the classroom, what Barr and Dreeben (1983) refer to as the "remainder." Accordingly, to keep this "remainder" occupied, teachers apparently plan the number of questions, exercises, and problems for the work portion of the class period with their faster students in mind. Specifically, they choose the length of the assignment so that the fastest students will likely not complete it too far in advance, thereby posing a possible classroom management issue. Unfortunately, their slower students find this length overwhelming and frustrating (Anderson & Pigford, 1987).

Given the nature of classroom instruction, then, chances are that some students will achieve mastery earlier than others. Furthermore, these differences among students may change from one unit to the next. So provisions must be made for those failing to achieve mastery within the allocated time and consideration given to those who achieve mastery the first time the unit test is administered. These provisions and considerations are included in the supplementary instruction plan.

In many respects the provision of corrective instruction is the heart and soul of mastery learning. The attentional, presentational, involvement, and encouragement problems are common to all teachers and all instructional approaches. Similarly, the provision of corrective feedback within *lessons or class periods* is a common practice of many teachers. The planning and delivery of corrective instruction within *units*, however, is unique to mastery learning. In fact, we would go so far as to say that without planned opportunities for corrective instruction there is no mastery learning.

Because of the importance attached to the provision of corrective supplementary instruction in mastery learning, much has already been written concerning its nature and function. For example, Anderson and Jones (1981) note:

> To be maximally effective ... correctives should be based on the nature of the errors and misunderstandings identified on the [unit] tests. Such errors and misunderstandings can provide clues as to why students performed poorly on [the] tests and, as a consequence, clues as to how instruction might be improved. (p. 135)

Similarly, Block and Anderson (1975) describe the instructional nature of these plans:

> We have one cardinal rule for the selection of correctives for a particular ... unit. *They must teach the same material as does your [original] plan for the unit, but they must do so in ways that differ from this plan.* In other words, the correctives should not only supplement the [original] instruction, but should provide some alternatives to it. Since the point of

most [original] plans of instruction is to *present* the materials to be learned and to *involve* students in its learning, this rule means the following. Your correctives should present the unit's material in ways that differ from the way your [original instructional] plan will present it. They should also involve students in learning the unit's material in ways that differ from the way your [original instructional] plan will involve them. (p. 33)

Finally, some errors and misunderstandings may be common to fairly large groups of learners, whereas others may be unique to two or three learners. The more common an error or misunderstanding is, the more likely a problem exists in the original instructional plan. Errors or misunderstandings made by a very few students, by contrast, typically indicate a learning weakness on their part. In line with this distinction between common and unique errors and misunderstandings, Block and Anderson (1975) classify general types of correctives in terms of "whether they can be used for *individual* learners or a *group* of learners" (pp. 33–34).

In general, then, the development of corrective supplementary plans requires that teachers consider several issues. "How can I link my supplementary instructional plan with specific content, processes, and objectives?" "In designing the plans, how can I provide different forms or methods of presentation and different ways of involving my students?" "Which of the content elements and objectives on the unit test will likely require group correctives, and which will require individual correctives?"

Providing Corrective Instruction.   For correctives to function as intended, they must be linked to specific errors and misunderstandings. Simply reteaching the entire unit in the hope that those who didn't "get it" the first time will get it the second or third time will likely not be cost-effective. Indeed, such unfocused or untargeted corrective instruction is no better than no corrective instruction at all (Rochester, 1982). Consequently, teachers need to "provide specific corrective activities for each of the items, or clusters of items, on the [unit] tests. In this way, the learner engages in activities which are the most relevant to his particular misunderstandings" (Anderson & Block, 1977, p. 179).

To foster this linkage between corrective activities and clusters of items pertaining to a particular unit goal, they must first comprehend the range of possible correctives. Barber (1985), Block and Anderson (1975), and Guskey (1985c) have all developed lists of possible correctives. Block and Anderson categorize their correctives in terms of two dimensions: (1) whether they are to be used by individuals or in groups and (2) whether they are novel ways to present the material or involve or encourage the students in learning. Guskey classifies his correctives in terms of whether they can be used (1) with the teacher, (2) with a friend, or (3) by oneself. Barber's correctives are differentiated in terms of their (1) input (for example, view or observe, read, or listen) and (2) output (make or construct, verbalize, or write). Naturally, some teachers' outputs could be inputs and vice versa.

Since Barber's correctives are in many ways the most comprehensive, they are displayed in Table 4.5. Note the incredible variety of ways in which Barber suggests any classroom material might be taught.

Based on a knowledge of the various types of correctives that are possible, now the teachers can assemble what Anderson and Block (1977) term a "corrective sheet" for each specific unit. An illustration for the history unit described previously is shown in Table 4.6. Note that the left-hand column of the corrective sheet includes summary statements of the goals, and clusters of items pertaining to specific content elements or objectives of each. In the next column the primary source of information pertaining to each of the content elements or objectives is given. Appropriate sources of information might include videotapes, audiotapes, filmstrips, written materials (textbooks, workbooks, handouts), peer study groups, and reteaching by the teacher. For ease of reference particular sources of information to be used in the supplementary plan can be coded by indicating first the unit number and then the number of that particular source. Thus "videotape 4.1" refers to videotape 1 in unit 4. Note that the same source of information is often appropriate for more than one cluster of items, that is, more than one content element or objective.

The third column indicates whether the source of information is to be used individually or in groups. Three codes are used for entries in this column : *I* (individual), *S* (small group), or *W* (whole class). In general, this column should be completed after the original instructional plan has been implemented and the student performance on the unit test examined. Reteaching to the whole class or small groups is generally used for content elements and objectives that, according to the unit test results, groups of students had difficulty learning. Similarly, individual correctives are most applicable to content elements and objectives that, based on the unit test results, only a few students had difficulty learning.

The fourth column indicates the assignments that should be completed as part of the corrective instructional process in order to check on the adequacy of the learning vis-à-vis the specific content elements and objectives. These assignments should be drawn from the collection developed for each course-level goal. Once again, for ease of reference these assignments can be coded to indicate unit number and assignment number.

Once a unit corrective sheet has been prepared, teachers must determine the logistics of corrective instruction. In general, there are three

TABLE 4.5. STUDENT ACTIVITY OPTIONS FOR ACHIEVING OBJECTIVE

Input Suggestions			Output Suggestions		
View/Observe	**Read**	**Listen**	**Make/Construct**	**Verbalize**	**Write**
Visuals	*Materials*	*Media*	*Materials*	*Verbalizations*	*Written Performance*
bulletin boards	books	radio	diorama	oral report	theme
banners	comic books	records	collage	panel	research paper
postars	pamphlets	TV	scroll	debate	report
transparencies	posters	*Verbalizations*	sand painting	discussion	workbook answers
slides	newspapers	speeches	diary	brainstorming	blackboard
films/filmstrips	bulletin boards	lectures	pictograph	oral questions and	problems
flashcards	flashcards	debates	maps	answers	poems, essays, etc.
TV	reports	discussions	models	*Solve*	*Perform*
graphs	wall grafitti	dramatic/interpre-	timelines	puzzles	simulation
Community Events	letters	tive readings	paintings	mazes	role play
field trips	*Smell/Taste/Touch*	interviews	food	problems	sociodrama
dramatic	objects	*Try/Do/Use*	clothing	equations	concert
presentations	textures	games	bulletin boards	games	pantomine
	food	experiments	banners	riddles	interpretive reading
	temperatures	exercises	graphs		drama
	chemicals	manipulative	word wall		
		materials	drawings		
			Presentations		
			films		
			filmstrips		
			tapes		

Source: Barber, 1985, p. I GH-4.

187

TABLE 4.6. CORRECTIVE SHEET FOR A SAMPLE HISTORY UNIT

Unit: 4
Unit Title: The U.S. Constitution

Goal and Test	Source of Information	Individual or Group	Assignment Items
1. Development of Constitution			
Item 1	Filmstrip 4.1	I	4.1
Items 2–3	Filmstrip 4.1	I	4.1
Items 4–5	Filmstrip 4.1	I	4.1
Items 6–8	Reteaching	W	4.1
Items 9–10	Filmstrip 4.1	I	4.1
2. Interpreting Constitution			
Items 11, 12, 26	Videotape 4.1	I	4.2
Items 13–15, 27	Reteaching	W	4.2
Items 16, 17, 28	Videotape 4.1	I	4.2
Items 18, 19, 29	Videotape 4.1	I	4.2
Item 20	Handout 4.1	I	4.3
Items 21–23	Study session	S	4.3
Items 24–25	Handout 4.2	I	4.4
Items 30–32	Text, pp. 317–18; 340–42; 424; 568	I	4.4
3. Significance of Constitution			
Items 33–34	Videotape 4.1	I	4.2
Items 35–36	Study session	S	4.5
Items 37–38	Study session	S	4.5
Items 39–40	Study session	S	4.5

locations for corrective instruction: in class, in school but out of class, and out of school. Corrective activities that require teacher input (such as reteaching) quite obviously must take place either in class or in school. Similarly, small group study sessions, learning centers or laboratories, and other activities that require objects or materials that must remain in schools (for example, computers, academic games) must be used either in class or in school. Out-of-school activities typically include those in text-books, workbooks, and learning kits. Depending on the home situation, out-of-school activities may include flashcards, individual tutoring (with parents or friends), and computers.

Quite obviously, the time costs involved in mastery learning can be reduced if the bulk of corrective activities can be performed out of class and out of school. If out-of-class and, particularly, out-of-school activities are to be functional, however, educators must attend to several points. First, schools must be organized flexibly. Teachers must allow students to work on out-of-class assignments during the work portion of their class period. Time before and after school must be made available for students who need additional help.

Second, linkages between schools and homes must be established or strengthened. Specifically, school personnel must ensure that resources needed to help students overcome errors and misunderstandings are available. In this regard, Smith (1982) provides several useful suggestions.

1. Homework assignments should be linked to specific textbook pages on which they are discussed and illustrated.
2. More time should be spent on directions and explanations pertaining to the homework assignment. These may include an example of how one question is to be answered or how one exercise or problem is to be completed.
3. Educators can convey their sense of urgency for student mastery during PTA meetings or school visitations. Subsequent written or oral communications between teachers and parents will also help parents work successfully to assist their children's learning.

In addition, "homework hotlines" can be set up for students whose home environment is not conducive to parent supervision of homework. Such hotlines permit such students to communicate via telephone with people who are able to provide necessary homework assistance.

Returning to the history unit, we would suggest that 3 days be spent implementing the supplementary instructional plan. Since, as has been mentioned, the original instructional plan for this hypothetical unit required 21 class periods, the supplementary instructional plan would be approximately 15% as long. Typically, the time needed to implement a supplementary plan will be about 10% to 20% of the time spent implementing the original plan. In fact, Bloom (1974) suggested 20% as an upper limit for supplementary plans.

During this 3-day period we would recommend the following approach. On day 1 the teacher would review the unit test and reteach content elements and objectives that require whole class instruction. On day 2 content elements and objectives requiring small group work would be emphasized. On day 3 the focus would be on content elements and objectives requiring individual work. Obviously, rigid adherence to this schedule is inappropriate. For example, the whole class instruction may "spill over" into the second day. Similarly, students requiring little in the way of group work may begin their individual work on the second day. Nonetheless, the general strategy of moving from whole class to small group to individual emphases during the implementation of the supplementary instructional plan seems most efficient.

Providing Enrichment Activities.   One of the most frequent questions raised by teachers contemplating mastery learning is, "What do we do with the students who achieve mastery after original instruction while we work with the students who need more time and help to master unit goals?" Several answers to this question have been proposed.

As has been mentioned, some educators suggest that all corrective instruction, once planned, be provided out of class or out of school, that is, that corrective instruction be given during students' and teachers' "free time" (study hall, before school, after school, or at home). Others suggest that as students get older, the responsibility for correcting their errors and misunderstandings should be shifted to them alone. In either case these procedures would ensure that faster students do not stay in "neutral" while in-class time is spent on correction. They can progress from one unit to the next essentially upon completion of each unit's formative test.

For several reasons we consider this progression inappropriate, especially early in the mastery learning experience. First, many teachers and most students do not want to give up their free time for correction. As a consequence, both teachers and students may likely see corrective instruction as a punishment rather than an essential of school life. Second, solely out-of-class correction limits the kinds of correctives that can be provided. The corrective instruction then tends to be "more of the same," violating Block and Anderson's (1975) cardinal principle (see page 184). Third, out-of-class and especially out-of-school correction assumes that students can work through the sources of information on their own. Quite likely, students who need corrective instruction on a particular unit are the least likely to be able to learn on their own, unless they have siblings or adults who can provide appropriate explanations and examples. Finally, such out-of-class correction frequently requires students to work on learning activities for the last unit at the same time that the activities for the next unit are beginning. Attempting to overcome previous difficulties while at the same time trying to attend to and learn new knowledge and skills is quite difficult for most people.

A second answer to the question of what to do with the students who master the goals after original instruction is to allow them to move on to subsequent units. Thus while students requiring corrective instruction for one unit receive it in class, those who do not begin the original instructional plan for the next unit. Indeed, this idea lies at the heart of the thinking of many outcome-based education advocates (for example, Cohen and Spady) and many educators who favor individually based, self-paced mastery programs (such as Keller, Postlethwait, and Rubin).

As reasonable as this plan seems on the surface, however, it too poses some potential headaches. First, it can result in an increasing number of within-class groupings of students. Based on the results of the test administered during the first unit, two groups are formed, the "masters" and the "not yet masters." On unit 2, the masters from unit 1 may split into two groups again. If the nonmasters from unit 1 have not caught up, we now have three groups: nonmasters (1), masters (1)–nonmasters (2), and masters (1 and 2). And on unit 3 and every subsequent unit this fractionation process is likely to continue to occur. The net effect will be a whole series of student groups. Eventually, the teacher must wait for some groups to catch up or face a classroom management nightmare.

This "fast forward" approach can wreak havoc with the structure of the course and ultimately the entire curriculum. In the course, additional units must be prepared so that the so-called fastest students do not "run out" of content, processes, objectives, and course-level goals. In the curriculum, concerns for the relationship across sequential courses must be addressed. Students completing additional units in earlier courses may be overprepared for subsequent courses, a state of affairs resulting in boredom on the part of students and frustration on the part of teachers. Since, one may argue, courses impose artificial boundaries on a virtually limitless sequence of units, a "continuous progress" curriculum might be developed where students move from unit to unit independent of course, grade level, or age level. But such a curriculum requires a number of significant organizational and structural changes, and the history of the their success is not a happy one.

A third answer to the question of what to do with students achieving mastery after original instruction, and the one we favor, is to provide them with a variety of enrichment activities in which they can engage while students who have not yet achieved mastery are engaged in corrective instruction. These enrichments cannot be construed as busywork. They must be pedagogically and educationally sound.

Anderson and Jones (1981) recommend four major types of activities to use with these mastery students. First, they may engage in tutoring, thereby becoming another resource within the corrective instructional plan. Such tutoring can be a valuable learning experience (Bloom, 1976; Ellson, 1976), but students must "(a) be willing to serve as tutors, (b) have specific tutorial materials available, and (c) be trained in tutoring" (Anderson & Jones, 1981, p. 136).

Second, students can engage in work in other subject areas or "free work." Most students receive a large number of assignments in a variety of different subject areas every day. Many relish the opportunity to complete these assignments during school time rather than at home. If no assignments are available, students should be encouraged to engage in recreational reading or sustained silent reading. In a world that places such a premium on verbal ability and fluency, time spent on reading is never wasted.

Third, students can engage in independent projects. These projects usually take the form of contract learning. Students are require to complete a project form indicating "(a) what is to be learned, (b) how it is to be learned, and (c) how they are to demonstrate what they have learned. An estimated time needed should also be [included]" (Anderson & Jones, 1981, p. 136).

Finally, students can engage in horizontal enrichment. In many ways, fast forwarding or continuous progress curriculums are examples of vertical enrichment, in that the emphasis is on acquiring greater rather than broader knowledge. In contrast, horizontal enrichment activities emphasize breadth of knowledge within a particular topic or content element. Anderson and Jones (1981) present an example of horizontal enrichment in the context of a science unit containing two objectives, classifying turtles and classifying lizards:

> Opportunities for horizontal enrichment would center around questions such as:
>
> 1. Draw a picture of a tizard (an animal that is part turtle and part lizard).
> 2. Write a story (compose a song) about a turtle and a lizard. Make sure that the setting of the story (song) is based on what you know about appropriate environments for turtles and lizards.
> 3. Find as many interesting facts/oddities about turtles/lizards as possible. Write them in a form appropriate for a "book of lists."
> 4. Suppose a lizard lost its tail (or a turtle lost its shell). Describe the adaptations the lizard (turtle) would have to make in order to survive....
>
> [Such] enrichment activities are limitless.... Once a good set of such activities have been developed, they can be typed on file cards or on typing paper and laminated. (p. 136)

The concept of horizontal enrichment also applies to out-of-school activities and learning. Students may be asked to capture a lizard or a turtle and bring it to class. They may also be encouraged to photograph the various lizards and turtles at a nearby zoo.

Two final points pertaining to the development and use of enrichment activities and materials must be made. First, there is a tendency on the part of some teachers to make enrichment activities and materials "exciting" and "interesting" so that students will willingly engage in them. By comparison, corrective activities and materials often become mundane and tedious. Enrichment, then, becomes associated with fun and play, while correctives become associated with drudgery and work. Our intent is that the distinction between correctives and enrichment not parallel the oft-made distinction between the "good" and "poor" learners. In fact, all students are likely to need correctives at least on certain occasions during a course. Consequently, concerns for student interest and excitement should be paramount in the design of both corrective and enrichment activities and materials.

Second, the use of enrichment activities and materials has been criticized by some theorists (such as Arlin, 1982) as a means of "holding back" students who could benefit most from constant exposure to new content and material. We admit that the benefits of enrichment can be debated for eons. We believe that enrichment, particularly when it involves in-depth study or the teaching of the material to others, permits a greater understanding of the topic and content being learned. Such understanding seems necessary for higher levels of processing (analysis, synthesis, and evaluation) to occur. In addition, we believe that such enrichment (even when coupled with necessary repetition) results in the automaticity that Bloom (1986) suggests is necessary for extreme talent to develop and flourish in individuals. Such automaticity, "the hands and feet of genius," is rarely accomplished by a brief exposure to, and minimal understanding of, great amounts of knowledge and information.

TEACHING FOR MASTERY

In simplest terms, teaching for mastery involves carrying out the plans made while planning for mastery. Unfortunately, life in classrooms is not simple. Here teachers also confront a series of questions. What can be done to ensure that students are aware of and knowledgeable about mastery learning? How can material to be learned be presented in such a way so as to increase the likelihood that most students will learn? How can students be involved in learning and encouraged to put forth the effort necessary for them to learn? How can the results of assignments and tests be used to help students overcome identified errors and misunderstandings? How can the classroom be managed in such a way that students who need help are provided it, but not at the expense of those who are ready to move on? Teaching for mastery involves at least four major activities: (1) orienting the students, (2) delivering the plan, (3) monitoring how the plan is unfolding in the classroom, and (4) making decisions based on the information obtained from the monitoring.

Orientation Activities

A great deal of research has pointed to the significance of the first week or two of the term or school year (Evertson & Emmer, 1982). During this time the overall climate of the classroom is established, and the rules and routines governing appropriate and inappropriate behavior are presented, rehearsed, and, from the students' perspective, "tested" (Allen, 1986). Both teachers and students are engaged in what Airasian (1984) refers to as "sizing up assessment," or "getting to know you."

During this time students should be oriented to mastery learning. Specifically, teachers should carefully delineate the responsibilities they will assume and those they expect students to assume. They need to communicate to the students the course-level goals, the grading procedure, the use of the diagnostic progress tests, and the use of corrective and enrichment activities (Anderson & Block, 1977).

As part of his orientation activities, for example, Schroeder (1982) distributes a letter to the students in his senior English class. Here are some excerpts from this letter:

> Under the concepts of Mastery Learning, the scope and sequence of the curriculum is developed in a hierarchical pattern. *Each skill learned is used to learn all subsequent skills....* The teacher/learner must know exactly what is to be mastered for each task before teaching/learning begins. In addition, ... mastery of an assigned task, if not mastered in the initial presentation, may [be achieved] through the use of additional practice or as the learner begins to use the assigned task to develop subsequent and related tasks.
>
> Under Mastery Learning, *the teacher has the primary responsibility of teaching.* In fulfilling his assigned responsibilities, the teacher should believe that almost all students can learn if given adequate instruction, that all students are deserving of the right to learn, and that the ultimate goal of teaching is to ensure that all students do in fact learn.... Every student needs to feel that the teacher wants him to learn and that the teacher is willing to help him learn.
>
> Under Mastery Learning, *the student has the primary responsibility of learning.* The student must be willing to be called a master learner—a successful student—and must be willing to admit that he can indeed learn by being willing to spend the time required and to complete the practice required.
>
> Mastery Learning is a *cooperative effort among all of us—each of you helping each of you and me helping each of you.* In a way, Mastery Learning makes each of us responsible for each of us. Since I believe that one of the best ways to demonstrate mastery is to teach someone else to master, any method used to learn is acceptable—even having one of your fellow learners teach you. Since I believe that each of you is capable of learning and since I know that I am responsible enough to teach you, I have established Mastery at 95 per cent. (pp. 16–17)

During the orientation session, teachers should also inform students of several important aspects of mastery learning. First, students will be graded on the basis of their performances on summative tests. Second, they will be graded based on their performances vis-à-vis mastery performance standards, not relative to the test performances of their peers. Third, all students who achieve these standards will receive appropriate grade rewards (A's); there is no fixed number of these rewards. Fourth, throughout the course, students will be given a series of unit tests intended to promote and pace their learning. Fifth, based partly on the results of these tests, students will be given extra time and help as they need to master the course-level goals (Block & Anderson, 1975).

Because many students have not been expected to learn or learn well prior to their entry into mastery learning, some of the orientation activities should focus on students' affective characteristics (Conner et al., 1986). During the orientation period, teachers should try to transfer their "can do" attitude or sense of efficacy to their students.

Furthermore, teachers should exhibit behaviors or engage in teaching practices that convey high expectations. This can occur in a number of ways. Conner and colleagues (1986), for example, suggest that teachers convey their expectations to students through their use of time (time is valuable and must not be wasted), their stating of goals (rather than page numbers or exercises to be completed), the type of questions they ask (Under what circumstances? How can you tell? What evidence can you find? Why?), and the amount of time they wait for answers or elaborations of initial answers (a short wait time implies low expectations). We have listed some of these expectations in Table 4.7.

Many students may not be able to assume responsibility initially; after all, they may not have been asked to do so before. Yet teachers should not become frustrated by students' initial failures to act responsibly. Just like most cognitive abilities, the students' ability to assume responsibility must be encouraged, fostered, and practiced.

Finally, students must experience success early in the course. The old saw that "nothing succeeds like success" clearly applies to classroom learning. Most students, especially veterans, realize that content and objectives become increasingly difficult during the term or year. As a consequence, initial failure in a course will likely have severe negative effects on the students' attitudes, self-confidence, and classroom behavior over the duration of the course.

Barber (1986) graphically represents the the repetitive nature of initial failure in a course or in school in what she refers to as a "failure cycle of learning," illustrated in Figure 4.1. One of the primary purposes of mastery learning is to break this failure cycle, to ensure success, and thus to increase self-concept, motivation, classroom behavior, and task accomplishment (that is, achievement). Some of the ways in which mastery breaks this cycle may be found in Figure 4.2 (Barber, 1985). If the failure cycle is to be broken, however, it must be at least "cracked" early in the

TABLE 4.7. CONVEYING EXPECTATIONS

	Teacher Behaviors That Convey High Expectations	Teacher Behaviors That Convey Low Expectations
Use of time	Start on time Few interruptions Demand that students be on task Specific, challenging time limits	Start late, end early Many interruptions Allow students to be off tasks Open-ended time limits

Goal stating, summarizing	Goal statements:
	   frequent
	   clear
	   specific
	   challenging
	Summaries: frequent
		Goal statements:
		   infrequent
		   unclear
		   general
		   unenthusiastic
		Summaries: infrequent

Input	Lots of input High proportion of new material Challenging work	Little input Little new material; much review Easy work
Types of questions	More questions More higher-order questions	Few questions Rote questions
Wait time, pursuing questions	Wait 3–6 seconds after a question Pursue if answer is wrong or incomplete	Wait under 1 second Move on if answer is wrong or incomplete
Encouraging students to express confusion	Set climate where students aren't afraid to ask Give students a clear sense of what they are supposed to be learning	Climate where students are afraid of looking stupid No clear sense of what they are supposed to be learning
Feedback	Frequent Immediate Differentiated Specific	Infrequent Delayed Undifferentiated Vague
Nonverbals	Facial expression Eye contact Use of names	Dull or negative expression Little eye contact Limited action zone

term or school year; few students bring a wait-and-see attitude to their coursework.

In summary, orientation activities are essential if teachers and students are to play the game of learning according to the same rules. Rules governing expectations, sanctions, and rewards should be made clear at the start of each course or school year. In many respects, the success of the orientation activities holds the key for the overall success of teaching for mastery.

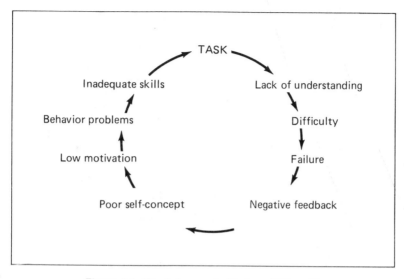

Figure 4.1. The failure cycle (Barber, 1986, p. 5)

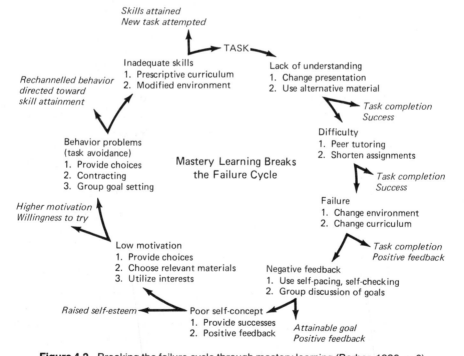

Figure 4.2. Breaking the failure cycle through mastery learning (Barber, 1986, p. 6)

Delivering the Plan

Since learning units are the focus of instructional planning within mastery learning, it is not surprising that most suggestions concerning teaching for mastery have pertained to them. Anderson and Jones (1981), for example, compiled a 14-step procedure for teaching mastery based primarily on the suggestions of Block and Anderson (1975) and Anderson and Block (1977). Based on these writings and other considerations, the following sequence of steps is recommended for teaching for mastery.

1. Inform students of the unit goals.
2. Give students an overview of the original instructional plan for the unit. Tell students how the material will be presented and what study strategies they might use to complement the proposed teaching approach.
3. Announce the date of the unit test and the standard(s) on the test that will indicate mastery of the unit goals.
4. Implement the daily lesson plans, paying particular attention to ways in which the plans enable you solve the attentional, presentational, involvement, and encouragement problems mentioned earlier.
5. On the designated date, administer the unit diagnostic progress test. (Based on information gathered while monitoring the plan, the administration of the unit test may be moved up or back a few days.)
6. Based on the test results, identify students who have and have not mastered the unit goals. Also identify specific content elements and objectives that may account for nonmastery.
7. Publicly acknowledge students who achieved mastery. Meet with them briefly to discuss your expectations for them during the time devoted to supplementary instruction.
8. Review the test results with the nonmasters, focusing on items many students answered incorrectly. Give nonmasters an overview of the supplementary instructional plan.
9. Implement the supplementary instructional plan, again monitoring the reactions of students.
10. Examine the performance of these students on the assignments in the supplementary instructional plan vis-à-vis the unit goals. If necessary or advisable, administer a parallel form of the unit test.
11. Publicly acknowledge students who have achieved mastery in view of the information obtained from the assignments or tests.
12. After all units in a particular marking period have been completed, administer the summative test for that marking period.

Barber (1986) has developed a flowchart (see Figure 4.3) that represents schematically the process of teaching for mastery learning. In essence, the flowchart is identical to our listing of steps. Two differences require some comment, however: the presence of optional tests at the beginning of the unit and the elaboration of the daily lessons.

Barber includes two optional tests at the beginning of each unit, one to assess students' prior learning necessary or useful for mastery of that unit and another to assess students' mastery of material in the unit to be taught. Both tests have advantages and disadvantages.

The major advantage is that these tests provide useful information about student learning prior to the teaching of the unit. The corresponding disadvantage is that the information, if collected, must be used. It makes no sense to have the information and then continue with "business as usual," that is, teach the entire unit to all students whether they're ready or not or whether they need it or not. Quite clearly, if all students possess the necessary prior learning, and if no students have mastered any or all portions of the unit, teachers should conduct "business as usual." However, if all students possess the necessary prior learning and if all students have mastered all portions of the unit, teachers should move to the next unit. And if no students either possess the necessary prior learning or have mastered any portions of the unit, teachers should not begin the unit.

Several variations on these themes are obvious. Some students may not possess the necessary prior learning. Others may have demonstrated mastery of the unit goals on the pretest. What to do with them? Should you conduct a brief review of this prior learning for all students? Should you conduct a brief review for only the students who need it, allowing the rest of the students to move on? Should you permit those who have demonstrated mastery on the pretest to skip that unit and move on to the next? If your answer to either question is yes, at least two potential problems must be addressed.

First, since you cannot be in three places at the same time, you have to devise alternative methods of presenting either the review, the new material contained in the present unit, or the new material contained in the subsequent unit. If, for example, the review material is on computer software and sufficient hardware is available and if the group moving to the next unit spends some time working on the prior-learning test and pretest for that unit, you can work with the group beginning the current unit and the problem is solved, at least temporarily.

Second, as we have already suggested, you have to anticipate the eventual formation of a fairly large number of groups. Ultimately, after several units, you could have as many groups as there are students in the class.

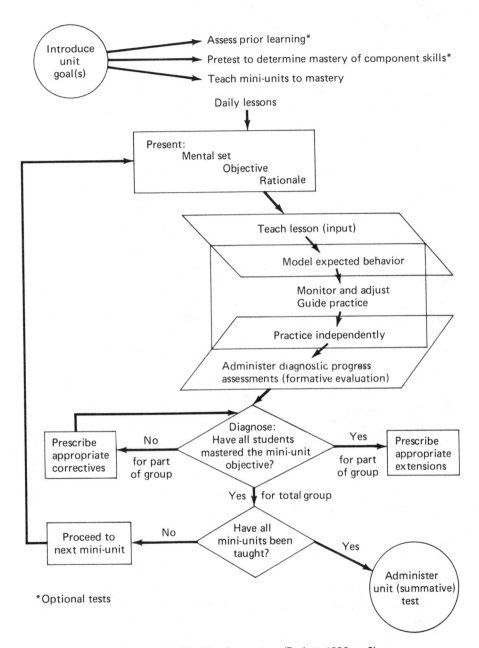

Figure 4.3. Teaching for mastery (Barber, 1986, p. 8)

Because of these and other complexities introduced by Barber's suggestion that teachers gather pretest data on a unit-by-unit basis, let us suggest another alternative. You could pretest at the beginning of the course. Fairly comprehensive course-level pretests designed primarily to assess relevant prior learning could be prepared. Portions of such tests could in turn be linked to a series of relatively short review units. Based on average student performance on each portion, decisions could then be made as to whether to include the various units in the course. Once a decision to include a unit has been made, all students will receive original instruction on it. We believe that a brief review of the material contained in these units certainly will not hurt, and perhaps will help, even students whose performance on the relevant portions of the test was quite high.

We propose this alternative for two reasons. First, it reduces the overall testing time in mastery learning. Second, and perhaps more important, our proposal reduces the overall amount of time spent in review, with a resultant increase in the amount of new content covered.

A second difference between Barber's flowchart and our list of steps involved in teaching for mastery resides in Barber's expansion of the daily lesson plans. Barber's expansion, in fact, closely resembles the lesson structure advocated by Hunter (1984).

Quite clearly, the Hunter lesson structure is compatible with mastery learning. But so are others, such as Good, Grouws, and Ebmeier's (1983) "active mathematics teaching" and Stallings's (1980) "interactive teaching," Adler's (1984) Padaiea proposals and Stodolsky's (1984) work groups, Johnson and Johnson's (1983) cooperative learning groups, and Slavin's (1983) student teams.

Our point is that no one particular lesson structure is sufficient for mastery learning. The proper structure of lessons will depend on factors such as subject matter and age of students. Many different lesson structures other than Hunter's are therefore compatible with mastery learning and likely to be workable in certain conditions. Since the emphasis in mastery learning is on ends (outcomes) rather than means (methods), we would choose to err on the side of inclusion of available lesson structures or methods of lesson delivery rather than exclusion.

In summary, the delivery of the plan requires the application of a series of steps. These steps are guides to action, not demands for particular action. Since the focus in mastery learning is on the learning unit, we have recommended implementation procedures that also apply to this level. More precise recommendations can be and have been offered concerning the proper structure or delivery of the daily lesson. But we have purposely avoided supporting these recommendations so as not to exclude any of the wide variety of thoughtful, potentially useful conceptualizations of the structure and delivery of lessons that currently exist.

Monitoring the Plan

At several points in our 12-step mastery teaching sequence, teachers are asked to monitor the implementation of the plan; that is, they are asked to collect evidence as to how the plan is going. When this evidence is collected and made public, both teachers and students become aware of whether the plans are functioning properly and whether students are learning as expected. As a consequence, evidence, rather than assumptions or opinions, is used to decide whether adjustments in the plan or in its delivery are needed.

Monitoring can occur at a variety of levels or stages in the teaching-learning process. Teachers can monitor students' reactions to specific explanations by watching them. Do they shrug their shoulders? Do they turn to other students? Do they nod their heads? Such monitoring is facilitated by the formation of steering groups as mentioned earlier. If no such reactions are forthcoming, teachers can attempt to stimulate such reactions by asking questions such as "OK?" "Does everyone understand?" or "Any questions?"

If teachers are unsatisfied with the reactions elicited by these global questions, they may choose to ask more specific questions about content, processes, or objectives. And they may address these questions to specific students. Such questions allow teachers to monitor the learning of students in general ("Who can tell me the major difference between fractions and decimals?") or of specific students ("Jean, can you tell me the major difference between fractions and decimals?").

Assignments also give teachers information whereby they can monitor student learning. Such assignments are a way of life in elementary school and for subjects at all school levels. Based on student performance on these assignments, teachers acquire an understanding of which students are not doing well and which content elements and objectives are not being learned by large numbers of students. If assignments are of high quality and are given on a regular basis, they provide useful sources of daily information.

Finally, unit tests can give teachers information on student learning relative to the major unit goals. Once again, such information is useful in differentiating what is being learned well and what is not. It is also useful in differentiating who is learning well and who is not. Based on unit test performance, students can then be categorized into those who require correction and those who need enrichment.

In general, the earlier that monitoring indicates that something is amiss, the better. If students fail to understand a series of explanations over several days, poor performance on assignments and unit tests can be expected. One exception to this generalization concerns content, processes, objectives, and unit goals that simply require a certain amount of time and thought in order to be learned—"things that must be fostered" rather than "things that can be taught," in the words of J. L. Green. The teacher is primarily responsible for the latter things, and the time needed to teach and learn is relatively short. Students are primarily responsible for the former things, since they require longer periods of time to learn. Daily monitoring may indicate that no progress has been made. In many ways daily monitoring in this case is like watching grass grow—it simply takes time.

The frequency of monitoring, then, depends on the nature of what is being monitored. Once again, some thought must be given to the amount of time students are likely to need to demonstrate any progress with respect to the content, process, objective, or goal being learned. If the goal being pursued is one in which progress should be noted at regular intervals, regular monitoring is advisable. If the goal being pursued is one of the "gone today, there tomorrow" variety, monitoring at regular intervals could be both misleading and frustrating.

Independent of the time or stage at which we monitor progress, the need for monitoring is central to successful implementation of mastery learning. Without information, instructional decisions are difficult if not impossible. The adoption of mastery learning implies that teachers will engage in monitoring at least near the end of each learning unit and in most cases on a more regular basis. The proper interpretation of the evidence gleaned from such monitoring activities depends in large part on understanding the length of time needed to learn. It is to the issue of proper interpretation that we now turn.

Making Instructional Decisions

As was the case of data collected from pretests or tests of prior learning, evidence collected by monitoring requires that something be done with it. Teachers often use this evidence to make decisions about individual students. "Manny didn't finish his assignment." "Juanita isn't paying attention." "Lucas really understands what we're talking about." "Tabitha doesn't belong in this class."

From a mastery learning point of view, the evidence should be used to make instructional decisions. "Should I try a different approach to teaching this material?" "Do they need more time on this topic, or should we move on?" "They look confused. I wonder if a few more examples would clarify the main points?" "Is this material simply too difficult for them?"

This shift from decisions about students to decisions about instruction is not easy for many teachers, especially those who hold the belief that the responsibility for learning rests primarily with the students. Nonetheless, it is absolutely necessary for teachers intent on teaching for mastery. It is important to remember, though, that this shift does not place the entire burden of responsibility for learning on the teachers. Rather, it begins to establish a healthy balance between the students and the teachers. As Schroeder (1982) pointed out in the letter to his students, mastery learning implies a shared responsibility—"We're all in this together!" The teaching-learning relationship should not be adversarial, with both sides ascribing blame for poor learning to members of the other side: "slow" learners versus "bad" teachers. Sometimes teachers do give simply awful explanations; sometimes students just aren't paying attention. Sometimes teachers assign too difficult or too much material; sometimes students don't work to the best of their ability.

To make some instructional decisions, it will be necessary to try to find out why the evidence is as it is. What is really going on here? Two types of follow-ups are useful. First, teachers can ask students probing questions, urge them to express misunderstandings and confusion, and encourage them to ask questions when they do not understand. Although many teachers will say they already do this, one study found that the rate of teacher questions to students was one per minute; the rate of student questions to teachers was one per *month*.

Second, with the advent of videotape capabilities, a technique referred to as stimulated recall can be used to help teachers develop skills in examining their own teaching. Videotapes of their teaching can be played back while teachers watch themselves and analyze their performance. If two cameras are available, a split-screen effect can be used to allow teachers to observe student reactions to various portions of the lesson. In this way teachers become consciously aware of their own behavior and activities, as well as the reactions of their students. Cruickshank (1985) calls such teaching "reflective."

The ability to make sound instructional decisions based on available evidence is a characteristic of excellent teachers. Even excellent teachers are not excellent all the time. What sets them apart from their peers, though, is a willingness to assume greater responsibility for excellent learning on the part of their students and to learn from their experiences, both positive and negative. For these teachers, teaching for mastery is a journey, not a destination.

GRADING FOR MASTERY

Finally, in grading for mastery, teachers must address three major questions. What can be done to ensure that the grades assigned reflect what students have actually learned, rather than how they stand relative to other students? How can the available data be translated into meaningful grades for students? How can differences in the rate of learning be taken into consideration in assigning these grades?

Much has been written in the mastery learning literature about defining, planning, and teaching for mastery. Unfortunately, little has been said about grading for it. Block and Anderson (1975), for example, devote about 4 pages in their 86-page book to the topic. Similarly, Guskey (1985c) spends about 2 of his 143 pages of basic text on "grading summative examinations" and doesn't mention grading at all in 86 pages of sample mastery learning materials. Finally, in the Levine (1985a) volume, issues involved in grading for mastery were mentioned by two authors (Smith and Robb) and consumed a mere two paragraphs of almost 300 pages of text.

Equally unfortunate, the limited advice on the topic is inconsistent. Block and Anderson (1975), for example, suggest that the course grade be based solely on the final course test. Guskey (1985c) suggests that it is usually "unwise to use the score from a single summative examination as the *only* grading criterion" (p. 86). Furthermore, Guskey asserts:

> Mastery learning does not require that *only* summative examination results be counted in determining students' grades. Certainly these examination results are very important and are usually weighted heavily. But many teachers also include a variety of other criteria in assigning grades. Some count homework assignments, marks on special projects, or participation in class sessions. So long as these criteria are clearly specified and communicated to students, and students are given explicit directions and guidance as they work to attain these criteria, they are likely to be appropriate in a mastery learning environment. (p. 86)

Smith (1985), in contrast, asserts:

> Students tend to perform very well on the more comprehensive summative examinations, lessening the teacher's need to have to score and record countless class assignments, some of which exist solely to protect students from the perceived tyranny of the more comprehensive examinations. (p. 247)

Suffice it to say that issues involved in grading for mastery have been treated sparingly and that differences of opinion exist as to how the data on student learning should be translated into the assignment of student grades. But what, then, do we make of the following quote?

> Grading is a pivotal issue in the implementation of [mastery learning] because grades are major tools in a district's credentialing, reward, control, opportunity, and motivation systems. (Spady, 1987, pp. 7–8)

If grades in fact influence the credentialing, reward, control, opportunity, and motivation systems in schools and districts, is it possible to change the nature of schooling without changing the grading procedures and systems that are used? We think not.

The Significance of Grades

Tucked away as a response to a "frequently asked question," Block and Anderson (1975) talk about the significance of grades. They respond to the question "Why grade at all?" by first suggesting that teachers typically have no choice in the matter. They then continue by offering "two good reasons to continue grading."

> One reason is the nature of our society. Like it or not, grades are the primary currency of exchange for many of the goods, services, and privileges that our society has to offer individuals. Grades can be exchanged for such diverse entities as cash (when parents pay their children a dollar for each "A"), parental approval, teacher approval, peer approval privileges (e.g., the opportunity to work in the library by oneself), and the opportunity for higher education and a good-paying job. To deprive students of grades, then, is to possibly deprive them of our society's goods, services, and privileges.
>
> A second reason is habit. Students are used to receiving grades and they are used to teachers giving them. Some students, in fact, even equate grades with learning. To deprive students of grades, therefore, is to ask them to break a deeply ingrained habit. And, for some students, it is to face the frightening possibility that they will have no way of knowing whether they have in fact learned. (p. 81)

Spady (1987) has examined the act of grading in somewhat more detail. Spady suggests that teachers assign grades for one or more of the following reasons.

Teachers assign grades as "judgments about the quality of [students'] work, behavior, attitudes, learning, and performance" (p. 8). Because of the number of available grading categories, however, grades for work and performance or behavior and attitudes may be combined, resulting in confusion as to the meaning of the grade.

Teachers also assign grades to "motivate and control students" (p. 4). For example, teachers may tell their students if they don't turn in homework, if they are caught cheating, or if they complete a project late, they will get a lower grade. (Students, believing that turnabout is fair play, are often heard to ask, "Will we be graded on this?" The assumption of this question is that if we won't be graded on this work, we likely won't do it, or if we do it, we won't do it very well.)

Teachers assign grades to "label students for certification and selection purposes" (p. 4). Honor rolls and dean's lists are commonplace. High school rank (based exclusively on grades) is used extensively in making college admission decisions. A certain number of failing grades often results in exclusion of students from extracurricular activities.

Finally, teachers assign grades to "uphold our meaning of standards" (p. 5). Somehow the distribution of teachers' grades gets translated into the standards that teachers hold. For example, the standards of teachers who assign mostly A's are typically questioned; concerns for "lowered standards," "lax grading," or "grade inflation" echo through the halls and, perhaps, beyond, into the community.

Although all these reasons underlie the practice of assigning grades, Spady suggests that none of them is the primary reason: "Mostly, however, I think that we grade out of habit, believing that the educational process and system require the labelling of students. They don't, of course, but beliefs die hard, especially when no one questions their validity" (p. 8).

Two points should be clear from the discussion so far. First, like it or not, grades have had a great deal of significance over the past century or two. Because of their significance, real or otherwise, they are "pivotal issues in the implementation of mastery learning." Robb (1985) provides a wonderful example of the way in which district grading policies can have a negative effect on mastery learning.

> Columbus district policy required that students reading below in the basal receive a grade no higher than C in reading. At Kent [Intermediate School in Columbus], initially, many students were making excellent progress in the mastery learning program, and were reading more effectively. Yet because they were still below level in their basal, they were limited to a grade of D or at best C. The grading system became a disincentive to students. (p. 265)

For students to believe they can learn or to continue to learn well, their learning must be translated into the proper currency—grades.

Second, despite the significance of grading, the assignment of grades has become habitual. The amount of thought apparently given to what grades actually mean and what procedure should be used to assign them parallels the paucity of writing about them as evidenced earlier. Thus teachers intent on mastery learning must do two things. They must re-examine their philosophy of grading, and they must develop a fair, impartial, defensible grading procedure.

The Meaning of Grades

If you consider almost any elementary school report card, you come face to face with the three primary areas in which teachers assign grades: conduct, effort, and achievement. In general, conduct grades reflect students' behavior vis-à-vis classroom rules and expectations. Appropriate behavior is rewarded with an S for "satisfactory," inappropriate behavior with a U for "unsatisfactory," and prototypically "good" or "proper" behavior with an E for "excellent."

Effort grades reflect the amount or intensity of student involvement in learning. Most of the grading evidence used comes from student activity during the work portion of the lesson or class period, during which students are expected to work on assignments. Additional evidence comes from the number of in-class or homework assignments actually completed. If students are off task a great deal during the work portion or fail to complete or hand in requisite assignments, an effort grade of U for "unsatisfactory" is assigned. If they are mostly on task and complete most assignments, though, an effort grade of S for "satisfactory" is assigned. In some cases they can even be so devotedly on task and assignment-conscious that an effort grade of E, for "exemplary," is assigned.

Note that in the case of both conduct and effort, only three gradations are typically used to differentiate among students: excellence (which is assigned for exemplary or prototypical behavior), satisfactory (whch is assigned for behavior at or above the acceptable standard), and unsatisfactory (which is assigned for behavior consistently below the acceptable).

Note that the grades assigned for conduct and effort are *absolute*, not *relative*. Conduct grades are assigned based on a comparison of that student's behavior with the classroom rules and expectations, not with the behavior of other classmates. Similarly, effort grades reflect how much work is actually expended by each student. Was the student on task 90% of the time? Did the student complete all but two of the assignments during a marking period? Again, notice that this evidence ("90%," "all but two") reflects student behavior independent of the behavior of other students in the class.

To be sure, teachers may use their wealth of knowledge of, say, fourth-grade students to set meaningful standards concerning conduct (for example, how much misbehavior just seems to be a part of a fourth grader?) and effort (how many homework assignments typically get lost?), but they *use this knowledge to set standards at somewhat less than the perfection they expect.* Consequently, deliberations about a particular student's conduct and effort grades are rarely, if ever, made with visions of the conduct and effort of other students in the class in mind.

In contrast to the meaning of conduct and effort grades, the meaning of achievement grades is confusing and typically ambiguous. The extent of this confusion and ambiguity is reflected in a series of questions raised about achievement grades in virtually every school setting. Do they reflect academic learning only, or are effort or conduct considered by teachers when assigning them? Do they denote academic learning in an absolute sense or relative to the academic learning of other students in the class? Do they indicate the *amount*, the *complexity*, or the *quality* of learning that occurred? How does the wealth of available evidence about student learning (daily assignments, quizzes, tests) get translated into achievement grades? Let us consider each of these questions briefly, then return to a discussion of the meaning of grading in mastery learning.

Achievement, Effort, and Conduct.   The clear delineations among achievement, effort, and conduct included on elementary school report cards blur on many secondary school report cards. While conduct and achievement grades generally continue to be assigned, effort grades may or may not be. When effort grades are not assigned, concerns for effort are often included in the assignment of the achievement grade. Some teachers, for example, express difficulty of giving an A grade to a student who learns well but is "lazy." Other teachers express discomfort in assigning an F grade to a student who has learned absolutely nothing but who "tries very hard."

Even when three separate grading categories exist on a report, this does not guarantee that these categories will be kept separate in the teacher's mind. The halo effect is well known and documented (Brophy & Good, 1974). Teachers quite likely form general impressions of their students, therefore, and label "good" students by some combination of conduct, effort, and achievement. The meaning of the achievement grade these students receive is thus obscured.

Absolute versus Relative Grades.   Although conduct and effort grades both represent absolute judgments of student behavior, achievement grades may reflect absolute judgments, relative judgments, or quite typically both. Relative judgments, in particular, are justifiable because of the variety of specific functions that achievement grades, and usually only achievement grades, serve.

Consider, for example, their "sorting and selecting" function (Spady, 1987). Somehow the significance of being on the honor roll or dean's list is diminished if all students are so designated. As a consequence, high school rank is in essence a *forced* sorting of students (with the exception of tied ranks). In a class of 300 students, ranks of 1 to 300 are assigned regardless of whether the grade average ranges from 3.0 (a grade of B) to 4.0 (A) or from 1.0 (D) to 4.0.

Relative comparisons among students are also useful in complying with regulations pertaining to "record keeping" and "upholding standards." As has been mentioned, disproportionate numbers of any single gradation on the grading scale are cause for careful scrutiny of teachers and grading practices.

In any case, the assignment of grades on relative and absolute considerations, coupled with the multiple functions typically served by grades, results in a confusion and ambiguity. There are numerous ways of getting a grade of A. Furthermore, the best answer to the question as to what a grade means is "It depends."

Amount, Complexity, or Quality.   The learning of students can be differentiated in many ways. Traditional ways include the subject matter being learned and the taxonomic level at which the learning occurs. Differences in the achievement grades assigned can therefore reflect any or all of the basic differences in learning. We have found it useful to emphasize three differences in learning that are easily translatable into differences in achievement grades: amount, complexity, and quality.

Many teachers assign grades on the amount of learning (or more precisely, the amount of work done). Students who learn more (that is, complete more work) receive higher grades. Many self-paced instructional programs use this approach to grading.

Other teachers assign grades based primarily on the complexity of learning (or again more precisely, the complexity or difficulty of work done). The Columbus district policy for assigning reading grades mentioned earlier (Robb, 1985) approximates this type of grade assignment. Since reading textbooks are written at different levels of difficulty, students with these textbooks are expected to read less complex material. As a consequence, these students' grades in reading cannot exceed C.

Still other teachers assign grades based largely on the quality of learning. Such an approach is the stock-in-trade of many teachers of high school woodworking, especially the introductory course levels. Students in these introductory courses are often expected to complete, in order, a finite number of projects (such as a chest of drawers). Since students work on the same project during the same time period, grading cannot be based on either the amount or complexity of learning. However, as anyone who has spent time in a woodworking shop can attest, differences in the quality of workmanship are evident. Thus grades quite obviously reflect these differences in quality.

The choice of grading on amount, complexity, or quality may depend in part on the age level of students or the subject matter being taught. The philosophy of grading inherent in the school district or instructional program quite likely plays a part in the choice.

Evidence and Grades.   When most teachers are asked by students, parents, or school administrators to defend the grades they assign, they take out their grade books or students' folders that hold the work completed during the marking period. Thus teachers use *evidence* to justify (and presumably to determine) achievement grades. Like judges in a courtroom, teachers must decide what evidence to consider, what evidence is admissible, and how the accumulation of evidence should be weighted.

Some college and university professors use performance on midterm and final examinations as their sole sources of evidence. Only such examinations provide admissible evidence, and the evidence from these two tests is equally weighted. Other college and university professors include class participation, essays and themes, and journal abstracts in their grading scheme (along with the aforementioned examinations) and devise a fairly complicated weighting scheme to combine all this information (for example, class participation counts 10%; journal abstracts, 20%; essays and themes, 20%; and examinations, 50%).

Similar grading systems are in place in elementary and secondary classrooms and school districts throughout this country. In Jackson, Mississippi, for example, course grades are determined by students' performances on daily work and unit tests. Nothing else is to be considered. Furthermore, the unit tests account for 80% of the grade, while daily work accounts for 20% (Fortenberry, 1986). In other school districts, the exact sources of evidence and the precise formula for weighting the sources of evidence are both left to individual classroom teachers.

Grading in Mastery Learning

The general philosophy of grading in mastery learning has been stated concisely by Block and Anderson (1975).

> We do not want to throw out grades, but we do want a student's grade to accurately reflect what he has and has not learned rather than just how well he has learned relative to his peers. We feel that as long as students must constantly judge themselves against the learning of their peers they can never develop their own personal performance standards nor can they experience the pure pleasure of meeting such standards. (p. 83)
> In a mastery learning situation, the grades one receives are correlated with what the student has learned in an absolute sense.... Grades in a mastery learning situation, therefore, reflect the students' learning alone. (p. 81)

The implications of this philosophy for practice can be seen by reexamining the four issues just raised about the meaning of grades.

Achievement, Effort, and Conduct.   In mastery learning, achievement grades should be based on learning only. Effort and conduct should be excluded from deliberations concerning the assignment of achievement grades. If effort and conduct are important, *independent* grades for each should be given.

Interestingly, related research reveals that when students are graded on learning alone, increased student effort and conduct follow. Students learn from such grading that paying attention to the relevant sources of information and putting forth the necessary effort really counts. And from this knowledge comes an understanding that if they pay attention and put forth the effort, they have the ability to learn. Once this effort-ability link is made by students, it is difficult to keep students off task.

Absolute versus Relative Grades.   In mastery learning, achievement grades should be absolute, not relative. Again, quoting from Block and Anderson (1975): "In mastery learning a student is graded for learning and not graded for with whom he learned. We believe that grading for learning can trigger the students' intrinsic or internal motives to learn" (p. 82).

What do we mean by absolute? We mean two things. First, the grading standards should be defined in terms of expected student achievement, not in terms of achievement relative to whomever takes the tests. Ideally, such standards should clearly separate students into two groups—those who have achieved the learning of interest and those who have not and are in the process of such achievement. Second, the grading standards should be fixed prior to the teaching-learning process and are not allowed to vary following instruction; that is, the standards should not be altered after the teaching process so as to compensate for less than expected learning. Such fixed and preset standards make grading a foresightful rather than hindsightful activity. They also making grading a thoughtful rather than thoughtless exercise (Block & Burns, 1981).

Amount, Complexity, or Quality.   In mastery learning, the emphasis is clearly on quality. Grading based on amount has likely contributed to students' concerns for "getting done" rather than developing "understanding" (Anderson, 1984). Grading based on amount also capitalizes on the fact that differences in aptitude are simply translated into differences in rate of learning (Carroll, 1963). Consequently, a teacher who grades on amount is essentially grading on aptitude, not achievement. Such grades reflect what students brought to the course and classroom at least as much as what they left with.

If you doubt this contention, conduct the following activity. Using whatever information you have available (student records, initial impressions, daily assignments), assign a grade to each student in your class at the end of the second week of the course. Based on this grade, rank the students (from 1 to the number of students in your class). Write the students' names, grades, and rank on a slip of paper, place in an envelope, seal it, and store it somewhere where you will remember it. At the end of the course, after you have assigned final course grades, retrieve the envelope. Open it and compare the course grades actually assigned and the order of the students with those in the envelope.

Now let us turn to the issue of grading on complexity. We believe that complexity should be more of a curricular issue than a grading one. Quite clearly, course-level and unit goals should be of appropriate degrees of complexity for the students enrolled or likely to enroll. To devise goals without concern for the proper level of complexity would do a disservice to the students; the course would likely be "too easy" or "too hard." This obvious fact leads, however, to a different view of complexity or difficulty than is currently held by many educators. Curricular content cannot be placed on a continuum of difficulty independent of the students for whom it is intended. Rather, complexity must be discussed in terms of the students for whom the course is intended.

In this view, complexity is the difference between the learning demands of the curricular content and the present learning capabilities of the students themselves. Thus, from this viewpoint, one can have complex content or complex goals taught at every grade level and for different types of students within every grade level. In short, as Bruner (1966) has argued, it should be possible to teach anything in an intellectually honest form at any age level.

In contrast with grades based on amount and complexity, grades based on quality are grades based on excellence in learning. With the possible exception of salespersons, amount has seldom been equated with excellence. Note, however, that even in this instance amount is simply a result of high quality in presentation or interpersonal relations. Complexity is also associated with excellence, but in a likewise indirect fashion. Quality on simple tasks is not valued as highly as on more complex ones. In fact, some would argue that some minimum level of complexity must be reached before the term *quality* would even apply. At the same time, however, even paintings by number differ in their quality.

In conclusion, then, mastery learning implies that grades are to be based solely on the quality of learning. Quality is more important than amount; complexity should be designed into the curriculum.

Evidence and Grades.   We now come to the area of greatest disagreement. What evidence should be used in determining which grades to assign to which students? At least two major points should be considered in answering this question.

First, performance on summative tests rather than formative tests or daily assignments should be used to assign grades to students. To use formative tests is contrary to their very function.

> Formative tests are intended to provide evidence that can be used to monitor (rather than evaluate) student learning so that quality of instruction decisions (not quality of learning decisions) can be made. (Anderson & Block, 1985, p. 3226).

We discourage the use of daily assignments in the determination of course grades for several reasons. First, as we noted earlier in this chapter, the relationship between performance on daily assignments and unit or course tests has remained questionable since the time of Morrison. Second, daily assignments typically are means to an end rather than ends in themselves. That is, they are intended to help students learn, not to judge their learning. Third, students in effective mastery learning programs tend to perform well on the summative tests, thus "lessening the teacher's need to have to score and record countless class assignments" (Smith, 1985, p. 247).

Second, since grades must be assigned periodically throughout the year, multiple summative tests should be developed and administered. With respect to these summative tests, several recommendations can be offered.

1. Summative tests should be comprehensive and cumulative. That is, they should emphasize the major course goals and should include items or questions pertaining to the most important goals up to the point at which the tests are administered. This suggestion means that if you choose to use midterm and final examinations, the former would cover the first half of the course and the latter would cover the entire course (not just the second half).

2. A blueprint or "table of specifications" for each summative test should be developed (see Block & Anderson, 1975, pp. 12–21, and Guskey, 1985c, pp. 23–31, for expanded discussions of tables of specifications and their use). At a minimum, this blueprint should indicate which course-level goals are to be included on the summative test. Such a blueprint is needed simply because far more content, objectives, and goals have been addressed during instruction than can conceivably be included on any single summative test.

3. Once blueprints have been developed, teachers should search through the questions, problems, and exercises they have collected

for each course-level goal. They must be sure to select the most important, probing, or thought-provoking questions, problems, and exercises that have not been used previously or have been used long enough ago that their answers or solutions cannot be remembered.

4. When multiple summative tests are prepared and administered, final summative tests should still be used, if for no other reason than to judge the overall quality of the course in fostering student retention. As mentioned throughout this book, mastery learning pertains to learning of the whole, not just the parts. Perhaps, in a four-quarter course, then, students' performance on the final summative test can contribute one-half of the the final course grade (with the four quarter grades contributing the other half). In this way improved learning over the duration of the course can be recognized and rewarded.

Assigning Grades

In the strictest interpretation of mastery learning, students have either mastered the course goals or they have not. We know, however, that some students have mastered some of the goals and some have not. What can we do with these students? Two options seem available. First, course grades can be assigned based on the number of course goals mastered. That is, 90% of goals mastered equals an A, 80% a B, and so on. In point of fact, this approach was initially preferred (Block & Anderson, 1975). We now prefer the second option, namely, assigning "incompletes" to students who fail to achieve mastery on the requisite number of course goals associated with an excellent grade. The selection of the second option requires that administrators and teachers consider the possibility of initiating an "open transcript" (Champlin, 1981), "one that allows students to demonstrate and receive credit for improved levels of performance at any time" (Anderson & Block, 1985, p. 3226).

Summary

The grades students receive can stand for any number of things. Regardless of what they stand for, they are enormously important in the lives of students. They can be exchanged for any number of present or future goods, services, or privileges.

In mastery learning, grades should stand for student learning, and student learning alone. In this regard, grades should represent the quality of student learning in an absolute rather than relative sense. The evidence used to assign grades should come from performance on carefully planned, summative tests; performance on formative tests and daily assignments should be excluded from course grading. These summative tests should be both comprehensive and cumulative; that is, they should emphasize the most important goals and should attempt to sum up student learning to that point in time. If several summative tests are to be used in a course, the weighting among them should be determined (with the final summative tests weighted somewhat more heavily). Finally, the length of time students have to demonstrate mastery on any particular summative test or in any specific course should be determined in advance. If time is flexible, the concept of open transcript should be explored; if time is fixed, the number of goals to be mastered to qualify for grades of A, B, C, and so on should be specified.

Like all four of the major tasks confronting teachers intent on successfully implementing mastery learning, grading for mastery is of critical importance. A final quote from Spady (1987) attests to the importance of properly carrying out this task.

> While students may enter school wanting to learn, most of them leave school wanting good grades instead. Somehow I believe that we, rather than they, are responsible for that distortion and the cynicism and lack of genuine motivation for learning that it fosters. (p. 11)

For mastery learning to be successful, the desire to learn must be fostered or rekindled as necessary. An approach to grading for mastery, such as that outlined here, should trigger that desire.

CHAPTER 5

What Do I Believe
about Mastery Learning?

In the preceding chapters we have regaled you with the theory, research, and practice of mastery learning. The purpose of these chapters has been to lead you to consider the adoption of mastery learning ideas for classroom, school, or school district use. The bulk of this discussion has revolved around empirical issues in mastery learning and the kind of technical leadership that the implementation of mastery learning will require of interested educators.

There is another side to leadership in mastery learning, however, that does not involve either data or technical matters. For want of a better term, we will call this moral leadership. As Foshay (1973) and more recently Sarason (1983) suggest, it is belief systems and the unarticulated assumptions from which these systems derive, not data or technical support structures, that ultimately drive all that we do in schools. It is to the belief system of mastery learning, therefore, that we must turn in closing this volume. Without the implementation and institutionalization of this belief system, all the data and all the technical support in the world will not keep your mastery learning experiment afloat. Indeed, we have never really seen a mastery learning program fail for technical reasons, but we have seen them fail repeatedly for belief ones. The technical problems are usually just the tip of a larger belief system iceberg.

In developing the mastery learning belief system, we shall return to the four major educational public policy issues that were raised at the start of this book—the matters of excellence and equity in learning and economy and excitement in teaching. We may preview our system by saying that we believe that virtually all students can be equal and excellent in their learning, learning rate, and self-confidence and that this equal excellence or "equalence" can be generated with existing resources, especially if staff are treated more humanely.

THE MASTERY LEARNING BELIEF SYSTEM

Beliefs about Excellence in Student Learning

We believe that each student, with a few exceptions, is capable of learning excellently, swiftly, and self-confidently,[1] To achieve this capability the student must master not only certain learning *products* but certain learning *processes*.

One product is the same levels of learning that have historically characterized our best students. Pragmatically speaking, this means we expect from the student A-level learning; it does not mean B, C, D, P ("pass"), or S ("satisfactory") learning. We reject B and C levels of learning as being indicative of excellence because these levels typically connote good or mediocre learning at best. Likewise, we reject D, P, and S levels of learning as being indicative of excellence because these levels typically connote the absence of failure in learning rather than the presence of real learning success.

The second product is the same types of learning that have historically characterized our best students. This means several things. First, the student will be asked to master not only certain intellectual outcomes but also certain emotional and behavioral ones. Our excellent learners, for example, would be expected to master outcomes from affective, psycho-motor, and interpersonal taxonomies as well as cognitive ones. Second, the students will be asked to master not only the lower-order aspects of these outcomes but higher-order aspects too. Our excellent learners, for example, would be pressed to master advanced and intermediate, not just elementary topics; elective, not just required topics; "open" topics where the compendium of knowledge, skills, appreciations, and understandings is constantly in flux as well as "closed" topics where this compendium is more stable; and topics that require creative, not just smart problem solving. Third, the students would be asked to master future-oriented as well as present-oriented outcomes. Our excellent students, for example, might be asked to master not only the three R's but also the three C's of communication, cooperation, and caring.

---

[1] The section headed "The Mastery Learning Belief System" is adapted from Block (1985) by permission.

The one process is the same learning-to-learn skills that have historically characterized our best students. As we argued in Chapter 2, learning to learn demands that each student accept appropriate personal responsibility for learning. Accordingly, we expect the student to learn how to assume greater *self-care* for learning. Note that we say greater, not total. We still assume that one of our chief instructional responsibilities is to do everything that we can as educators to help students learn. But even we will eventually exhaust our instructional possibilities. At that point the instructional ball is out of our hands. We must generate students who *want* to take this ball and run.

Learning to learn also demands that the student acquire appropriate personal "response-ability" for learning. Accordingly, we eventually expect each student to learn how to assume greater *self-treatment* of learning. We expect that students will begin to define their own mastery learning outcomes and standards, to develop their own instructional sequences for attaining these outcomes to standard, to plan and execute their own mastery learning instruction for each unit in the sequence (including original instruction, feedback, correction, and enrichment techniques), and to conduct their own summative evaluations. Again, we are not assuming that students will always have to treat themselves; indeed, sometimes self-treatment is not only unnecessary but also dangerous. But we do want students who *can* treat themselves when and if the situation arises, as it must in much of out-of-class and postschool life.

Last, learning to learn demands that students acquire appropriate personal "respond-ability" for learning. It is not enough to have students who can and want to assume greater self-direction for their learning when necessary. Ultimately, we must have a student who *does* assume this direction. Accordingly, we expect each student to develop greater skills in the *self-assessment* of their learning. Assessment, along with measurement and evaluation, is one of three major schools of testing that have dominated educational thinking (Bloom, 1970). It is the only school of testing to be equally concerned, however, with learner growth as well as learning growth. By teaching students to engage in self-assessment, we are inviting them to look at the relationship between what they intellectually can and emotionally want to do as learners and what they behaviorally do do in their learning. Out of this self-examination we expect better and better alignments of actions with thought and feelings.

Beliefs about Equity in Student Learning

Besides pursuing excellence in student learning, we believe that we must pursue equity too. We believe that virtually all students can learn equally excellently, equally swiftly, and equally self-confidently. Consequently, we expect all students to attain the same distribution of learning products and processes that has historically characterized our best students. Our excellent students would be heterogeneously grouped to master these products and processes. They would not be homogeneously grouped in any way to ensure that some students master different products and processes.

Obviously, we believe in equity in terms of student learning outcomes, not in terms of student learning opportunities. Indeed, to attain outcome equity we are willing to provide unequal treatment in terms of learning opportunities and learning time for some students and especially for those who historically have been the "have-nots" in the teaching-learning process. We do not care whether these have-nots come from groups where teaching and learning discrimination is based on such differences as race, sex, or social class or from groups where the discrimination is based on educational constructs such as ability and effort.

Beliefs about Economy in Teaching

We further believe that equal excellence or what Block (1985) calls "equalence" in student learning can be pursued using existing resources. Indeed, we have seen equalence pursued in school districts throughout this country for literally pennies in proportion to their existing budgets. These programs have wisely used mastery learning ideas to articulate and orchestrate existing nonhuman and, especially, human resources.

One economical way to pursue equalence is to employ an evolutionary, not a revolutionary staff development strategy. Rather than trying at the outset to change radically the nature of the school organizations or the human beings with which we deal, equalence advocates must initially accept schools and their staffs as they are and try to move them toward where they want to be. For example, we ask our clients to work in the realm between what *should be* the case and what they know *is* the case at their school. We call this the realm of "can be." For example, if we believe that students ought to graded on only a 2-point system of excellence or of excellence in the making and we are dealing with a school system that has a 5-point system A, B, C, D, and F, we find ways that their A's can initially index excellence and their B, C, D, or F's can initially indicate various degrees of excellence in the making. If we believe that instruction ought to be more tutorlike but are faced with a group-based instructional situation, we find ways that group-based instruction can be made more tutorial. We always try to remember that the "can be's" of one year are the "is's" of the next year. So next year what is will be closer to what should be.

A second economical way to pursue equalence is by focusing on altering things that can be altered. Equalence advocates must constantly be trying to figure out ways to redefine apparently unsolvable problems in solvable terms.

One basic tenet of many mastery learning staff development programs, for example, seems to be that program administrators want every teacher to participate regardless of interest in or acceptance of mastery learning ideas. Implicit in this tenet seems to be the bootstrap notion that some teachers need staff development more than others and that if staff developers can somehow get this "deadwood" to sprout, everybody else will follow suit. Often, however, these people have good reasons for rejecting any new set of teaching and learning ideas. Targeting an entire staff development program to them can absorb abnormally large and frustrating amounts of time and energy and threaten the success of the overall program.

We therefore encourage program leaders to use a differentiated, rather than a whole staff development approach. This approach focuses initially on really interested "livewood" teachers and temporarily ignores "deadwood" ones. After all, if you cannot make a program go with really interested people, you are not going to get the ideas to go at all. Interested people will be able to test whether the ideas work at a given site, under the site's particular teaching and learning conditions. If they do, the initial participants will share these ideas with other potentially interested colleagues. This combination of really interested and potentially interested "livewood" teachers can generate critical mass at a school site regarding a particular set of teaching and learning ideas and become a powerful lever for "deadwood" change. Now, however, the lever is collegial peer pressure, not administrative fiat.

The final, and in many ways the most powerful, economical way to pursue equalence is by focusing on the prevention of student learning problems rather than their remediation. As Block (1983) has already indicated in the newsletter of the Network of Outcome-based Schools:

> I believe it is time for a fundamental change of course in the design of group-based mastery learning programs. Rather than designing these programs to be solely remedial in nature, I propose that we also begin to design them to be more *preventative* in nature too. . . .
>
> I view preventative group-based mastery learning strategies as treating all students' learning problems as if they were potentially chronic and degenerative. Such strategies would, therefore, get to students earlier in their careers and would stay with them throughout. They would have as their goal learning maintenance and promotion, much as preventative strategies in public health have as their goals health maintenance and promotion. I believe that we need instructional programs that tell students not only what to do after they have developed particular learning

problems, but also what to do to prevent these problems to begin with. (pp. 23–24)

This call for the design of more preventive instructional programs parallels a similar call by colleagues in public health areas such as medicine and dentistry, where it has been noted that vast amounts of public dollars are needlessly spent on remediation when small amounts could be spent on prevention with the same effect. Consider, for example, the cost of a dental crown versus the cost of flossing.

To this point in our educational history, however, most instructional interventions have had a remedial quality about them. Again, we have no ax to grind about the use of such remedial instructional systems. Our point is that when one adds the power of prevention to the power of remediation one gets the most cost-effective learning results for the public's expenditure.

Beliefs about Excitement in Teaching

We believe that equalence can be economically pursued by making an explicit commitment to rely heavily on existing human resources rather than on new nonhuman ones. At the heart of this commitment should be humane techniques that reaffirm teachers' self-worth and power.

One exciting way to pursue equalence is to be optimistic about each teacher's capacity to teach well, swiftly, and self-confidently. This means staff development programs that use mastery learning ideas to teach teachers for equalence in their teaching, just as teachers will teach students for equalence in learning.

A second exciting way to pursue equalence is to be acceptant of teachers as craftspersons. To our mind, a craft is somewhere between a science and an art. Craftspersons, like scientists, are expected to do things day in and day out that will replicate a particular product or process. Like artists, however, craftspersons are typically given freedom to do these things in ways that fit their current predilections and skills. Accepting teachers as craftspersons thus means regarding teachers as people who can consistently perform the critical instructional functions—say, feedback and correction—required to produce equalence but who must be given some freedom to do so in ways with which they are are conversant and comfortable. Craftspersons will flourish, of course, in teacher-centered staff development programs, not materials-centered ones. The latter programs tend to insult the craftperson's scientific artistry and send implicit and explicit messages to program participants that they are largely assumed to be incapable of conducting their own pedagogical affairs. Indeed, these programs are often touted by their developers as being teacher-proof. The former programs, however, recognize and develop the craftsperson's scientific artistry and send just the reverse messages. In fact, they build heavily on the teacher's already existing skill repertoires, supplement them as necessary, and orchestrate new skills with old ones within the mastery teaching-learning scaffolding.

A final exciting way to pursue equalence involves empowering school staffs to exercise their craft. This empowering means treating teachers as grass-roots public policymakers who have the personal power to change a school system from the bottom up and allowing them most of the critical teaching and learning decisions. It also means that school site and central office administrators can often adopt a stance of "benign neglect" about the teachers' improvement efforts. Administrators may "deflect" inside and outside attempts to tamper with these efforts so as to protect their development. But they must not directly touch the teachers' efforts until there really is something to touch.

To summarize, we believe that it is possible for virtually all students to be excellent and equal as learners. We further believe that this equalence can be economically attained using existing resources, the most exciting of which are teachers.

SOME CRITICAL CONCERNS ABOUT THE
MASTERY LEARNING BELIEF SYSTEM

Not surprisingly, these particular beliefs and the belief system they form have come under substantial fire. To elaborate why we believe as we do, let us share some of this fire and briefly react to it.

Excellence Concerns

Our beliefs that excellence ought to be defined in terms of certain learning products and processes has prompted the following major concerns. Colleagues point out several failings in our defining excellence for each student in terms of the types and levels of learning characteristic of our best students. They say we are being unrealistic and fail to realize how tough it is to design an instructional program targeted to producing A students. They say we are reintroducing the fuzzy-wuzzies of the humanistic educational experience of the 1960s and 1970s. They say we are not being staunch basic skills advocates. Moreover, they say that in defining excellence for each student in terms of the learning-to-learn characteristics of our best students, we are reversing our earlier position that the student's sole burden for learning must be lightened.

We respect these concerns but believe our colleagues are wrong. We clearly recognize the difficulty of designing an instructional system targeted to obtaining A levels of learning from all students. However, we would rather encourage the design of a teaching and learning system that shoots high and falls short than one that shoots short to begin with. Our experience has been that every time we have been realistic and cut the A levels of learning expected of a fledgling mastery system, the system has yielded less excellent learning than when we have been unrealistic and not cut our standards.

We are also not trying to reincarnate the neohumanistic experience of the past two decades. We are simply pointing out that historically our best students not only could intellectually undertake the learning challenges they faced at school, but they also emotionally wanted to and behaviorally did undertake these challenges. Moreover, we are suggesting that it is possible to teach emotional and behavioral skills in such a way that students are challenged, not coddled, and given responsibility, not license. Philadelphia's remarkable mastery learning program is an excellent case in point (see Conner et al., 1986).

We are strong basic skills advocates too. But rather than just looking to the present to define what is basic, we also look to the future. This futurist orientation on basic skills has been forged in the caldron of painful experience. This experience has taught us that our best students constantly seem to acquire school learning outcomes that keep them on the edge of cultural, political, economic, social, and spiritual progress. And it has taught us that it takes time to design any successful instructional program that can keep students at that edge and additional time for any student to complete that program. We estimate that it takes at least 5 to 6 years to finely tune a K–12 mastery learning program. This means that it will take until the mid-1990s to finely tune a program initiated today and until at least 2006 for this program to yield its first graduates. If we want these graduates to be on the leading edge of progress in their post–high school world, we must consider what might be basic in that world of 2006. We simply cannot afford the luxury of assuming that those intellectual, emotional, and behavioral skills that are basic now will be basic then.

Finally, we still believe that teachers must help lighten students' burden of learning. In our early writings, however, we suggested that if teachers were more responsible, "response-able," and "respond-able" in their teaching, students would be pressed to be likewise in their learning. We have learned, though, that pressing students to be more responsible, "response-able," and "respond-able" is one matter; getting them to assume this burden, especially in the teacher's absence, is another. Mastery learning teachers must do more than just drop this burden in each student's lap; they must also teach the learning-to-learn skills students need to assume this burden.

Equity Concerns

Our beliefs about equalence in student learning, especially about equalence in learning rates, have clearly concerned many of our colleagues even more than our views about excellence. They seem to have two major concerns. First, do not these beliefs deny what everyone knows about individual differences in learners? Second, even if they do not deny individual differences in learners, will not the attainment of equalence actually lead to mediocrity, not excellence in learning—to homogeneity, not diversity in learners? Let us address both issues.

Our belief about equalence does not deny the existence of individual differences in learners. Indeed, as psychologists, we share with most educators an abiding belief that each learner, while alike in some respects, is different in many others. As educators, however, we do not share many psychologists' assumption that because students differ as learners, they must also differ in their learning outcomes.

One reason for not sharing this assumption is technical and comes out of recent research on school and classroom effects. This research is beginning to explode the myth of individual differences in learners as being a major drawback to their learning, learning rate, and learning self-confidence. In particular, the research begins to suggest that many observed student learning outcome differences may be due to social context differences in schools and classrooms and not to individual differences in learners at all. Moreover, the research is beginning to reveal how educators have historically masked school- and classroom-induced social context differences in the guise of individual differences such as sex, race, social class, ability, and effort. Such a guise serves very well, of course, to shift responsibility for poor learning, slow learning rate, and low learning self-confidence from factors inside the school to ones outside it. In other words, learner differences become a perfect scapegoat for within- and between-school teaching differences.

A second reason for not sharing the assumption that individual differences in learners must translate into individual differences in learning outcomes is an ethical one. Even if the assumption were partially true, we would still not let it get in the way of helping virtually all students to learn excellently, swiftly, and self-confidently. Like ophthalmologists who daily face real individual differences in eyesight and yet must try to help people see, we would still search to find some temporary or permanent prostheses so that students with certain individual differences could learn by artificial means what students with other individual differences appear to learn naturally.

We would do so because we believe that most educational institutions' current response to perceived individual differences in learners has been to create a panoply of homogeneous human kennels based on various students' perceived strengths or weaknesses (Bridges, 1986). Some of these kennels are formal, like special education, Chapter 1, academically talented, college, and vocational tracks. Others are informal, like reading groups.

The problem with these kennels is not that their homogeneity is mean-spirited. The problem is that some kennels are better equipped than others, and they are still kennels, with restricted entrance and exit. Each kennel therefore effectively provides a separate curriculum for its inmates whereby each inmate is given the opportunity to acquire only a particular kind of cultural capital in terms of special knowledge, skills, appreciation, and understandings. Unless one finds oneself in the right compound to begin with—unless one has the "right stuff" in terms of school-perceived individual differences—one may have little or no real opportunity to acquire the capital our best students have historically been allowed to attain.

Just as we believe that our views about equalence in learning outcomes do not deny individual differences in learning but simply try to assure that some people's individuality is not given unwarranted advantages over other people's individuality, we also believe that our views about equalence do not lead to mediocrity and homogeneity. On the contrary, we believe they lead to excellence and true human diversity.

We have been struck, in reading about the development of exceptionally talented human beings, that genius in most fields of human endeavor does not leap from nothingness. Rather it springs out of mastery of a practically understood, though perhaps theoretically undefined, foundation of basic, field-relevant intellectual, emotional, and behavioral skills. Geniuses in the arts (such as Picasso and Mozart) and in the sciences (such as Einstein), for example, appear to have already mastered the accepted parameters of their fields before they started to transform these parameters.

We have also been struck that individuals who have mastered the accepted parameters of a field are as diverse as can be in what they do with this mastery. Unlike most of us, who choose to do a limited variety of things because we perceive we are incompetent to do more, these people choose to do a broad variety of things because they perceive they are competent to do just about anything at all. In short, their diversity appears to be based on their general educational competence, whereas ours, as the Peter principle reminds us, is based on our general educational incompetence.

In saying that we pursue equalence, we are saying that we envision a social order whose diversity is predicated on the general excellence of the many rather than the special excellence of a few. We believe that a general educational foundation is required for excellence in the bulk of the various vocational and avocational fields that students pursue upon graduation.

And when virtually all students have acquired this foundation of excellence, we believe they will show the same kinds of true diversity in their vocational and avocational choices as geniuses have historically shown. These choices will be made on the basis of their general educational competence, too.

Economy Concerns

Just as our beliefs about equalence have caused controversy, our beliefs about economy have raised eyebrows. Colleagues have been especially concerned about the apparent gap between the radicalness of our ideas on equalence in learning and the conservativeness of our ideas on economy in teaching. We are not bothered by the gap at all.

At the heart of our colleagues' concerns seems to lie the idea that current resources will not do, no matter how they are orchestrated, and that radical change in school requires substantially new resources. We do not share their pessimism about our current resources, especially our human ones; in fact, as we have indicated, we have great faith that our current human resources are more than enough. Nor do we share their optimism about new resources, for we have watched how such resources tend to be used. Most of them seem to go into the structures that frame the teaching and learning process; only a minority seem to go into the process itself. California, for example, has recently reinvested over $1 billion in its schools, but only a small fraction of that money has been earmarked for directly improving teaching and learning; the bulk, in fact, has gone for improving structures and other programs only indirectly related to the teaching and learning process. Now we are not so naive as to disbelieve that certain physical structures make certain teaching and learning processes easier, but we are naive enough to believe that the structures we currently have are not sufficiently problematic to preclude the pursuit of equalence.

No, new resources are not the answer. Better use of existing resources is. Perhaps if we can better orchestrate existing resources to pursue equalence now, we will be in a politically stronger position to go after new resources in the future.

Excitement Concerns

Our views about staff development have also drawn fire, especially from colleagues who believe in commercially developed, materials-based approaches to staff development or in the administrator's role as a strong instructional leader. Both sets of colleagues wonder whether we believe they have any place in staff development and renewal.

Our answer is yes, they do have a place. It is a matter of when they assume their place. We believe that both sets of colleagues have important roles to play *after* teacher-based and teacher-as-instructional-leader approaches have gotten the pursuit of equalence off the ground.

Giving teachers time to build on their existing skill base and to exert instructional leadership from the bottom up gives teachers a critical stake in the implementation of a new set of teaching and learning ideas. As this stake grows under conditions of benign administrator neglect, we have found that teacher-centered staff development programs invariably find the need to begin incorporating some materials-centered staff development input. We have also found that bottom-up programs invariably find the need for some top-down help. Giving teachers a real initial stake in the success of a new set of teaching and learning ideas therefore helps them appreciate materials-based and top-down instructional leadership gambits that they might have ignored or resented without the stake.

REACTION TO THESE CONCERNS

What has been our overall reaction to these concerns? Frankly, we have been amazed by the sincere conviction with which they have been expressed and by the pessimism about human capacity to learn and teach that much of this conviction reveals. Whereas we optimistically believe that virtually all students can learn for equalence and virtually all teachers can teach for equalence too, apparently many critics believe just the reverse. Indeed, their concerns are frequently prefaced with statements that steadfastly assert that some students learn more poorly, more slowly, and less confidently than others and that teachers cannot change this natural state of affairs.

Let us conclude this chapter, therefore, by speculating about the nature of the impasse between our sincere optimism about human capacity to learn and teach for equalence and our critics' equally sincere pessimism. We believe that the heart of the impasse lies in what Sarason (1983) calls our "unarticulated assumptions":

> When an institution appears over time to be resistant to change *and* improvement from within and without, with money and without money, the effort sometimes powered by passionate sincerity and sometimes by the needs of image-making; when critics and school personnel are licking their wounds, hardly able to generate energy to reenter the fray, left only with the hope that the passage of time will somehow bring improvements, does this not suggest that both critics and educators share some blind spots—that there is something in their basic assumptions that they are unable to identify and whose silent existence is part of the explanation for the present malaise and impasse? In raising this possibility, we

are not suggesting that identifying or confronting these assumptions will disperse the confusion or lead to a peace treaty among the combatants, allowing us all to move together to the improvement of education. On the contrary, it is a characteristic of widely held but unarticulated assumptions that they serve the purpose of defining and bulwarking individual and societal perceptions of what is right, natural, and proper. These assumptions are not learned in the sense that we learn to drive a car, but they are absorbed by us, become part of us, in the course of our socialization. (pp. 25–26)

In the case of our critics and us, these unarticulated assumptions pivot around a set of pessimistic ideas about human beings and human technology deeply imbedded in the very roots of modern American public education. We reject these ideas; our critics, we believe, tacitly accept them. These are the ideas of Charles Darwin, especially as these ideas were interpreted and institutionalized in American public education by Spencer and the proponents of social Darwinism (for more on social Darwinism, see Cremin, 1961).

Central to Darwinian thinking, of course, was the assumption that human beings living in naturally occurring environments, like all other biological species, evolve according to the laws of natural selection; therefore, some human beings would be naturally more fit for certain environments than other human beings. Social Darwinists decided to elaborate on this assumption. Rather than just letting nature simply take her course in separating fit humans from unfit ones, they decided to help Mother Nature along. In particular, they urged the creation of particular social environments to help the natural selection process. Our public schools, in particular, were charged with the responsibility of creating educational environments wherein our most naturally academically talented students could be identified and sorted from their less talented peers.

Generally speaking, public school educators responded to this charge by developing an impressive sorting process wherein the natural learning talents of some students were repeatedly and systematically pitted in stiffer and stiffer competitions against the talents of other students. Central to this process was one operating assumption: The process must reify, not challenge, the basic notion that only a few students probably had the right academic stuff. So certain curriculum, teaching, and administrative procedures were elaborated allowing individual differences in learners to pursue their natural course. And certain testing procedures were implemented enabling individual differences in learners to be measured meritocratically and translated into individual differences in learning outcomes. Collectively and effectively, these procedures made school learning into a sequence of progressively more competitive races, each designed to spread its entering student field around the track depending on their natural learning talents. Those who won, placed, or showed in their respective learning races were then allowed to race again against their counterparts from the other learning races. The also-rans from each race were formally and informally allowed to drop by the wayside via a whole host of regular and remedial instructional programs.

In saying that we reject Darwinian conceptions of humans and social Darwinian conceptions of how humans should be educated that many of our critics may tacitly accept, we are not saying, as Sarason (1983) notes, that recognizing this fact will necessarily resolve our differences. We are asking, however, for our critics, and especially educators who share their pessimism about human capacity to teach and learn, to take a fresh look at the modern public educational value—and costs—of Darwinian and social Darwinian ideas.

After all, Darwin conducted his research over a century ago. At that time it still made some sense to talk about humans living in naturally occurring environments. And such environments were indeed bound by laws of ecology, which invariably point to natural limits of human talent. The presence of such limits made public educators' concerns about the identification and selection of our most talented human beings at least understandable.

Today, however, humans live less and less in naturally occurring environments and more and more in human-made ones. In human-made environments, the laws of technology, in the sense of the old Greek word *technos*, "human know-how," not the laws of ecology, hold sway. And these laws invariably point not to any natural limits of human talents but to the technological possibilities of transcending these limits. At this time, therefore, public educators' concern should not be with the identification and selection of the talented few but with the development of the talented many.

Abandoning Darwinian and social Darwinian thinking in education will, we believe, allow us to move forward to forms of high human technology that will help humans transcend their former natural limits. After all, the essence of any such technology is to simulate for all persons with human devices what natural devices have provided for a few. And in assembling this technology we will be able to address what McMurrin (1971) has termed the "great task of education" in an era of rapid technological change: "to guarantee the progress that assures us the full benefits of an advancing technology and yet to preserve and enhance the humane quality of a civilization whose humanity is threatened by that technology" (p. 12).

Let us summarize this book with two images that capture much of our feelings about the power of belief systems and instructional improvement and our optimism about human capacity to teach and learn, regardless of natural endowments. We say "feelings" because we concur with the well-known and now departed environmentalist and scientist René Dubos:

> Most scientists might not admit the role of emotions in their research. They would say that it's an interest in the intellectual aspect of the problem that motivates them. I don't believe it. I think most of us do something because at a certain moment in our lives we have been profoundly impressed in an emotional way by some event. We overlook in every thing we do the importance of deep emotional responses that, at a critical period, focus our interests in a certain direction.

The mastery learning movement, we believe, is at one of those critical periods.

Our first image comes from the second movie in the *Star Wars* trilogy, *The Empire Strikes Back*. The image is powerful for the rebel alliance, after an initial success, finds on its back the educational equivalent of a board of education, state department of education, federal agencies, judges, lawyers, and politicians all rolled into one—The Empire. And the Empire even has an all-purpose hatchet man, Darth Vader.

The image is that of Luke Skywalker, the hero, being trained in the ways of the "force" by the ancient Jedi master Yoda. When Luke's ship starts to sink in the swamp, he attempts to save it by using his fledgling Jedi skills. After the ship temporarily rises, only then to fall still deeper into the swamp, Luke stalks past Yoda and says in frustration and failure, "I don't believe it." Yoda responds, "That is why you fail," and proceeds to rescue the ship.

Luke, of course, learned the relationship between beliefs and failure and went on to enormous success in the third movie in the trilogy. As a direct result of his beliefs, he was even able to persuade Darth Vader, his long-lost father, to get religion, recant his sins, and go to Jedi heaven.[2] We wonder, though, given the current interest in mastery learning and its initial success, how many practitioners will choose to use mastery learning ideas and practices, raise their student learning slightly, and then let the learning slide deeper into the swamp simply because they did not really believe the ideas and practices in the first place.

The second image comes from the movie *Chariots of Fire* and is poignant because it comes from England, a country with an educational system that is highly elitist, though outwardly meritocratic, and deeply pessimistic about most humans' capacities to transcend their natural backgrounds. The image is also poignant because it involves representatives of two groups, Arabs and Jews, whose natural capacities for physical,

---

[2] We are indebted to Arthur Mallory, former commissioner of education for the state of Missouri, for this observation.

cultural, and spiritual survival have been sorely challenged in recent years.

The image is the scene where the Jewish sprinter, who had not lost a competition until college, is summoned before his college's administrators for hiring an Arab coach to improve his running style. Essentially, the young man is paternally chastised for running with the aid of instruction instead of only his own natural resources. But when pressed to cease his unnatural educational program, the sprinter responds to his conservative critics, "I, sir, believe in the pursuit of excellence; the future lies with me." And indeed it did, for the young man went on to win an Olympic medal in the 100-yard dash.

Those of us who pursue excellence and equity in student learning with economy and excitement in teaching question the ideological hegemony of Darwinian and social Darwinian thought. Like the sprinter, we believe the future is with us!

APPENDIX

Mastery Learning
People and Resources

This appendix contains some of the basic human and nonhuman resources to which you can turn to learn more about mastery learning. As with any list, we have probably inadvertently omitted some valuable people, places, and things. If your name, site, or writings do not appear here, please forgive us. Why not contact us about your work and experiences? We plan to update this resource list periodically and would be happy to acknowledge you.

James H. Block
Department of Education
University of California
Santa Barbara, CA 93106
(805) 961-3301

ORGANIZATIONS

Far West Laboratory for Educational
    Research and Development
Robert Burns and Nikola Filby
Support for Outcome-based Education
    Project
1855 Folsom Street
San Francisco, CA 94103
(415) 565-3169

Northwest Regional Educational
    Laboratory
Goal-based Education Program
Robert Blum and Jocelyn Butler
300 S.W. Sixth Avenue
Portland, OR 97204
(503) 248-6800

The Network for Outcome-based
  Schools
Johnson City Central Schools
666 Reynolds Road
Johnson City, NY 13700
(607) 729-9211

Outcomes Associates
P.O. Box 1046
Monroe, WA 98272
(206) 743-9000

CONSULTANTS AND SITES

The following are a few of the many persons and sites interested in mastery learning ideas and practices. To help you use the following list, we have arranged the entries by region of the country and would encourage you to try local contacts before trying more distant ones. In many cases this strategy will enable you to tap in to a whole variety of people, places, and things in your local area. We have used the letter *C* to denote mastery learning consultants, *S* to denote sites, and *RC* to denote regional coordinators for the Network of Outcome-based Schools. In several cases certain consultants are associated with commercial programs of mastery learning in reading and mathematics; we have used the letter *M* to denote these individuals. We include these consultants because of their general expertise in mastery learning. We do not endorse any mastery learning programs in the content areas in this appendix.

Northeast: New England States, New Jersey, New York, Pennsylvania, and Eastern Canadian Provinces

Anita Cimino (C)
Teacher Resource Specialist
United Federation of Teachers'
  Teacher Center
ATP 346
1400 Pennsylvania Avenue
Brooklyn, NY 11239
(718) 642-3135

Kathy Conner (S)
Karen Scholnick
Philadelphia Mastery Learning
  Program
Affective Education Program/
  Instructional Projects
Room 321
Board of Education
21st Street and Parkway
Philadelphia, PA 19103
(215) 299-7776

John DeCaro (S)
Superintendent
Ellwood City Area School District
501 Crescent Avenue
Ellwood City, PA 16117
(412) 752-1591

Ken Hood (C)
Assistant Dean
College of Education
311 Waterman Building
University of Vermont
Burlington, VT 05405-0160
(802) 656-3424

Howard Goodrow (S)
Superintendent
Windsor Central Supervisory Union
Woodstock, VT 05091
(802) 457-1213

Lewis Grell (S)
Superintendent
Hamburg Central School District
5305 Abbott Road
Hamburg, NY 14705
(716) 649-6850

Terence Keegan (S)
Coordinator of Instructional Programs
Fox Chapel Area School District
611 Field Club Road
Pittsburgh, PA 15238
(412) 963-9600

Albert Mamary (C, S, RC)
Superintendent
Larry Rowe
Assistant Superintendent
Johnson City Central Schools
666 Reynolds Road
Johnson City, NY 13790
(607) 729-9211

Mary Ann McAllister (S)
Attleboro Public Schools
Attleboro, MA 02703
(617) 222-0012

Donald Robb (C, M)
36 York Street
Andover, MA 01810
(617) 475-1968

Stephen Rubin (S, C, M)
Assistant Superintendent
New Canaan Public Schools
156 South Avenue
New Canaan, CT 06840
(203) 966-9575

Dick Shands (S)
Superintendent
Frontier Central School District
54432 Bayview Road
Hamburg, NY 14075
(716) 649-6001

Robert Shanes (S)
Coordinator of Mastery Learning
Room 837
Division of High Schools
New York City Community School
    District 19
110 Livingston Street
Brooklyn, NY 11201
(718) 596-4008

William J. Smith (S)
Assistant Superintendent for
    Instruction
East Islip School District
8 Laurel Avenue
East Islip, NY 11730
(516) 581-1600

David A. Squires (C, S)
Supervisor of Curriculum and Staff
    Development
Red Bank Public Schools
Administration Building
76 Branch Avenue
Red Bank, NJ 07701
(201) 758-1510

Tom Rusk Vickery (C)
Professor
Syracuse University
P.O. Box 456
Syracuse, NY 13210
(315) 423-3343

Leon Weisman (S)
Director of Language Arts
New York City Community School
    District 19
557 Pennsylvania Avenue
Brooklyn, NY 11207
(718) 257-6900

Middle Atlantic: Washington, DC; Delaware; Kentucky; Maryland; Virginia; and West Virginia

Carol Barber (C, S)
434 Granada Drive
Chesapeake, VA 23320
(804) 436-2250

Joseph Basile (RC)
Director of Educational Program
  Development
West Virginia Department of
  Education
Building 6, Capitol Complex
Charleston, WV 25305
(607) 729-1722

Reginald Elliott (S)
Executive Director
D.C. Street Academy
10th Street and Monroe Street NE
Washington, DC 20017
(202) 576-7006

Thomas R. Guskey (C)
Professor
College of Education
University of Kentucky
Lexington, KY 40506
(606) 257-8666

Joan Kozlovsky (C, S)
Principal
Oakleigh Elementary School
4730 Clermont Mill Road
Pylesville, MD 21132
(301) 665-2670

Southeast: Florida, Georgia, North Carolina, and South Carolina

Lorin Anderson (C)
Professor
Educational Leadership and Policy
College of Education
University of South Carolina
Columbia, SC 29208
(803) 777-5205

John T. Burks (S, RC)
Superintendent
Social Circle City Schools
P.O. Box 428
Social Circle, GA 30279
(404) 464-2611

James Okey (C)
Professor
Department of Science Education
University of Georgia
212 Aderhold Hall
Athens, GA 30602
(404) 542-1763

Gregg Strasler (C)
121 Whitwood Circle
Columbia, SC 29210
(803) 758-8825

Deep South: Alabama, Arkansas, Louisiana, Mississippi, and Tennessee

Elizabeth Donnelly (S)
Principal
Crump Elementary School
4405 Crump Avenue
Memphis, TN 38115
(901) 795-8873

Robert Fortenberry (S)
Superintendent
P.O. Box 2338
Jackson Public Schools
Jackson, MS 39205
(601) 354-0372

Glen Hymel (C)
Professor
Department of Psychology
Loyola University
6363 St. Charles Avenue
New Orleans, LA 70118
(504) 865-3257

Jeanne P. Phillips (S, RC)
Assistant Superintendent
Meridian Public Schools
P.O. Box 31
Meridian, MS 39301
(601) 483-6271

Julian Prince (S)
Tupelo Municipal Separate School
  District
P.O. Box 557
Tupelo, MS 38802
(601) 842-1464

Eastern Great Lakes: Indiana, Michigan, Ohio, and Ontario

Pat Decker (S)
Principal
Van Raalte School
461 Van Raalte Avenue
Holland, MI 49423
(616) 392-3836

Helen Efthim (C, S)
Research Associate
Center for Research, Evaluation, and
  Information Services
School District, City of Pontiac
44 State Street
Pontiac, MI 48053
(313) 857-8427

John M. Hoben (S, RC)
Superintendent
Plymouth-Canton School District
454 South Harvey Street
Plymouth, MI 48170
(313) 451-3140

James Klucher (S)
Assistant Superintendent/Elementary
  Education
James Costanza
Assistant Superintendent/Secondary
  Education
Mentor Public Schools
6451 Center Street
Mentor, OH 44060
(216) 255-4444

Marilyn March (S)
Director of Curriculum and Instruction
Lafayette School Corporation
2300 Cason Street
Lafayette, IN 47904
(317) 448-4640

Ken Pendleton (S)
Principal
Kent Elementary School
Columbus, OH 43205
(614) 252-4997

Norma Rogers (S)
Director of Reading
Monroe County Community School
  Corporation
315 North Drive
Bloomington, IN 47401
(812) 339-3489

Doris Ryan (C)
Professor
Ontario Institute for the Study of
  Education
252 West Bloor Street
Toronto, Ontario M5S 1V6
(416) 923-6641

Western Great Lakes: Illinois, Iowa, Minnesota, Missouri, and Wisconsin

Robert Bortnick (C)
Assistant Superintendent
Elk Grove School District 59
2123 South Arlington Heights Road
Arlington Heights, IL 60005
(312) 593-4328

Kathleen Fitzpatrick (C, S)
Assistant Superintendent
Township High School District 214
799 West Kensington Street
Mt. Prospect, IL 60056
(312) 259-5300

Karl O. Gandt (S, RC)
Superintendent
Union Ridge Elementary District
4600 North Oak Park Avenue
Harwood Heights, IL 60656
(312) 867-5822

Richard King (S)
Department of Elementary and
  Secondary Education
Missouri State Department of
  Education
P.O. Box 480
Jefferson City, MO 65102
(314) 751-2625

Daniel Levine (C)
Professor
Department of Education
University of Missouri
5100 Rockhill Road
Kansas City, MO 64110
(816) 276-2251

Plains: Kansas, Nebraska, North Dakota, South Dakota, and Manitoba

Jesse Kirksey (S)
Principal
Border-Starr Elementary School
Kansas City, KS 64113
(816) 444-0077

Ronald Meyer (S)
Department of Instructional Services
Omaha Public Schools
3902 Davenport Street
Omaha, NE 68131
(402) 554-6260

Mountain: Colorado, Montana, Utah, Wyoming, and Saskatchewan

George W. Bailey (C)
Bailey, Rogers & Associates
2317 South 5th Avenue
Cheyenne, WY 82007
(307) 637-7109

Jack Burr (S)
Director
Central Utah Educational Services
188 West Center Street
Richfield, UT 84701
(801) 896-4469

Harvie Guest (C, S)
Northglenn Junior High School
1123 Muriel Drive
Northglenn, CO 80233
(303) 452-2921

Ethna Reid (C, S, M)
Director
Exemplary Center for Reading
  Instruction
3310 South 2700 East
Salt Lake City, UT 84109
(801) 486-5083

Dick Rogers (S)
Principal
Conrad Ball Junior High
2660 North Monroe Street
Loveland, CO 80537
(303) 669-3550

Bill Meador (S)
Superintendent
Grand School District
264 South 4th Street East
Moab, UT 84532
(801) 259-6212

Carla Santorno (C, S)
Principal
Harrington Elementary School
3230 East 38th Avenue
Denver, CO 80205
(303) 333-4293

Caryl Thomason (S)
Director of Staff Development
Harrison School District
1060 Harrison Road
Colorado Springs, CO 80906
(303) 576-8360

Brent Thorne (S)
Assistant Superintendent
North Sanpete School District
41 West Main Street
Mt. Pleasant, UT 84647
(801) 462-2485

John Tuft (S)
Superintendent
Sevier School District
195 East 5th Street North
Richfield, UT 84701
(801) 896-4406

Lyle Wright (C)
Utah State Office of Education
250 East 5th Street South
Salt Lake City, UT 84111
(801) 533-5061

Southwest: New Mexico, Oklahoma, and Texas

John Champlin (C, RC)
Outcomes, Inc.
1805 Bangor Street
Lubbock, TX 79416
(806) 799-1837

Diane Leggert (S)
Director of Staff Development
Fort Worth School District
5208 North Hampshire
Fort Worth, TX 76112
(817) 336-8311

D. Leverman (S)
Director of Elementary Education
San Felipe-Del Rio School District
P.O. Drawer 420128
Del Rio, TX 78842
(512) 774-3521

Manda Lively (S)
Director of Instruction
Willis School District
204 West Rogers
Willis, TX 77378
(409) 856-4571

Pacific Northwest: Alaska, Idaho, Oregon, Washington, Alberta, and British Columbia

Daisy Arredondo (C)
4119-124th Avenue SE
Suite 305
Bellevue, WA 98006
(206) 643-4463

Robert E. Blum (C, RC)
Director, Goal-based Education
  Program
Northwest Regional Educational
  Laboratory
300 Southwest 6th Avenue
Portland, OR 97204
(503) 248-6800

Leroy Casagranda (C)
Professor
College of Education
Montana State University
Bozeman, MT 59717
(406) 994-5953

Charlotte Danielson (C)
Outcomes Associates
P.O. Box 1046
Monroe, WA 98272
(206) 743-9000

Thomas M. Everett (S)
Learning Specialist
Colstrip Public Schools
Colstrip, MT 59323
(406) 748-3602

Rob Foster (C)
8700 Camden Crescent
Richmond, British Columbia V7C 3G4
(604) 271-3247

Spike Jorgensen (S)
Superintendent
Alaska-Gateway School District
P.O. Box 226
Tok, AL 99780
(907) 883-5151

Suzanne Simonson (C, S)
Principal
Mariner High School
10604 26th Drive S.E.
Everett, WA 98204
(206) 337-6035

Ron Wick (S)
Principal
Explorer Elementary School
9600 Sharon Drive
Everett, WA 98204
(206) 356-1250

Pacific Southwest: Arizona, California, and Nevada

James H. Block (C)
Professor
Department of Education
University of California
Santa Barbara, CA 93106
(805) 961-3301

Sharon Bolster (C, S)
Arizona Department of Education
1535 West Jefferson Street
Phoeniz, AZ 85007
(602) 255-5567

Robert Burns (C, S)
Far West Regional Laboratory for
  Educational Research and
  Development
1855 Folsom Street
San Francisco, CA 94103
(415) 565-3269

S. Alan Cohen (C, M)
Professor
University of San Francisco
School of Education
Ignatian Heights
San Francisco, CA 94117
(415) 666-6289

Richard Escott (S)
Superintendent
Yamhill Education Service District
800 East 2nd Street
McMinnville, OR 97128
(503) 472-1431

Jeannine Goenne (S)
Principal
Lampton Elementary School
14716 Elmcroft Avenue
Norwalk, CA 90650
(213) 868-0865

Nancy Hill (S)
Principal
Cleveland Elementary School
123 Alameda Padre Serra
Santa Barbara, CA 93103
(805) 963-4331

Joan Hyman (C)
Professor
School of Education
University of San Francisco
Ignatian Heights
San Francisco, CA 94117
(415) 666-6289

Jean Kelleman (S)
Principal
Washington Elementary School
Bellflower, CA 90706
(213) 925-6603

Richard Miller (C)
Associate Superintendent for
    Educational Services
Port Hueneme School District
354 North 3rd Street
Port Hueneme, CA 93041
(805) 488-3588

Margaret Oda (C)
Deputy Superintendent of Instruction
Hawaii State Department of Education
1390 Miller Street
Honolulu, HI 96813
(808) 548-6911

William G. Spady (C, RC)
President
The Spady Consulting Group
14 Whitman Court
San Carlos, CA 94070
(415) 592-7053

Herbert Wadley (S)
Associate Superintendent
Campbell Public Schools
155 North 3rd Street
Campbell, CA 95008
(408) 371-0960

James Weyand (C)
Coordinator
College of Education
University of Arizona
Tucson, AZ 85721
(602) 621-1527

AVAILABLE MATERIALS

Written References, for Further Reading

Block, J. (Ed.). *Mastery Learning: Theory and Practice.* New York: Holt, Rinehart and Winston, 1971.

Block, J. (Ed.). *Schools, Society, and Mastery Learning*. New York: Holt, Rinehart and Winston, 1974.

Block, J., & Anderson, L. *Mastery Learning and Classroom Instruction*. New York: Macmillan, 1975.

Bloom, B. S. *Human Characteristics and School Learning*. New York: McGraw-Hill, 1976.

Bloom, B. S. *All Our Children Learning*. New York: McGraw-Hill, 1981.

Bloom, B. S., Hastings, J. T., & Madaus, G. F. *Handbook on Formative and Summative Evaluation of Student Learning*. New York: McGraw-Hill, 1971.

Blum, R. (Ed.). *Effective Schooling Practices: A Research Synthesis*. Portland, OR: Northwest Regional Educational Laboratory, 1984.

Brandt, R. (Special issue on mastery learning). *Educational Leadership, 37*(2), 1979.

Burns, R. *Models of Instructional Organization: A Casebook on Mastery Learning and Outcome-based Education*. San Francisco, CA: Far West Regional Laboratory for Educational Research and Development, 1987.

Carroll, J. B. "A Model of School Learning." *Teachers College Record, 64*, 723–733, 1963.

Far West Regional Educational Laboratory. *Outcome-based Instructional Systems: Practice and Primer*. San Francisco, CA: Far West Regional Laboratory for Educational Research and Development, 1984.

Guskey, T. R. *Implementing Mastery Learning*. Belmont, CA: Wadsworth, 1985.

Horton, L. *Mastery Learning*. Bloomington, IN: Phi Delta Kappa Educational Foundation, 1981.

Hunter, M. *Mastery Teaching*. El Segundo, CA: TIP Publications, 1984.

Hymel, G. M. *Mastery Learning: A Comprehensive Bibliography*. New Orleans: Clearinghouse on Mastery Learning, Loyola Center for Educational Improvement, Loyola University, 1982.

Kojimoto, C., & Burns, R. *People and Resources in Mastery Learning and Outcome-based Education*. San Francisco, CA: Far West Regional Laboratory for Educational Research and Development, 1986.

Lee, J. F., Jr., & Pruitt, K. W. *Providing for Individual Differences in Student Learning: A Mastery Learning Approach*. Springfield, IL: Thomas, 1984.

Levine, D. U. (Ed.). *Improving Student Achievement through Mastery Learning Programs*. San Francisco: Jossey-Bass, 1985.

Network for Outcome Based Schools. *Outcomes*, each issue.

Outcomes Associates. *The Exchange*, each issue.

Torshen, K. P. *The Mastery Approach to Competency-based Education*. Orlando, FL: Academic Press, 1977.

Training Manuals

Barber, C. *Mastery Learning Training Manual*. Price, UT: Southeastern Education Service Center, 1985.

Cimino, A. *Centering on Mastery Learning in Your Classroom: A Handbook for an Approach to an Alternative Learning Strategy*. New York: New York City Teacher Centers Consortium, n.d.

Danielson, C. *Practitioner's Implementation Handbooks*. Monroe, WA: Outcomes Associates, 1986.

The Mastery Learning Manual. Philadelphia, School District of Philadelphia. 1986.

Squires, D. A. *Training Manual for Unit Development*. Phoenix, AZ: Arizona Department of Education, 1987.

Audiovisual Materials

Block, J. H. *Belief Systems and Instructional Improvement: A Lesson in Mastery Learning*. Dayton, OH: Institute for the Development of Educational Activities, 1986.

A videotape that develops the belief system of mastery learning.

Cohen, S. A. *Mastery Learning Systems*. Novato, CA: S. Alan Cohen Associates, n.d.

A classroom microcomputer system to manage outcome-based, mastery learning, competency-based instructional programs at the classroom level using a 48K, two-disk machine.

Guskey, T. *Mastery Learning*. Alexandria, VA: American Association for Supervision and Curriculum Development, 1983.

An audiocassette introduction to mastery learning.

Okey, J. R., & Ciesla, J. L. *Mastery Teaching*. Bloomington: National Center for the Development of Training Materials in Teacher Education, Indiana University, 1975.

An integrated written, audio, and visual introduction to mastery learning.

Rubin, S. E., & Spady, W. G. *Outcome-based Education: Success for All* and *Taking the First Steps to Success*. Redwood City, CA: Spady Consulting Group, 1986.

Success for All is a 50-minute presentation defining outcome-based education, its effectiveness, exemplary implementation practices, and steps for getting started; *Taking the First Steps to Success* outlines one district's implementation of OBE. Accompanying the videotapes is an Implementation Manual, which provides practical suggestions for districts beginning the OBE process.

School District No. 12, Adams County, CO: *CMI 3000*. n.d.

A computer-based system for managing all aspects of mastery learning.

References

Abrams, J. B. (1985). Making outcome-based education work. *Educational Leadership*, *43*(1), 30–32.

Adler, M. (1984). *The Padaiea proposal*. New York: Macmillan.

Airasian, P. W. (1969). *Formative evaluation instruments: A construction and validation of tests to evaluate learning over short time periods*. Unpublished doctoral dissertation, University of Chicago.

Airasian, P. W. (1984). *Classroom assessment and educational improvement*. Paper presented at the conference Classroom Assessment: A Key to Educational Excellence, Northwest Regional Educational Laboratory, Portland, Oregon.

Allen, J. D. (1986). Classroom management: Students' perspectives, goals, and strategies. *American Educational Research Journal*, *23*, 437–459.

Ames, C., & Ames R. (1984a). Systems of student and teacher motivation: Qualitative definition. *Journal of Educational Psychology*, *76*, 535–556.

Ames, R. E., & Ames, C. (Eds.). (1984b). *Research on motivation in education* (Vol. 1): *Student motivation*. Orlando, FL: Academic Press.

Anderson, L. M. (1984). The environment of instruction: The function of seatwork in a commercially developed curriculum. In G. G. Duffy, L. Roehler, & J. Mason (Eds.), *Comprehension instruction*. White Plains, NY: Longman.

Anderson, L. M., Evertson, C., & Emmer, E. (1980). Dimensions of classroom management derived from recent research. *Journal of Curriculum Studies*, *12*, 193–223.

Anderson, L. W. (1973). *Time and school learning*. Unpublished doctoral dissertation, University of Chicago.

Anderson, L. W. (1975). Student involvement in learning and school achievement. *California Journal of Educational Research*, *26*, 53–62.

Anderson, L. W. (1976a). *The effects of a mastery learning program on selected cognitive, affective, and interpersonal variables in grades 1 through 6.* Paper presented at the annual meeting of the American Educational Research Association, San Francisco.

Anderson, L. W. (1976b). An empirical investigation of individual differences in time to learn. *Journal of Educational Psychology, 68,* 226–233.

Anderson, L. W. (1981). A functional analysis of mastery learning. *Outcomes, 1*(2), 1–3.

Anderson, L. W. (1985a). A retrospective and prospective view of Bloom's "Learning for Mastery." In M. C. Wang and H. J. Walberg (Eds.), *Adapting instruction to individual differences.* Berkeley: McCutchan.

Anderson, L. W. (1985b). Review of *Improving student achievement through mastery learning programs. Educational Technology, 25*(9), 56–58.

Anderson, L. W. (1985c). Time and timing. In C. Fischer and D. Berliner (Eds.), *Perspectives on instructional time.* White Plains, NY: Longman.

Anderson, L. W. (1986). Research on teaching and educational effectiveness. *NASSP Curriculum Report, 15*(4), 1–6.

Anderson, L. W., & Block, J. H. (1977). Mastery learning. In D. Treffinger et al. (Eds.), *Handbook on teaching educational psychology.* Orlando, FL: Academic Press.

Anderson, L. W., & Block, J. H. (1985). The mastery learning model of instruction. In T. Husen & T. N. Postlethwaite (Eds.), *International encyclopedia of education.* Oxford, England: Pergamon Press.

Anderson, L. W., & Jones, B. F. (1981). Designing instructional strategies which facilitate learning for mastery. *Educational Psychologist, 16,* 121–138.

Anderson, L. W., & Pigford, A. (1987). *When assignments drive Chapter 1 instruction.* Paper presented at the annual meeting of the American Educational Research Association, Washington, DC.

Angoff, W. H. (1971). Scales, norms, and equivalent scores. In R. L. Thorndike (Ed.), *Educational measurement* (2nd ed.). Washington, DC: American Council on Education.

Apple, M. (1979). *Ideology and curriculum.* London: Routledge & Kegan Paul.

Arlin, M. (1973). *Rate and rate variance trends under mastery learning.* Unpublished doctoral dissertation, University of Chicago.

Arlin, M. (1982). Teacher responses to student time differences in mastery learning. *American Journal of Education, 90,* 334–352.

Arlin, M. (1984). Time, equality, and mastery learning. *Review of Educational Research, 54,* 65–87.

Arlin, M., & Webster, J. (1983). Time costs of mastery learning. *Journal of Educational Psychology, 75,* 187–195.

Arter, J. A., & Estes, G. D. (1984). *A guide to item banking in education* (2nd ed.). Portland, OR: Northwest Regional Educational Laboratory.

Arter, J. A., & Estes, G. D. (1985). *Item banking for local test development: Practitioner's handbook.* Portland, OR: Northwest Regional Educational Laboratory.

Bandura, A. (1977). Self-efficacy: Towards a unifying theory of behavioral change. *Psychological Review, 84,* 191–215.

Bangert, R. L., Kulik, J., & Kulik, C.-L. (1983). Individualized systems of instruction in secondary schools. *Review of Educational Research*, *53*, 143–158.

Barber, C. (1982). Mastery learning in the Denver public schools. *Outcomes*, *2*(1), 12–15.

Barber, C. (1985). *Mastery learning training manual*. Price, UT: Southeastern Education Service Center.

Barber, C. (1986). Outcome-based education/mastery learning: What is it? Why do it? *Outcomes*, *5*(3), 1–9.

Barker, R. G., & Gump, P. V. (Eds.). (1964). *Big school, small school*. Stanford, CA: Stanford University Press.

Barr, R., & Dreeben, R. (1983). *How schools work*. Chicago: University of Chicago Press.

Bauchner, J., & Loucks, S. (1982). *Building administrators and their role in the improvement process*. Paper presented at the annual meeting of the American Educational Research Association, New York.

Berman, P., & McLaughlin, M. (1978). *Federal programs supporting educational change* (Vol. 3): *Implementing and sustaining innovations*. Santa Monica, CA: Rand Corp.

Blakemore, C. L. (1985). Mastery learning: An effective technique for the physical education teacher. *Outcomes*, *4*(4), 6–8.

Block, J. H. (1970). *The effects of various levels of performance on selected cognitive, affective, and time variables*. Unpublished doctoral dissertation, University of Chicago.

Block, J. H. (Ed.). (1971). *Mastery learning: Theory and practice*. New York: Holt, Rinehart and Winston.

Block, J. H. (1972). Student learning and the setting of mastery performance standards. *Educational Horizons*, *50*, 183–191.

Block, J. H. (1974a). Mastery learning in the classroom: An overview of recent research. In J. Block (Ed.), *Schools, society, and mastery learning*. New York: Holt, Rinehart and Winston.

Block, J. H. (Ed.). (1974b). *Schools, society, and mastery learning*. New York: Holt, Rinehart and Winston.

Block, J. H. (1977). Motivation, evaluation, and mastery learning. *UCLA Educator*, *19*, 31–36.

Block, J. H. (1978a). Learning for competence. *Victorian Institute of Educational Research Bulletin*, *40*, 27–43.

Block, J. H. (1978b). Standards and criteria: A response. *Journal of Educational Measurement*, *15*, 291–295.

Block, J. H. (1979). Mastery learning: The current state of the craft. *Educational Leadership*, *37*(2), 114–117.

Block, J. H. (1980). Promoting excellence through mastery learning. *Theory into Practice*, *19*(1), 66–74.

Block, J. H. (1983). Learning rates and mastery learning. *Outcomes*, *2*(3), 18–25.

Block, J. H. (1984). Making school learning activities more playlike: Flow and mastery learning. *Outcomes*, *3*(2), 21–29.

Block, J. H. (1985). Belief systems and mastery learning. *Outcomes, 4*(2), 1–13.

Block, J. H., & Anderson, L. W. (1975). *Mastery learning in classroom instruction*. New York: Macmillan.

Block, J. H., & Burns, R. B. (1976). Mastery learning. In L. Shulman (Ed.), *Review of research in education* (Vol. 4). Itasca, IL: Peacock.

Block, J. H., & Burns, R. B. (1981). Student evaluation: A mastery learning perspective. In A. Levy and D. Nevo (Eds.), *Evaluation roles in education.* London: Gordon & Breach.

Block, J. H., & Cantlay, L. (1979). *Self-mastery.* Paper presented at the annual meeting of the American Educational Research Association, San Francisco.

Block, J. H., & King, N. R. (1987). *School play.* New York: Garland Press.

Block, J. H., & Tierney, M. (1974). An exploration of two correction procedures used in mastery learning approaches to instruction. *Journal of Educational Psychology, 66,* 962–967.

Bloom, B. S. (Ed.). (1956). *Taxonomy of educational objectives. Handbook I: The cognitive domain.* White Plains, N.Y.: Longman.

Bloom, B. S. (1968). Learning for mastery. *Evaluation Comment, 1*(2), 1–12.

Bloom, B. S. (1970). Toward a theory of testing which includes measurement-evaluation-assessment. In M. C. Wittrock & D. E. Wiley (Eds.), *The evaluation of instruction.* New York: Holt, Rinehart and Winston.

Bloom, B. S. (1971). Affective consequences of school achievement. In J. H. Block (Ed.), *Mastery learning: Theory and practice.* New York: Holt, Rinehart and Winston.

Bloom, B. S. (1974). An introduction to mastery learning theory. In J. H. Block (Ed.), *Schools, society, and mastery learning.* New York: Holt, Rinehart and Winston.

Bloom, B. S. (1976). *Human characteristics and school learning.* New York: McGraw-Hill.

Bloom, B. S. (1981). *All our children learning.* New York: McGraw-Hill.

Bloom, B. S. (1984). The search for methods of group instruction as effective as one-to-one tutoring. *Educational Leadership, 41*(8), 4–18.

Bloom, B. S. (1985). *Developing talent in young people.* New York: Ballantine.

Bloom, B. S. (1986). "The hands and feet of genius": Automaticity. *Educational Leadership, 43*(5), 70–77.

Bloom, B. S., Hastings, J. T., & Madaus, G. F. (1971). *Handbook on formative and summative evaluation of student learning.* New York: McGraw-Hill.

Blum, R. E., & Butler, J. A. (1985a). Effective schooling practices synthesized by NWREL goal-based education program. *Outcomes, 4*(2), 29–30.

Blum, R. E., & Butler, J. A. (1985b). Managing improvement by profiling. *Eductional Leadership, 42*(6), 54–58.

Bridges, E. M. (1986). *The incompetent teacher.* Philadelphia: Falmer Press.

Brookover, W. B., & Lezotte, L. W. (1979). *Changes in school characteristics coincident with changes in student achievement.* Occasional Paper No. 17. East Lansing: Michigan State University, Institute for Research on Teaching.

Brookover, W. B., Beamer, L., Efthim, H., Hathaway, D., Lezotte, L., Miller, S., Passalacqua, J., & Tornatzky, L. (1982). *Creating effective schools: An inservice program for enhancing school climate and achievement.* Holmes Beach, FL: Learning Publications, Inc.

Brophy, J. E. (1981). Teacher praise: A functional analysis. *Review of Educational Research, 51,* 5–32.

Brophy, J. E., & Good, T. L. (1974). *Teacher-student relationships: Causes and consequences*. New York: Holt, Rinehart and Winston.

Brophy, J. E., & Good, T. L. (1986). Teacher behavior and student achievement. In M. C. Wittrock (Ed.), *Handbook of research on teaching* (3rd ed.). New York: Macmillan.

Brownell, W. (1948). Criteria of learning in educational research. *Journal of Educational Psychology*, *39*, 170–182.

Bruner, J. S. (1966). *Toward a theory of instruction*. Cambridge, MA: Harvard University Press.

Burns, R. B. (1979). Mastery learning: does it work? *Educational Leadership*, *37*(2), 110–113.

Burns, R. B. (1984). The process and content of teaching: A conceptual framework. *Evaluation in Education*, *8*(2), 95–112.

Burns, R. B. (1986). Accumulating the accumulated evidence on mastery learning. *Outcomes*, *5*(2), 4–10.

Burns, R. B., Spady, W. G., & Filby, N. (1986). Defining features of outcome-based education. San Francisco, CA: Far West Regional Educational Laboratory.

Carroll, J. B. (1963). A model of school learning. *Teachers College Record*, *64*, 723–733.

Carroll, J. B. (1964). Words, meanings, and concepts. *Harvard Educational Review*, *34*, 178–202.

Carroll, J. B. (1971). Problems of measurement related to the concept of mastery learning. In J. H. Block (Ed.), *Mastery learning: Theory and practice*. New York: Holt, Rinehart and Winston.

Carroll, J. B. (1985). The model of school learning: Progress of an idea. In L. W. Anderson (Ed.), *Perspectives on school learning*. Hillsdale, NJ: Erlbaum.

Champlin, J. R. (1981). Is creating an outcome-based program worth the extra effort? A superintendent's perspective. *Outcomes*, *1*(2), 4–8.

Champlin, J. R., & Mamary, A. (1982). Johnson City's philosophical principles and practices. *Outcomes*, *2*(1), 22–23.

Champlin, J. R. (1983). Four phases in creating and managing an outcome-based program. *Outcomes*, *3*(1), 28–41.

Champlin, J. R. (1987). Leadership: A change agent's view. In L. T. Sheive & M. B. Schoenheit (Eds.), *Leadership: Examining the elusive*. Washington, DC: Association for Supervision and Curriculum Development.

Chan, K. S. (1981). *The interaction of aptitude with mastery versus non-mastery instruction: Effects on reading comprehension of grade three students*. Unpublished doctoral dissertation, University of Western Australia.

Chandler, T. A. (1973). *Utilization of a contract approach in a graduate educational psychology course*. Paper presented at the annual meeting of the American Educational Research Association, New Orleans.

Chrispeels, J., & Meaney, D. (1985). *Building effective schools: Assessing, planning, implementing*. San Diego: San Diego County Office of Education.

Cohen, S. A. (1983). Implications of psychological research on mastery learning. *Outcomes*, *2*(4), 18–24.

Cohen, S. A. (1986). *Implications of instructional alignment research*. Studies in Evaluation Research and Instructional Design, School of Education, University of San Francisco.

Cohen, S. A., Hyman, J. S., & Stone, R. (1985). Comparing learning rates of lower with higher aptitude students in mastery learning: A test of Bloom's proposition. *Outcomes*, *4*(3), 11–18.

Conner, K., Hairston, J., Hill, I., Kopple, H., Marshall, J., Scholnick, K., & Shulman, M. (1985). Using formative testing at the classroom, school, and district levels. *Educational Leadership*, *43*(2), 63–67.

Conner, K., Hill, I., Kopple, H., Marshall, J., Scholnick, K., Shulman, M., & Sloan, E. (1986). Mastery learning in Philadelphia: Cognitive and affective dimensions. Adapted from Bloom, B. S. (1956). Taxonomy of educational objectives. Handbook I: Cognitive domain. White Plains, NY: Longman.

Conyers, J. G. (1985). Denver public schools and standards of excellence. *Outcomes*, *4*(3), 19–27.

Corbett, H. D., & D'Amico, J. J. (1986). No more heroes: Creating systems to support change. *Educational Leadership*, *44*(1), 70–72.

Covington, M. (1984). The motive for self-worth. In R. E. Ames & C. Ames (Eds.), *Research on motivation in education* (Vol. 1): *Student motivation*. Orlando, FL: Academic Press.

Cremin, L. A. (1961). *The transformation of the school*. New York: Vintage Books.

Cronbach, L. J. (1972). [Review of *Mastery learning: Theory and practice*.] *International Review of Education*, *18*, 250–252.

Cronbach, L. J., & Snow, R. W. (1977). *Aptitudes and instructional methods*. New York: Irvington.

Cruickshank, D. (1985). *Models for the preparation of America's teachers*. Bloomington, IN: Phi Delta Kappa Educational Foundation.

Csikszentmihalyi, M., & McCormack, J. (1986). The influence of teachers. *Phi Delta Kappan*, *67*, 415–419.

Current, R. N., DeConde, A., & Dante, H. L. (1967). *United States history*. Glenview, IL: Scott, Foresman.

Dahloff, U. S. (1971). *Ability grouping, content validity, and curriculum process analysis*. New York: Teachers College Press.

Deci, E. L. (1980). *The psychology of self-determination*. Lexington, MA: Heath.

DelSeni, D. (1981). Mastery learning from the perspective of an intermediate school principal. *IMPACT on Instructional Improvement*, *17*, 25–31.

Dewey, J. (1938). *Experience and education*. New York: Collier.

Dolan, L. (1986). Mastery learning as a preventive strategy. *Outcomes*, *5*(2), 20–26.

Dolan, L., & Kellam, S. (1987). *Preliminary report of mastery learning interventions during first grade with cohort I students*. Baltimore, MD: Johns Hopkins University, Department of Mental Hygiene, Prevention Center.

Duby, P. B. (1980). *An investigation of the mediating role of causal attributions in school learning*. Unpublished doctoral dissertation, University of Chicago.

Dunkleberger, G. E., & Heikkinen, H. W. (1983). Mastery learning: Implications and practices. *Science Education*, *67*, 553–560.

Edmonds, R. (1978). *A discussion of the literature and issues related to effective schooling*. Paper presented at the National Conference on Urban Education, St. Louis.

Efthim, H. E. (1984). *Time for mastery*. Unpublished funding proposal.

Efthim, H. E. (1987). [Description of Crofoot School, Pontiac, MI.] Dissertation in progress, Union Graduate School.

Ellson, E. D. (1976). Tutoring. In N. L. Gage (Ed.), *The psychology of teaching methods*, 74th Yearbook of the National Society for the Study of Education, Part 1. Chicago: University of Chicago Press.

Evertson, C. M., & Emmer, E. T. (1982). Preventive classroom management. In D. Duke (Ed.), *Helping teachers manage classrooms*. Alexandria, VA: Association for Supervision and Curriculum Development.

Evertson, C. M., Emmer, E., & Brophy, J. (1980). Predictors of effective teaching in junior high mathematics classrooms. *Journal for Research in Mathematics Education, 11*, 167–168.

Faure, E., et al. (1972). *Learning to be: The world of education today and tomorrow*. Paris: UNESCO.

Feuerstein, R. (1980). *Instrumental enrichment: An intervention program for cognitive modifiability*. Baltimore: University Park Press.

Fielding, G., Schalock, M., Christensen, P., & Schalock, D. (1986). Implementing outcome-based instructional programs: The Valley Education Consortium's approach. *Outcomes, 5*(4), 14–22.

Finn, C. E. (1984). Toward strategic independence: Nine commandments for enhancing school effectiveness. *Phi Delta Kappan, 65*, 518–524.

Fitzpatrick, K. A., & Charters, W. W. (1986). *A study of staff development practices and organizational conditions related to instructional improvement in secondary schools*. Eugene: Center for Educational Policy and Management, College of Education, University of Oregon.

Fortenberry, R. (1986). Statement at hearing on H.R. 747, the Effective Schools Development in Education Act of 1985. Washington, DC: U.S. Government Printing Office.

Foshay, A. (1973). Sources of school practice. In J. I. Goodlad & H. Shane (Eds.), *The elementary school in the United States*, 72nd Yearbook of the National Society for the Study of Education, Part 2. Chicago: University of Chicago Press.

Gagné, R. M. (1968). Learning hierarchies. *Educational Psychologist, 6*, 1–9.

Gall, M., Fielding, G., Schalock, D., Charters, W., & Wiczinski, J. (1984). *Involving the principal in teachers' staff development: Effects on the quality of mathematics instruction in elementary schools*. Eugene: Center for Educational Policy and Management, University of Oregon.

Garner, W. T. (1973). *The identification of an educational production function by experimental means*. Unpublished doctoral dissertation, University of Chicago.

Gersten, R., & Carnine, D. (1981). *Administrative and supervisory support functions for the implementation of effective educational programs for low-income students*. Eugene: Center for Educational Policy and Management, University of Oregon.

Glass, G., McGaw, B., & Smith, M. (1981). *Meta-analysis of social research*. Beverly Hills, CA: Sage.

Glasnapp, D. R., Poggio, J. P., & Ory, J. C. (1975). *Cognitive and affective consequences of mastery and nonmastery instructional strategies*. Paper presented at the annual meeting of the American Educational Research Association, Washington, DC.

Good, T. L., & Grouws, D. A. (1979). The Missouri mathematics effectiveness project: An experimental study in fourth grade classrooms. *Journal of Educational Psychology, 71,* 355–362.

Good, T. L., & Stipek, D. (1983). Individual differences in the classroom: A psychological perspective. In G. Fenstermacher & J. I. Goodlad (Eds.), *Individual differences and the common curriculum,* 82nd Yearbook of the National Society for the Study of Education, Part 1. Chicago: University of Chicago Press.

Good, T. L., Grouws, D. A., & Ebmeier, H. (1983). *Active mathematics teaching.* White Plains, NY: Longman.

Goodlad, J. I. (1984). *A place called school.* New York: McGraw-Hill.

Grell, L. A. (1984). Why mastery learning? *Outcomes, 4*(1) 14–17.

Groff, P. (1974). Some criticisms of mastery learning. *Today's Education, 63,* 88–91.

Gruener, J. L. (1984). The nuts and bolts of getting started. *Outcomes, 3*(2), 39–42.

Guskey, T. R. (1984). The influence of change in instructional effectiveness upon the affective characteristics of teachers. *American Educational Research Journal, 21,* 245–259.

Guskey, T. R. (1985a). Bloom's mastery learning: A legacy for effectiveness. *Educational Horizons, 63,* 90–92.

Guskey, T. R. (1985b). The contribution of mastery learning. *Outcomes, 4*(3), 1–10.

Guskey, T. R. (1985c). *Implementing mastery learning.* Belmont, CA: Wadsworth.

Guskey, T. R. (1985d). Staff development and teacher change. *Educational Leadership, 42*(7), 57–60.

Guskey, T. R. (1987). Defining the essential elements of mastery learning. *Outcomes, 7*(1), 30–34.

Guskey, T. R., & Gates, S. L. (1985). *A synthesis of research on group-based mastery learning programs.* Paper presented at the annual meeting of the American Educational Research Association, Chicago.

Guskey, T. R., & Gates, S. L. (1986). Synthesis of research on the effects of mastery learning in elementary and secondary classrooms. *Educational Leadership, 43*(8), 73–80.

Guskey, T. R., & Monsaas, J. A. (1979). *Mastery learning in the city colleges of Chicago: A strategy for academic success.* Paper presented at the annual meeting of the AERA/SIG for Community-Junior College Research, Columbus, OH.

Guttman, L. (1969). Integration of test design and analysis. *Proceeedings of the 1969 Invitational Conference on Testing Problems.* Princeton, NJ: Educational Testing Service.

Hagans, R. (1986). Goal-based secondary schools: A summary of commonalities. *Outcomes, 5*(4), 23–32.

Hartwig, M. (1986). *The development and validation of an ethnographically based instrument to elicit students' perceptions of their classroom.* Unpublished doctoral dissertation, University of California, Santa Barbara.

Hedges, L., & Olkin, I. (1985). *Statistical methods for meta-analysis.* Orlando, FL: Academic Press.

Hively, W., Patterson, H. L., & Page, S. A. (1968). A "universe-defined" system of arithmetic achievement tests. *Journal of Educational Measurement, 5*, 275–290.

Hoben, J. M. (1981). Starting and managing an outcome-based curriculum. *Outcomes, 1*(2), 14–15.

Horton, L. (1981). *Mastery learning.* Bloomington, IN: Phi Delta Kappa.

House, E. R. (1984). Assumptions underlying evaluation methods. *Educational Researcher, 7*(3), 4–12.

Hunter, M. (1984). *Mastery teaching.* El Segundo, CA: TIP Publications.

Husen, T. & Postlethwaite, N. (Eds.). (1985). *International encyclopedia of education: research and studies.* London: Pergamon Press.

Hyman, J. L., & Cohen, S. A. (1979). "Learning for mastery: Ten conclusions after fifteen years. *Educational Leadership, 37*(2), 104–109.

Hymel, G. M. (1982). *Mastery learning: A comprehensive bibliography.* New Orleans: Clearinghouse on Mastery Learning, Loyola Center for Educational Improvement, Loyola University.

Hymel, G. M. (1986). A macro model for mastery learning, effective schools, and outcome-based schooling: An overview. *Outcomes, 5*(3), 31–36.

Johnson, D. W., & Johnson, R. T. (1983). The socialization and achievement crisis: Are cooperative learning experiences the solution? In L. Bickman (Ed.), *Applied social psychology Annual 4.* Beverly Hills, CA: Sage.

Jones, B. F. (1983). A checklist for effective mastery learning instruction and assessment. *Outcomes. 2*(4), 38–42.

Jones, B. F., Friedman, L. B., Tinzmann, M., & Cox, B. E. (1985). Guidelines for instruction-enriched mastery learning to improve comprehension. In D. U. Levine (Ed.), *Improving student achievement through mastery learning programs.* San Francisco: Jossey-Bass.

Jones, B. F., & Spady, W. G. (1985). Enhanced mastery learning and quality of instruction. In D. U. Levine (Ed.), *Improving student achievement through mastery learning programs.* San Francisco: Jossey-Bass.

Joyce, B. R., & Showers, B. (1983). *Power in staff development through research in training.* Washington, DC: Association for Supervision and Curriculum Development

Keller, F. S. (1968). Goodbye, teacher.... *Journal of Applied Behavioral Analysis, 1*, 79–89.

Kennedy, J., Cruickshank, D., Bush, A., & Myers, B. (1978). Additional investigations into the nature of teacher clarity. *Journal of Educational Research, 72*, 3–10.

Koehn, J. J. (1983). Mastery learning: Easier said than done. *Outcomes, 3*(1), 50–54.

Kounin, J. (1970). *Discipline and group management in classrooms.* New York: Holt, Rinehart and Winston.

Kounin, J. S., & Sherman, L. W. (1979). School environments as behavior settings. *Theory into Practice, 18*, 145–149.

Kozlovsky, J. D. (1986). Making mastery learning work: Part 2. District-level implementation of mastery learning. *Outcomes, 5*(2), 41–50.

Lee, J. F., Jr., & Pruitt, K. W. (1984). *Providing for individual differences in student learning: A mastery learning approach.* Springfield, IL: Thomas.

Leinhardt, G., & Leinhardt, S. (1980). Exploratory data analysis: New tools for the analysis of empirical data. *Review of Research in Education, 8*, 85–157.

Levin, H. M. (1987). Accelerated schools for disadvantaged students. *Educational Leadership*, *44*(6), 19–21.

Levine, D. U. (Ed.). (1985a). *Improving student achievement through mastery learning programs*. San Francisco: Jossey-Bass.

Levine, D. U. (1985b). A mini-description of initially unsuccessful attempts to introduce outcomes-based instruction. *Outcomes*, *4*(2), 15–19.

Lezotte, L., & Bancroft, B. (1986). School improvement based on effective schools research. *Outcomes*, *6*(1), 13–17.

Lieberman, A. (1986). Collaborative work. *Educational Leadership*, *43*(5), 4–8.

Light, R., & Pillemer, D. (1984). *Summing up: The science of reviewing research*. Cambridge, MA: Harvard University Press.

Little, J. W. (1981). *School success and staff development: The role of staff development in urban desegregated schools*. Boulder, CO: Center for Action Research, Inc.

Little, J. W. (1982). Norms of collegiality and experimentation: workplace conditions of school success. *American Educational Research Journal, 19*, 325–340.

Lortie, D. C. (1985). *Schoolteacher*. Chicago: University of Chicago Press.

Loucks, S. F., & Hall, G. E. (1979). *Implementing innovations in schools: A concerns-based approach*. Austin: Research and Development Center for Teacher Education, University of Texas.

Loucks-Horsley, S. F., & Hergert, L. F. (1985). *An action guide to school improvement*. Alexandria, VA: Association for Supervision and Curriculum Development and the NETWORK, Inc.

Louis, K. S. (1986). Reforming secondary schools: A critique and an agenda for administrators. *Educational Leadership*, *44*(1), 33–36.

Louis, K. S., Rosenblum, S., Molitor, J. A., Chabotar, K. J., Kelly, D., & Yin, R. K. (1981). *Strategies for knowledge use and school improvement: A summary*. Cambridge. MA: Abt Associates.

Mamary, A. (1986). *Mastery learning in the Johnson City schools*. Paper presented at the National Conference of the Network for Outcome-based Schools, Binghamton, NY.

Mamary, A., & Rowe, L. A. (1985). Flexible and heterogeneous instructional arrangements to facilitate mastery learning. In D. U. Levine (Ed.), *Improving student achievement through mastery learning programs*. San Francisco: Jossey-Bass.

Mastery Education Corp. (1985). *CMLR Profile, District 19, Brooklyn, New York*. Watertown, MA: Author.

McDonald, F. J. (1982). Mastery learning evaluation: Interim report. New York: New York City Board of Education.

McLaughlin, M. W., Pfeifer, R. S., Swanson-Owens, D., & Yee, S. (1986). Why teachers won't teach. *Phi Delta Kappan, 67*, 420–425.

McMurrin, S. M. (1971). Technology and education. In S. G. Tickton (Ed.), *To improve learning: An evaluation of instructional technology* (Vol. 2). New York: Bowker.

McNeil, J. D. (1969). Forces influencing curriculum. *Review of Educational Research, 39*, 293–318.

Merrill, M. D., Barton, K., & Wood, L. E. (1970). Specific review in learning a hierarchical imaginary science. *Journal of Educational Psychology*, *61*, 102–109.

Mevarech, Z. R. (n.d.). Instructional approaches to developing students' lower and higher mental processes. Unpublished paper.

Mevarech, Z. R. (1980). The role of teaching-learning strategies and feedback and corrective procedures in developing higher cognitive achievement. Unpublished doctoral dissertation, University of Chicago.

Miles, M. B. (1983). Unraveling the myth of institutionalization. *Educational Leadership*, *41*(3), 14–19.

Miller, S. K. (1983). *The J curve of conforming behavior: Implications of nonexposure in teacher education curricula.* Paper presented at the meeting of the American Association of Colleges for Teacher Education, Detroit.

Morrison, H. C. (1926). *The practice of teaching in the secondary school.* Chicago: University of Chicago Press.

Mueller, D. (1976). Mastery learning: Partly boon, partly boondoggle. *Teachers College Record*, *78*, 41–52.

National Education Association. (1986). *The conditions and resources of teaching.* Survey conducted by Organizational Analysis and Practice Inc.

Nedelsky, L. (1954). Absolute grading standards for objective tests. *Educational and Psychological Measurement*, *14*, 3–19.

Nicholls, J. G. (1979). Quality and equality in intellectual development: The role of motivation in education. *American Psychologist*, *34*, 1071–1084.

Nicholls, J. G. (1983). Conceptions of ability and achievement motivation: A theory and its implications for education. In E. Paris, G. Olson, & H. Stevenson (Eds.), *Learning and motivation in the classroom.* Hillsdale, NJ: Erlbaum.

Nicholls, J. G. (1984). Conceptions of ability and achievement motivation. In R. E. Ames & C. Ames (Eds.), *Research on motivation in education: Student motivation.* Orlando, FL: Academic Press.

Northwest Regional Educational Laboratory (1985). *Effective schooling practices: A research synthesis.* Portland, OR: Goal-based Education Program, Northwest Regional Educational Laboratory.

Okey, J. R. (1974). Altering teacher and pupil behavior with mastery teaching. *School Science and Mathematics*, *74*, 530–535.

Okey, J. R., & Ciesla, J. L. (1975). *Mastery teaching.* Bloomington: National Center for the Development of Training Materials in Teacher Education, Indiana University.

Olson, L. (1985). Proponents of mastery learning defend method after its rejection by Chicago. *Education Week*, *6*(42), 1, 30.

Olson, L. (1986, April 16). Report on 1986 NEA survey. *Education Week*, p. 1.

Paskal, D., Leverenz, D., Ruchgy, W., & Brandi, F. (1986). *Effective staff development: Program guidelines that pay off!* Wayne, MI: Wayne County Intermediate School District.

Peters, T. J., and Waterman, R. H. (1982). *In search of excellence: Lessons from America's best-run companies.* New York: Harper & Row.

Philadelphia Public Schools. (1980). [See under School District of Philadelphia.]

Poggio, J. (1976). *Long-term cognitive retention resulting from the mastery learning paradigm.* Paper presented at the annual meeting of the American Educational Research Association, San Francisco.

Popham, W. J. (1983). *Modern educational measurement.* Englewood Cliffs, NJ: Prentice-Hall.

Pringle, P. R. (1982). Developing outcome-based curriculum systems to improve students' learning. *Outcomes, 1*(4), 12–18.

Pringle, P. R. (1985). Establishing a management plan for implementing mastery learning. In D. U. Levine (Ed.), *Improving student achievement through mastery learning programs.* San Francisco: Jossey-Bass.

Reid, E. R. (1985). Preventing failure with effective instruction. *Outcomes, 4*(4), 18–23.

Resnick, L. B. (1976). Task analysis in instructional design. In D. Klahr (Ed.), *Cognition and instruction.* Hillsdale, NJ: Erlbaum.

Robb, D. W. (1985). Strategies for implementing successful mastery learning programs. In D. U. Levine (Ed.), *Improving student achievement through mastery learning programs.* San Francisco: Jossey-Bass.

Roberts, J. M. E., & Kenney, J. L. (1986). Making mastery learning work: Part 1. Overview of the Baltimore Project. *Outcomes, 5*(2), 28–40.

Roberts, J. M. E., Kenney, J. L., & Kozlovsky, J. D. (1986). Making mastery learning work: Part 3. Summary. *Outcomes, 5*(2), 51–53.

Rochester, M. (1982). *An analysis of the formative testing and corrective instruction components of LFM programs.* Unpublished doctoral dissertation, University of South Carolina.

Roid, G., & Haladyna, T. (1982). *A technology for test-item writing.* Orlando, FL: Academic Press.

Rosenshine, B. (1979). Content, time, and direct instruction. In P. Peterson & H. Walberg (Eds.), *Research on teaching: Concepts, findings, and implications.* Berkeley, CA: McCutchan.

Rosenshine, B. (1983). Teaching functions in instructional programs. *Elementary School Journal, 83*, 335–351.

Rosenshine, B. (1985). *The gaps and overlaps between mastery learning principles and master developers' instructional functions.* Paper presented at the annual meeting of the American Educational Research Association, Chicago.

Rosenshine, B., & Stephens, R. (1986). Teaching functions. In M. C. Wittrock (Ed.), *The handbook of research on teaching* (3rd ed.). New York: Macmillan.

Russell, J. S., & White, T. (1982). Linking behaviors and activities of secondary school principals to school effectiveness. Eugene: Center for Educational Policy and Management, University of Oregon.

Ryan, D. W. (1983). Redefining the roles of middle managers in outcome-based systems. *Outcomes, 2*(4), 26–33.

Ryan, D. W. (1985). Preactive and proactive supervision of mastery learning programs. In D. U. Levine (Ed.), *Improving student achievement through mastery learning programs.* San Francisco: Jossey-Bass.

Sarason, S. (1983). *Schooling in America: Scapegoat and salvation.* New York: Free Press.

School District No. 12, Adams County, CO. (1984). *CMI 3000.*

School District of Philadelphia. (1986). *The mastery learning manual.*

Schroeder, D. (1982). A letter to students in my senior English class. *Outcomes, 2*(2), 16–17.

Simonson, S. (1982). Mariner High Schools operating principles. *Outcomes, 2*(1),

17–21.

Simpson, E. L. (1976). *Humanistic education: An interpretation*. Cambridge, MA: Ballinger.

Sizer, T. R., & Powell, A. G. (1984). A study of high schools. *Outcomes, 3*(3), 16–22.

Slavin, R. E. (1983). *Cooperative learning*. White Plains, NY: Longman.

Slavin, R. E., & Karweit, N. (1984). Mastery learning and student teams: A factorial experiment in urban general mathematics classes. *American Educational Research Journal, 21*, 725–736.

Smith, M. I. (1968). *Teaching to specific objectives: Second progress report (evaluation of test data) for the development of a county-wide articulation in foreign language instruction through common measurement procedures*. Stanislaus, CA: Stanislaus County Schools Office.

Smith, R. M. (1984). Beyond mastery learning: Expanding the horizons of instructional management. *Outcomes, 3*(3), 6–9.

Smith, W. J. (1982). Is there "time" for mastery learning? *Outcomes, 2*(2), 27–29.

Smith, W. J. (1985). Incorporating testing and retesting into the teaching plan. In D. U. Levine (Ed.), *Improving student achievement through mastery learning programs*. San Francisco: Jossey-Bass.

Smith, W. J. (1986). The higher cognitive levels and test alignment. *Outcomes, 5*(3), 14–24.

Spady, W. G. (1974). The sociological implications of mastery learning. In J. H. Block (Ed.), *Schools, society, and mastery learning*. New York: Holt, Rinehart and Winston.

Spady, W. G. (1981). Outcome-based management: A sociological perspective. NIE-P-80-0194. Washington, DC: National Institute of Education.

Spady, W. G. (1982). Outcome-based instructional management: A sociological perspective. *Australian Journal of Education, 26*, 123–143.

Spady, W. G. (1985a). *Key philosophical principles of outcome-based education*. San Francisco, CA: Far West Regional Educational Laboratory.

Spady, W. G. (1985b). *Essential operational components of outcome-based education*. San Francisco, CA: Far West Regional Educational Laboratory.

Spady, W. G. (1987). On grades, grading, and school reform. *Outcomes, 6*(1), 7–12.

Spady, W. G., & Jones, B. F. (1985). Enhanced mastery learning and quality of instruction. In D. U. Levine (Ed.), *Improving student achievement through mastery learning programs*. San Francisco: Jossey-Bass.

Sparks, G. M. (1983). Synthesis of research on staff development for effective teaching. *Educational Leadership, 41*(3), 65–72.

Squires, D. A., Huitt, W. G., & Segars, J. K. (1983–1984). *Effective schools and classrooms: A research-based perspective*. Alexandria, VA: Association for Supervision and Curriculum Development.

Stallings, J. A. (1980). Allocated academic learning time revisited, or beyond time on task. *Educational Researcher, 9*, 11–16.

Stallings, J. A., & Stipek, D. (1986). Research on early childhood and elementary school teaching programs. In M. C. Wittrock (Ed.), *Handbook of research on teaching* (3rd ed.). New York: Macmillan.

Stodolsky, S. (1984). Frameworks for studying instructional processes in peer-work groups. In P. L. Peterson, L. C. Wilkinson, & M. Hallinan (Eds.), *The social context of instruction: Group organization and group processes.* Orlando, FL: Academic Press.

Talmage, H. (1975). *Systems of individualized education.* Berkeley, CA: McCutchan.

Torshen, K. P. (1977). *The mastery approach to competency-based education.* Orlando, FL: Academic Press.

Tukey, J. (1977). *Exploratory data analysis.* Reading, MA: Addison-Wesley.

Turner, B. (1986). Statement at hearing on H.R. 747, the Effective Schools Development in Education Act of 1985. Washington, DC: U.S. Government Printing Office.

Vickery, T. R. (1984). Data for the long haul. *Outcomes, 4*(1), 1–5.

Vickery, T. R. (1987). *Excellence in an outcome-driven school district: A validation study of the schools of Johnson City, New York.* Syracuse, NY: Syracuse University.

Walberg, H. J. (1984). Improving the productivity of America's schools. *Educational Leadership, 41*(8), 19–27.

Walberg, H. J. (1985). Examining the theory, practice, and outcomes of mastery learning. In D. U. Levine (Ed.), *Improving student achievement through mastery learning programs.* San Francisco: Jossey-Bass.

Walbesser, H. H., & Carter, H. (1968). Some methodological considerations of curriculum education research. *Educational Leadership, 26*(1), 53–64.

Wang, M. C., & Walberg, H. J. (Eds.). (1985). *Adapting instruction to individual differences.* Berkeley, CA: McCutchan.

Washburne, C. W. (1922). Educational measurements as a key to individualizing instruction and promotions. *Journal of Educational Research, 5,* 195–206.

Waxman, H., Wang, M. C., Anderson, K., and Walberg, H. J. (1985). *Adaptive education and student outcomes: A quantitative synthesis.* Pittsburgh: University of Pittsburgh, Learning Research and Development Center.

Weinstein, C. F., & Mayer, R. F. (1986). The teaching of learning strategies. In M. C. Wittrock (Ed.), *Handbook of research on teaching* (3rd ed.). New York: Macmillan.

Westerberg, T., & Stevick, J. (1985). Mastery learning at the high school level: a prescription for success. *Outcomes, 5*(1), 24–27.

White, R. T. (1979). Achievement, mastery, proficiency, competence. *Studies in Science Education, 6,* 1–22.

White, R. W. (1959). Motivation reconsidered: The concept of competence. *Psychological Review, 66,* 297–333.

Willett, J. J., Yamashita, J., & Anderson, R. (1983). A meta-analysis of instructional systems applied to science teaching. *Journal of Research in Science Teaching, 20,* 405–417.

Wittrock, M. C. (Ed.). (1986). *Handbook of research on teaching* (3rd ed.). New York: Macmillan.

Yinger, R. (1980). A study of teacher planning. *Elementary School Journal, 80,* 107–127.

Ziomek, R. L., & Wilson, M. (n.d.). *A proposed additional index to Glass' effect size estimator with application to mastery learning experiments.* Des Moines. IA: Department of Evaluation and Research, Des Moines Public Schools.

Index